Praise for Linux Pocket Guide

Linux Pocket Guide is a must-have book on every Linux user's desk, even in this digital age. It's like a collection of my favorite bookmarked manual pages that I keep revisiting for reference, but simpler to understand and easier to follow.

—*Abhishek Prakash,*
cofounder of It's FOSS

One of the beloved features of Linux environments is the assortment of small utilities that combine in wonderful ways to solve problems. This book distills that experience into an accessible reference. Even experienced readers will rediscover forgotten facets and incredible options on their favorite tools.

—*Jess Males, DevOps*
engineer, TriumphPay

This is such a handy reference! It somehow manages to be both thorough and concise.

—*Jerod Santo,*
changelog.com

4TH EDITION

Linux Pocket Guide

Daniel J. Barrett

Beijing · Boston · Farnham · Sebastopol · Tokyo

Linux Pocket Guide

by Daniel J. Barrett

Copyright © 2024 Daniel J. Barrett. All rights reserved.

Published by O'Reilly Media, Inc., 1005 Gravenstein Highway North, Sebastopol, CA 95472.

O'Reilly books may be purchased for educational, business, or sales promotional use. Online editions are also available for most titles (*https://oreilly.com*). For more information, contact our corporate/institutional sales department: 800-998-9938 or *corporate@oreilly.com*.

Acquisitions Editor: John Devins
Development Editor: Virginia Wilson
Production Editor: Ashley Stussy
Copyeditor: Stephanie English
Proofreader: Dwight Ramsey
Indexer: Daniel J. Barrett and BIM Creatives, LLC
Interior Designer: David Futato
Cover Designer: Karen Montgomery
Illustrator: Kate Dullea

March 2024:   Fourth Edition

Revision History for the Fourth Edition

    2024-03-01:   First Release
    2024-06-07:   Second Release

See *https://oreil.ly/lpg4eERR* for release details.

978-1-098-15796-8

[LSI]

Table of Contents

First Things First

Welcome to Linux! If you're a new user, this book can serve as a quick introduction, as well as a guide to common and practical commands. If you have Linux experience, feel free to skip the introductory material.

What's in This Book?

This book is a short guide, *not a comprehensive reference*. I cover important, useful aspects of Linux so you can work productively. I do not, however, present every single command and every last option (my apologies if your favorite was omitted), nor delve into detail about operating system internals. Short, sweet, and essential—that's our motto.

I focus on *commands*, those pesky little words you type on a command line to tell a Linux system what to do. Here's an example command that counts lines of text in a file, *myfile*:

```
wc -l myfile
```

This book covers important Linux commands for most users, such as ls (list files), grep (search for text), mplayer (play audio and video files), and df (measure free disk space). I touch only briefly on graphical environments like GNOME and KDE Plasma, each of which could fill a *Pocket Guide* by itself.

I've organized the material by function to provide a concise learning path. For example, to help you view the contents of a file, I introduce many file-viewing commands together: cat for short text files, less for longer ones, od for binary files, and so on. Then I explain each command in turn, briefly presenting its common uses and options.

I assume you have access to a Linux system and can log in. If not, it's easy to try out Linux on most computers. Just download and install a "live" Linux distribution onto a USB thumb drive and boot it. Examples are Ubuntu (*https://oreil.ly/ralRq*), Fedora (*https://oreil.ly/Y3QGZ*), and KNOPPIX (*https://oreil.ly/Byqeu*).

What's New in the Fourth Edition?

New commands
  I've added 50 new commands to this edition, such as git and svn for version control, split and column for text manipulation, pandoc and ffmpeg for file conversion, snap and flatpak for package management, mdadm, lvcreate, and zfs for fancy storage management, gpg for encryption, and many others.

Clearer organization
  I've reorganized the book into chapters on concepts, files, basic system administration, networking, and other topics.

Goodbye, ancient commands
  Some commands from previous editions of this book are mostly obsolete today, such as write and finger, or deprecated, such as ftp. I've replaced them with more relevant commands for modern Linux systems.

Conventions Used in This Book

Each command I present in this book begins with a standard heading. Figure P-1 shows the heading for ls, a command that lists the names and attributes of files. The heading demonstrates the command's general usage in a simple format:

```
ls [options] [files]
```

which means you'd type "ls" followed, if you choose, by options and then filenames. Don't type the square brackets "[" and "]" —they just indicate their contents are optional. Words in italics mean you have to fill in your own values, like names of actual files. If you see a vertical bar between options or arguments, perhaps grouped by parentheses:

```
(file | directory)
```

this indicates choice: you may supply either a filename or directory name as an argument.

---

ls   stdin **stdout** -file **-- opt --help --version**

```
ls [options] [files]
```

Figure P-1. Standard command heading

The standard heading shown in Figure P-1 also includes six properties of the command, printed in black (supported) or gray (unsupported):

stdin

> The command reads by default from standard input (i.e., your keyboard). See "Input, Output, and Redirection" on page 25.

stdout

> The command writes by default to standard output (i.e., your display). See "Input, Output, and Redirection" on page 25.

- file

> A single-dash argument (-), when provided as an input filename, tells the command to read from standard input rather than a disk file. Likewise, if the dash is supplied

as an output filename, the command writes to standard output. For example, the following wc command line reads the files *myfile* and *myfile2*, then standard input, then *myfile3*:

```
wc myfile myfile2 - myfile3
```

-- *opt*

A double-dash option (--) means "end of options": any strings appearing later on the command line are not treated as options. A double dash is sometimes necessary to work with a filename that begins with a dash, which otherwise would be (mistakenly) treated as an option. For example, if you have a file named *-dashfile*, the command wc -dashfile fails because the string -dashfile is treated as an (invalid) option. Run wc -- -dashfile to indicate -dashfile is a filename. If a command does not support "--", you can still work around the problem by prepending the current directory path "./" to the filename so the dash is no longer the first character:

```
wc ./-dashfile
```

--help

The option --help makes the command print a help message explaining proper usage, then exit.

--version

The option --version makes the command print its version information and exit.

Commands, Prompts, and Output

The Linux command line, or *shell*, prints a special symbol, called a *prompt*, when it's waiting for a command. In this book, the prompt is a right-facing arrow:

→

Prompts come in all shapes and sizes, depending on how your shell is configured. Your prompt might be a dollar sign

($), a combination of your computer name, username, and various symbols (myhost:~smith$), or something else. Every prompt means the same thing: the shell is ready for your next command.

When I show a command line in this book, some parts are meant to be typed by the user, and other parts are not (like the prompt and the command's output). I use boldface to identify the parts to type. Sometimes I add italic comments to explain what's going on:

```
→ wc -l myfile          The command to type at the prompt
18 myfile               The output it produces
```

Your Friend, the echo Command

In many of my examples, I print information to the screen with the echo command, which I formally describe in "Screen Output" on page 257. echo is one of the simplest commands—it merely prints its arguments on standard output, once those arguments have been processed by the shell:

```
→ echo My dog has fleas
My dog has fleas
→ echo My name is $USER          The shell variable USER
My name is smith
```

Long Command Lines

Sometimes, a command is longer than the width of a page, so I split it onto multiple lines. A final backslash character means "continued on the next line":

```
→ echo This is a long command that does not fit on \
  one line
This is a long command that does not fit on one line
```

If you enter one of my multiline commands in a running shell, feel free to break it up with backslashes as I did, or just type the whole command on one line without backslashes.

Keystrokes

I use certain symbols for keystrokes. The caret (^) means "hold down the Control key," usually labeled Ctrl. For example, ^D (Ctrl D) means "hold down the Ctrl key and type D." I also write ESC to mean "press and release the Escape key." Keys like Enter and the space bar should be self-explanatory.

Downloading the Practice Files

I've created a collection of files to help you practice with Linux. Download and install them on any Linux machine, and you can run most of the example commands in this book verbatim. To download them for the first time, run the following commands.[1] (Note that -O contains a capital O, not a zero.)

```
→ cd
→ curl -O https://linuxpocketguide.com/LPG4.tar.gz
→ tar -xf LPG4.tar.gz
```

The preceding commands create a directory named *linuxpocketguide* in your home directory. Visit this directory:

```
→ cd ~/linuxpocketguide
```

and run commands as you read the book. The output should match the book's except for local details like dates and usernames.

To re-download and install the practice files (say, if you've modified them), simply run the provided reset-lpg script:

```
→ cd ~/linuxpocketguide
→ bash reset-lpg
```

---

1 Or, if you are experienced with git and GitHub, download the files (*https://resources.oreilly.com/oreillymedia/linux_pocket_guide_4*) and skip the rest of my instructions. If you clone the repository and want to restore the files to their original state, don't run the reset-lpg script; run git reset --hard instead.

If you've placed the practice files in a different directory, supply it to `reset-lpg`. The following command creates or refreshes the directory */tmp/practice/linuxpocketguide*:

→ bash reset-lpg /tmp/practice

Conventions Used in This Book

The following typographical conventions are used in this book:

Italic

Indicates new terms, URLs, email addresses, filenames, and file extensions.

`Constant width`

Used for program listings, as well as within paragraphs to refer to program elements such as variable or function names, databases, data types, environment variables, statements, and keywords.

`Constant width bold`

Shows commands or other text that should be typed literally by the user.

`Constant width italic`

Shows text that should be replaced with user-supplied values or by values determined by context.

TIP

This element signifies a tip or suggestion.

NOTE

This element signifies a general note.

O'Reilly Online Learning

O'REILLY®   For more than 40 years, *O'Reilly Media* has provided technology and business training, knowledge, and insight to help companies succeed.

Our unique network of experts and innovators share their knowledge and expertise through books, articles, and our online learning platform. O'Reilly's online learning platform gives you on-demand access to live training courses, in-depth learning paths, interactive coding environments, and a vast collection of text and video from O'Reilly and 200+ other publishers. For more information, visit *https://oreilly.com*.

How to Contact Us

Please address comments and questions concerning this book to the publisher:

O'Reilly Media, Inc.
1005 Gravenstein Highway North
Sebastopol, CA 95472
800-889-8969 (in the United States or Canada)
707-827-7019 (international or local)
707-829-0104 (fax)
support@oreilly.com
https://www.oreilly.com/about/contact.html

We have a web page for this book, where we list errata, examples, and any additional information. You can access this page at *https://oreil.ly/linux-pocket-guide-4e*.

For news and information about our books and courses, visit *https://oreilly.com*.

Find us on LinkedIn: *https://linkedin.com/company/oreilly-media*.

Watch us on YouTube: *https://youtube.com/oreillymedia*.

Acknowledgments

I am so grateful to the many readers who purchased the first three editions of this book over the past 20(!) years, making the fourth edition possible. My heartfelt thanks also go to my editor Virginia Wilson, acquisitions editor John Devins, the O'Reilly production team, my awesome technical reviewers (Abhishek Prakash, Dan Ritter, Doron Beit-Halahmi, Ethan Schwartz, and Jess Males), Maggie Johnson at Google, and Kerry and Lesley Minnear at Alucard Music. And all my love to my wonderful family, Lisa, Sophia, Kay, and Luna.

CHAPTER 1

Essential Concepts

What's Linux?

Linux is a free, open source operating system (OS) that's an alternative to Microsoft Windows and Apple macOS. Linux powers most of the servers on the internet. It operates behind the scenes on every Android mobile phone and Chromebook, and on millions of network-connected devices like routers, firewalls, and robotic cow-milking systems (seriously). It also runs fine on desktop and laptop computers.

Linux has four major parts, shown in Figure 1-1:

The kernel
> Low-level software. It controls the hardware and basic functions like process scheduling and networking. Few users interact with the kernel directly.

Supplied programs
> Thousands of programs for file handling, text editing, software development, web browsing, audio, video, encryption, mathematics…you name it. These programs talk to the kernel. Programs that run on the command line are called *commands*.

The shell

A Linux program for running commands and displaying the results. Linux has an assortment of shells with different features. This book focuses on a shell called bash, which is often the default for user accounts. Some other shells are dash, fish, ksh (Korn shell), tcsh (TC shell, or T shell), zsh (Z shell), and to a lesser extent, busybox. All shells have similar functions, though their usage varies.

Graphical desktop environment (optional)

A UI with windows, menus, icons, mouse support, and other familiar GUI elements. Some popular environments are GNOME and KDE Plasma. Most applications built for GNOME can run in KDE and vice versa.[1]

This book focuses on the command-line parts of Linux, namely the supplied programs and the shell. Windows and macOS have command-line interfaces too (cmd and powershell on Windows, Terminal on the Mac), but most of their users stick with the GUI and might never see or need a command line. On Linux, the shell is critical. If you use Linux without the shell, you are missing out.

Linux is extremely configurable and comes in hundreds of varieties that serve different needs and tastes. Each variety is called a *distro* (short for "distribution"). All distros share some core components but may look different and include different programs and files. Some popular distros include Mint, Ubuntu, Manjaro, Arch, Gentoo, Red Hat, and OpenSUSE, among others. The core material in this book should apply to every distro.

---

1 GNOME, KDE, and other environments are built on a common windowing system that is either X or Wayland. To see which system you're using, run the command echo $XDG_SESSION_TYPE.

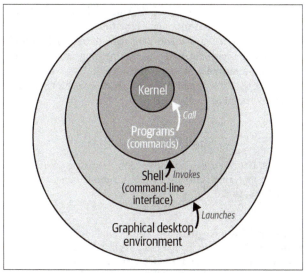

Figure 1-1. The four major parts of Linux, conceptually. Low-level kernel functions are called by programs, which are invoked in a shell, which can be launched by a graphical desktop.

Launching a Shell

Where do shells come from? Sometimes Linux will launch one for you automatically. This is often the case when you log in over a network using ssh or a similar tool. The first significant thing you see is a shell prompt awaiting your command.

Other times, you have to launch a shell manually. This is common when using a graphical desktop full of icons and menus with no shell in sight. In such cases, you need a GUI application called a *terminal* or *terminal program* that runs shells in a window. The sidebar "Shell Versus Terminal" on page 4 clarifies the difference between shells and terminals.

Every distro with a graphical desktop includes at least one terminal program, but you might have to hunt for it. Search for an application, icon, or menu item named Terminal, Konsole, xterm, gnome-terminal, uxterm, or something similar, and run it to open a terminal. Also try pressing Ctrl-Alt-t (hold the Control and Alt keys and press T), which opens a terminal in some environments.

Shell Versus Terminal

A shell is a command-line interface for launching Linux commands by typing plain text. It prints a prompt and waits for your command:

→

A terminal is a program that opens a window and presents a running shell, shown in Figure 1-2. It's like a graphical wrapper around a shell. A terminal adds menus, scrollbars, copy and paste, and other GUI features that support the shell.

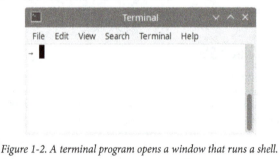

Figure 1-2. A terminal program opens a window that runs a shell.

Command-Line Warm-Up

To give you a feel for Linux, here are 10 simple commands to try right now in a shell. Type them *exactly*, including capital and small letters, spaces, and all symbols after the prompt. At the end of each command, press Enter.[2]

Display a calendar for November 2023:

```
→ cal nov 2023
    November 2023
Su Mo Tu We Th Fr Sa
          1  2  3  4
 5  6  7  8  9 10 11
12 13 14 15 16 17 18
19 20 21 22 23 24 25
26 27 28 29 30
```

List the contents of the */bin* directory, which contains many commands:

```
→ ls /bin
bash       less       rm
bunzip2    lessecho   rmdir
busybox    lessfile   rnano
⋮
```

Count the number of visible items in your home directory (represented here by a variable, HOME, that I discuss later):

```
→ ls $HOME | wc -l
8                        Your value may be different
```

See how much space is used on a partition of your hard disk:

```
→ df -h /
Filesystem  Size  Used Avail Use% Mounted on
/dev/sdb1    78G   30G   48G  61% /
```

Watch the processes running on your computer (press "q" to quit):

```
→ top -d1
```

---

2 If you see an error message "command not found," don't worry: a command probably isn't installed on your system. See "Installing Software Packages" on page 177.

Print the file */etc/hosts*, which contains names and addresses of computers, on your default printer if you have one set up:

```
→ lpr /etc/hosts
```

See how long you've been logged in:

```
→ last -1 $USER
smith   pts/7 :0   Tue Nov 10 20:12   still logged in
```

Download a file *sample.pdf* from this book's website to your current directory, without needing a web browser:

```
→ curl -O https://linuxpocketguide.com/sample.pdf
```

See who owns the domain name *oreilly.com* (press the space bar to move forward page by page, and press "q" to quit):

```
→ whois oreilly.com | less
Domain Name: OREILLY.COM
Registrar: GODADDY.COM, LLC
⋮
```

Finally, clear your terminal or screen:

```
→ clear
```

Congratulations, you are now a Linux user!

The Structure of Commands

A Linux command typically consists of a *program name* followed by *options* and *arguments*:

```
wc -l myfile
```

The program name (wc, short for "word count") refers to a program somewhere on disk that the shell locates and runs. Options, which usually begin with a dash, affect the behavior of the program. In the preceding command, the -l option tells wc to count lines and not words. The argument myfile specifies the file that wc should read and process.

Commands can have multiple options and arguments. Options may be given individually, or combined after a single dash:

```
wc -l -w myfile        Two individual options
wc -lw myfile          Combined options, same as -l -w
```

though some programs are quirky and do not recognize combined options. Multiple arguments are also OK:

```
wc -l myfile myfile2   Count lines in two files.
```

Options are not standardized. They may be a single dash and one character (say, -l), two dashes and a word (--lines), or several other formats. The same option may have different meanings to different programs: in the command wc -l, the option -l means "lines of text," but in ls -l it means "long output." Two programs also might use different options to mean the same thing, such as -q for "run quietly" versus -s for "run silently." Some options are followed by a value, such as -s 10, and space between them might not be required (-s10).

Arguments are usually filenames for input or output, but they can be other things too, like directory names, usernames, hostnames, IP addresses, regular expressions, or arbitrary strings.

A command that's just a single program with options and arguments is called a *simple command*. Here's a simple command that lists users who are logged into a Linux server:[3]

```
→ who
silver     :0      Sep 23 20:44
byrnes     pts/0   Sep 15 13:51
barrett    pts/1   Sep 22 21:15
silver     pts/2   Sep 22 21:18
```

A command can also invoke several programs at once and even connect programs so they interact. Here's a command that connects the output of who to the input of wc, which counts lines of text. The result is the number of lines in the output of who:

---

3 User "silver," who is listed twice, is running two interactive shells at once.

```
→ who | wc -l
4
```

The vertical bar, called a *pipe*, makes the connection between who and wc. Linux experts use these sorts of combined commands, called *pipelines*, all the time.

Commands can also include programming language constructs like variables, conditionals, and loops, which I cover in "Programming with Shell Scripts" on page 293. For example, a command might say, "run this program, write its output to a file of my choosing, and if any errors occur, send me an email with the results."

Users and Superusers

Linux is a multiuser OS: multiple people can run programs on a single Linux computer at the same time. On a given computer, each user is identified by a *username*, like smith or funkydance. Each user has a separate workspace of sorts (see "Home Directories" on page 11) so they don't interfere with one another.

A special user named *root*—the *superuser* or *administrator*—has the privileges to do anything at all on the system. The superuser can create, modify, or delete any file and run any program. Ordinary users are restricted: they can run most programs, but in general, they can't mess with other users' stuff.

Some commands in this book require superuser privileges. I precede these commands with sudo:

→ **sudo** *superuser command goes here*

WARNING

sudo gives you the power to destroy your Linux system.

I discuss sudo fully in "Becoming the Superuser" on page 143, but for now, all you need to know is that sudo gives you super-user powers and sometimes prompts for your password. For example, to count lines in a protected file called /etc/shadow, with and without sudo, you could run this command:

```
→ wc -l /etc/shadow                    This fails
wc: /etc/shadow: Permission denied
→ sudo wc -l /etc/shadow               Run with sudo
[sudo] password: xxxxxxxx
51 /etc/shadow                         It worked!
```

The Filesystem

To make use of any Linux system, you must become comfortable with Linux files and directories (a.k.a. folders), collectively called the *filesystem*. On a graphical desktop, files and directories are obvious on screen. In a command-line interface like the Linux shell, the same files and directories are still present but less visible, so at times you must remember which directory you are "in" and how it relates to other directories. You'll use shell commands like cd (change directory) to move between directories, and commands like pwd (print working directory) to keep track of where you are in the filesystem.

Let's cover some terminology. Linux files are collected into *directories*. The directories form a hierarchy, or *tree*, as in Figure 1-3. One directory may contain other directories, called *subdirectories*, which may themselves contain other files and subdirectories, and so on, into infinity. The topmost directory is called the *root directory* and is denoted by a slash (/).[4]

---

4 In Linux, *all* files and directories descend from the root. This is unlike Windows, in which different devices are accessed by drive letters.

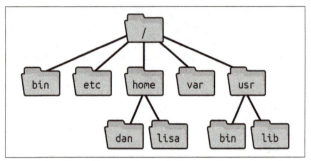

Figure 1-3. A Linux filesystem (partial). The root directory is at the top. The absolute path to the "dan" directory is /home/dan.

Linux refers to its files and directories using a "names and slashes" syntax called a *path*. For instance, the following path:

    /one/two/three/four

refers to the root directory /, which contains a directory called *one*, which contains a directory *two*, which contains a directory *three*, which contains a final file or directory, *four*. Any path that begins with a slash, which descends all the way from the root, is called an *absolute* path.

Paths don't have to be absolute—they can be relative to some directory other than the root. Figure 1-3 has two different directories named *bin*, whose absolute paths are /bin and /usr/bin. If you simply refer to "the *bin* directory," it's not clear which one you mean. You need more context. Any path that doesn't begin with a slash, like *bin*, is called a *relative* path.

To make sense of a relative path, you need to know "where you are" in the Linux filesystem. This location is called your *current directory* (sometimes called "working directory" or "current working directory").

Every shell has a current directory, and when you run commands in that shell, they operate relative to its current directory. For example, if your shell is "in" the directory /usr, and you refer to a relative path *bin*, it means /usr/bin. In general, if your current directory is */one/two/three*, a relative path *a/b/c* would imply the absolute path */one/two/three/a/b/c*.

Two special relative paths are named . (a single period, or "dot") and .. (two periods, or "dot dot"). "Dot" means your shell's current directory, and "dot dot" means its *parent* directory, one level above. So if your shell's current directory is */one/two/three*, then . refers to this directory and .. refers to */one/two*.

To travel from one directory to another, use the cd command, which changes your shell's current directory:

→ **cd /usr/local/bin**   *Enter the directory /usr/local/bin*

The previous cd command used an absolute path. You can make relative moves with cd as well:

→ **cd d**   *Enter subdirectory d of my current directory*
→ **cd ../mydir**   *Go up to my parent, then into directory mydir*

File and directory names may contain most characters you expect: capital and small letters,[5] numbers, periods, dashes, underscores, and most symbols (but not "/", which is reserved for separating directories). For efficiency, however, avoid spaces, asterisks, dollar signs, parentheses, and other characters that have special meaning to the shell. These characters require special treatment in filenames (see "Quoting" on page 28), which can be inconvenient or tedious.

Home Directories

Users' personal files are usually kept in the directory */home* (for ordinary users) or */root* (for the superuser). Your home directory is typically */home/<your-username>* (*/home/smith*, */home/funkydance*, etc.). There are several ways to visit or refer to your home directory:

---

5 Linux filenames are case-sensitive, so upper and lowercase letters are not equivalent.

cd

> With no arguments, the cd command returns you (i.e., sets the shell's current directory) to your home directory.

HOME *variable*

> The environment variable HOME (see "Shell Variables" on page 21) contains the name of your home directory:

```
→ echo $HOME          Print the directory name
/home/smith
→ cd $HOME/linuxpocketguide   Visit a subdirectory
```

~

> When used in place of a directory, a lone tilde is expanded by the shell to the name of your home directory.

```
→ echo ~              Print the directory name
/home/smith
→ cd ~/linuxpocketguide   Visit a subdirectory
```

> When the tilde is followed by a username (as in *~fred*), the shell expands this string to be the user's home directory:

```
→ cd ~fred            Visit Fred's home directory, if it exists
→ pwd                 The "print working directory" command
/home/fred
```

System Directories

A Linux system has tens of thousands of system directories. They contain OS files, applications, documentation, and just about everything except personal user files (which typically live in */home*).

Unless you're a system administrator, you'll rarely visit most system directories—but with a little knowledge you can understand or guess their purposes. Their names often contain three parts, as shown in Figure 1-4.

Figure 1-4. Directory scope, category, and application

Directory path part 1: scope

The *scope* of a directory path describes, at a high level, the purpose of an entire directory tree. Some common ones are:

/	(Pronounced "root") System files supplied with your distro
/usr	(Pronounced "user") More system files supplied with your distro
/usr/local	(Pronounced "user local") System files that are not supplied with your distro; they may be unique to your local Linux network or your individual computer

There isn't a clear distinction between / and */usr* in practice, but / is considered "lower level" and closer to the OS.

Directory path part 2: category

The *category* of a directory path in Figure 1-4 describes the types of files found in a directory. For example, if the category is *lib*, you can be reasonably sure that the directory contains *lib*rary files for programming. If the category is *bin*, the contents are usually *bin*ary files—executable programs.

When you precede a category like *bin* with a scope, you produce paths like */bin*, */usr/bin*, and */usr/local/bin*. A distro's most fundamental system programs like `ls` and `cat` are typically in */bin*, and other system programs are in */usr/bin*.[6] */usr/local/bin* contains locally installed programs not included in your distro. These are not hard-and-fast rules but typical cases.

---

6 Some distros no longer make these distinctions. Fedora, for example, makes */bin* a symbolic link to */usr/bin*.

Some common categories are as follows:

Categories for programs

bin	Programs (usually binary files)
sbin	Programs (usually binary files) for superusers
lib	Libraries of code used by programs

Categories for documentation

doc	Documentation
info	Documentation files for emacs's built-in help system
man	Documentation files (manual pages) displayed by the man command; the files are often compressed and are sprinkled with typesetting commands for man to interpret
share	Program-specific files, such as examples and installation instructions

Categories for configuration

etc	Configuration files for the system (and other miscellaneous stuff)
init.d	Configuration files for booting Linux
rc.d	Configuration files for booting Linux; also *rc1.d*, *rc2.d*, ...

Categories for programming

include	Header files for programming
src	Source code for programs

Categories for web files

cgi-bin	Scripts/programs that run on web pages
html	Web pages
public_html	Web pages, typically in users' home directories
www	Web pages

Categories for display

fonts	Fonts (surprise!)
X11	X window system files

Categories for hardware

dev   Device files for interfacing with disks and other hardware

media   Mount points: directories that provide access to disks

mnt   Mount points: directories that provide access to disks

Categories for runtime files

var   Files related to the state of the computer, updated frequently

lock   Lock files, created by programs to say, "I am running"; the existence of a lock file may prevent another program, or another instance of the same program, from performing an action

log   Logfiles that track important system events, containing error, warning, and informational messages

mail   Mailboxes for incoming email

run   PID files, which contain the IDs of running processes; these files are often consulted to track or kill particular processes

spool   Files queued or in transit, such as outgoing email, print jobs, and scheduled jobs

tmp   Temporary storage for programs and/or people to use

Directory path part 3: application

The application part of a directory path (Figure 1-4), if present, is usually the name of a program. For example, the directory */etc/systemd* has scope root (/), category *etc* (configuration files), and application *systemd*. Since *systemd* is a service for configuring Linux machines, a good guess is that */etc/systemd* contains configuration files for that service—and it does.

Kernel-Related Directories

Some directories support the Linux kernel, the lowest-level part of the Linux OS:

/boot

Files for booting the system. The kernel lives here, typically in */boot/vmlinuz* or a file of similar name.

/lost+found

Damaged files that were rescued by a disk recovery tool.

/proc

Files for currently running processes; for advanced users.

/sys

Files for kernel internals; for advanced users.

The files in */proc* and */sys* provide views into the running kernel and have special properties. Files in */proc* always appear to be zero-sized, read-only, and dated now, but their contents magically contain information about the Linux kernel:

```
→ ls -lG /proc/version
-r--r--r-- 1 root 0 Oct 3 22:55 /proc/version
→ cat /proc/version
Linux version 5.15.0-76-generic ...
```

Files in */sys* also have misleading sizes and magical contents:

```
→ ls -lG /sys/power/state
-rw-r--r-- 1 root 4096 Jul 8 06:12 /sys/power/state
→ cat /sys/power/state
freeze mem disk
```

/proc and */sys* are used mostly by system programs, but feel free to view them. Here are some examples:

/proc/ioports	A list of your computer's input/output hardware.
/proc/cpuinfo	Information about your computer's processors.
/proc/version	The OS version. The `uname` command prints the same information.
/proc/uptime	System uptime: seconds elapsed since the system was last booted. Run `uptime` for a more human-readable result.
/proc/NNN	Information about the Linux process with ID *NNN*, where *NNN* is a positive integer, such as */proc/13542*.

/proc/self	Information about the current process you're running; a symbolic link to a /proc/nnn file, automatically updated. Try running:

```
→ ls -l /proc/self
```

several times in a row, and /proc/self changes where it points.

File Permissions

A Linux system may have many user accounts. To maintain privacy and security, most users can access only *some* files on the system, not all. This access control is embodied in two questions:

Who has permission?
> Every file and directory has an *owner* who can do anything they want with it. Typically, a file's owner is the user who created it. A superuser can change a file's owner.
>
> Additionally, a predefined *group* of users may access a file. Groups are defined by the system administrator and I cover them in "Group Management" on page 174.
>
> Finally, a file or directory can be opened to *all users* who have accounts on the system. You'll also see this set of users called *the world* or simply *other*.

What kind of permission is granted?
> File owners, groups, and the world may each have permission to *read*, *write* (modify), and *execute* (run) particular files. Permissions also extend to directories, which users may read (view files within the directory), write (create and delete files within the directory), and execute (enter the directory with cd).

To see the ownership and permissions of a file named *myfile*, run ls -l, described in "Basic File Operations" on page 43:

```
→ ls -l myfile
-rw-r--r-- 1 smith smith  1168 Oct 28  2015 myfile
```

To see the ownership and permissions of a directory named *mydir*, add the `-d` option:

```
→ ls -ld mydir
drwxr-x--- 3 smith smith  4096 Jan 08 15:02 mydir
```

In the output, the file permissions are the 10 leftmost characters, a string of r (read), w (write), x (execute), other letters, and dashes. For example:

```
-rwxr-x---
```

Here's what these letters and symbols mean, briefly:

Position	Meaning
1	**File type:** - = file, d = directory, l = symbolic link, p = named pipe, c = character device, b = block device
2–4	**Permissions for the file's owner:** read (r), write (w), execute (x), or no permission (-).
5–7	**Permissions for the file's group:** r, w, x, -
8–10	**Permissions for all other users:** r, w, x, -

My example `-rwxr-x---` means a file that can be read, written, and executed by the owner; read and executed by the group, but not written; and not accessed at all by other users. To change the owner, group, or permissions, use the commands chown, chgrp, and chmod, respectively, as described in "Properties of Files" on page 65.

Selected Features of Bash

A shell does much more than simply run commands. It also *simplifies* the running of commands, thanks to powerful features: pattern matching for filenames, a "command history" to recall previous commands quickly, pipes to send the output of one command to the input of another, variables to store values for use by the shell, and more. Take the time to learn these features, and you will become faster and more productive with

Linux.[7] Let's skim the surface and introduce you to these useful tools. (For full documentation, run `info bash`.)

Which Shell Are You Running?

This book assumes that your shell is bash. To identify your shell, run:

```
→ echo $SHELL
/bin/bash
```

If your shell isn't bash and you wish to try it, run the command bash directly, because bash, like all shells, is just a program. (It's located at */bin/bash*.)

```
→ bash
```

Run the command `exit` when done to return to your regular shell. To change your default shell to bash, see the chsh command in "User Account Management" on page 170.

Pattern Matching

Pattern matching in the shell, sometimes called wildcards, is a shorthand to work with sets of files. For example, the pattern a* refers to files whose names begin with lowercase "a." The shell expands a pattern into the full set of filenames it matches. If you run:

```
→ ls a*
aardvark   adamantium   apple
```

the shell invisibly expands the pattern a* into the filenames that begin with "a" in your current directory, as if you had typed:

```
→ ls aardvark adamantium apple
```

ls never knows you used a pattern: it sees only the final list of filenames after expansion. This means *every* Linux program

---

7 Also see my follow-up book, *Efficient Linux at the Command Line* (*https://oreil.ly/mUP9M*), to grow your skills.

you launch from a shell, regardless of its origin, "works" with patterns and other shell features. This is a critically important point. A surprising number of Linux users think that programs expand their own file patterns on the command line. They don't. The shell does it *before the associated program even runs.*

Patterns never match two special characters: a leading period and the directory slash (/). These characters must be given literally. A pattern like .bas* matches *.bashrc*, and /etc/*conf matches all filenames ending in *conf* in the */etc* directory.

Dot Files

Filenames with a leading period, called *dot files*, are often hidden from view unless you explicitly request them. An example is the bash initialization file *.bashrc* in your home directory.

- ls omits dot files from directory listings, unless you provide the -a option.
- Pattern-matching characters in the shell do not match a leading period.

As a result, dot files are often called "hidden files."

Pattern	Meaning
*	Zero or more consecutive characters, except a leading dot or a directory slash.
?	Any single character, except a leading dot or a directory slash.
[*set*]	Any single character in the given set. It can be a sequence of characters, like [aeiouAEIOU] for all vowels, or a range with a dash, like [A-Z] for all capital letters, or a combination.
[!*set*]	Any single character *not* in the given set, such as [!0-9] to mean any nondigit.
[^*set*]	Same as [!*set*].

To match a literal dash in a character set, put it first or last so it's not part of a range. To include a literal closing square bracket in the set, put it first in the set, or escape it with a backslash (\]). To include a ^ or ! symbol literally, place it somewhere other than first in the set, or escape it.

Brace Expansion

Similar to file patterns, expressions with curly braces also expand to become multiple arguments to a command. The comma-separated expression:

```
{bubble,quick,merge}
```

expands first to bubble, then quick, and finally merge within a command line, like this:

```
→ echo {bubble,quick,merge}sort.java
bubblesort.java quicksort.java mergesort.java
```

NOTE

The key difference between braces and square brackets is that braces work with *any* strings, whereas square bracket expressions match only existing filenames.

Curly braces can also expand to a sequence of values in a range, if you separate the endpoints of the range with two dots (..):

```
→ echo {3..12}
3 4 5 6 7 8 9 10 11 12
→ echo {A..E}
A B C D E
→ echo file{1..5}.py
file1.py file2.py file3.py file4.py file5.py
```

Shell Variables

You can define variables in a shell and assign them values:

→ **MYVAR=3**   *Assign the value 3 to variable MYVAR*

To refer to a value, simply place a dollar sign in front of the variable name:

→ **echo $MYVAR**
3

The shell defines some standard variables when you log in:

Variable	Meaning
DISPLAY	The name of your X window display
HOME	Your home directory, such as */home/smith*
LOGNAME	Your login name, such as smith
MAIL	Your incoming mailbox, such as */var/spool/mail/smith*
OLDPWD	Your shell's previous directory, prior to the last cd command
PATH	Your shell search path: directories separated by colons
PWD	Your shell's current directory
SHELL	The path to your shell (e.g., */bin/bash*)
TERM	The type of your terminal (e.g., xterm or vt100)
USER	Your login name

Variables and their values are limited, by default, to the shell that defines them. To make a variable and its value available to other programs your shell invokes (i.e., subprocesses), use the export command:

→ **MYVAR=3**
→ **export MYVAR**

or the shorthand:

→ **export MYVAR=3**

Your exported variable is now called an *environment variable*. To go further and make a variable available to every new shell you run, not just subprocesses of your current shell, place the variable definition beforehand in a shell configuration file; see "Tailoring Shell Behavior" on page 40.

To list a shell's environment variables, run:

```
→ printenv
```

To set an environment variable just for the duration of one command, prepend *variable=value* to the command line:

```
→ printenv HOME
/home/smith
→ HOME=/home/sally printenv HOME
/home/sally
→ printenv HOME
/home/smith                    The original value is unaffected
```

Search Path

Programs may be scattered all over the Linux filesystem, mostly in directories like */bin* and */usr/bin*. When you run a command that invokes a program, somehow the shell must locate the program in the filesystem:

```
→ who          The shell must locate the "who" program to run it
```

The shell finds the program by consulting the value of the environment variable PATH, which is a list of directories separated by colons. This list is called the shell's *search path*.

```
→ echo $PATH
/usr/local/bin:/bin:/usr/bin      Search path with 3 directories
```

The shell looks for an executable file named who in each listed directory in sequence. If it locates who (say, in */usr/bin/who*), it executes the program, and also caches the location for next time (run hash --help for more on caching). Otherwise, it reports a failure:

```
bash: who: command not found
```

To print a command's location in your search path, run the type or which command:

```
→ type who
who is hashed (/usr/bin/who)          The output may vary:
who is /usr/bin/who                    This means "who" is cached
→ which who                            This means "who" isn't cached
/usr/bin/who
```

To add directories to your shell's search path temporarily, modify its PATH variable. For example, append */usr/sbin* to your shell's search path:

```
→ PATH=$PATH:/usr/sbin
→ echo $PATH
/usr/local/bin:/bin:/usr/bin:/usr/sbin
```

This change affects only the current shell. To make it stick, modify PATH in a bash configuration file, as explained in "Tailoring Shell Behavior" on page 40. Then log out and log back in, or run the configuration file by hand in each open shell window. For example:

```
→ . $HOME/.bashrc          If you modified $HOME/.bashrc
```

Aliases

The alias command defines a convenient shorthand for another command. For example, this alias:

```
→ alias ll='ls -lG'
```

defines a new command ll that runs ls -lG:

```
→ ll
total 436
-rw-r--r--      1 smith        3584 Oct 11 14:59 file1
-rwxr-xr-x      1 smith          72 Aug  6 23:04 file2
⋮
```

Define aliases in your *~/.bashrc* file (see "Tailoring Shell Behavior" on page 40) to make them available to future shells.[8] To list all your aliases, run alias. If you want more flexibility than

---

8 Some setups use *~/.bash_aliases* for this purpose.

aliases provide, see "Programming with Shell Scripts" on page 293, run info bash, and read up on "shell functions."

Built-in Commands

Most Linux commands are programs in the Linux filesystem. Examples are wc and who, which usually live in the directory */usr/bin*. The shell locates and runs them using the PATH variable, as I described in "Search Path" on page 23. Some other commands, however, are built-in features of the shell, known as *built-in commands*. You've seen several built-in commands in this chapter, such as cd, alias, and export. To determine whether a command is in the filesystem, a built-in command, or an alias, run the type command:

```
→ type wc cd ll            Print the types of these commands
wc is /usr/bin/wc          A program in the filesystem
cd is a shell builtin      A built-in shell command
ll is aliased to `ls -lG'  An alias
```

Input, Output, and Redirection

Most Linux commands accept input and/or produce output. Keyboard input is called *standard input* or *stdin*. Output to your display is called *standard output* or *stdout*. Error messages are treated specially and printed on *standard error* or *stderr*, which also is usually your display, but Linux separates stderr from stdout internally.[9]

The shell can redirect standard input, standard output, and standard error to and from files. In other words, any command that reads from standard input can have its input come from a file instead with the shell's < operator:

```
→ command < infile
```

---

9 For example, you can capture standard output in a file and still have standard error messages appear on screen.

Likewise, any command that writes to standard output can write to a file instead:

→ **command** > **outfile**   *Create/overwrite outfile*
→ **command** >> **outfile**   *Append to outfile*

A command that writes to standard error can have its error output redirected to a file as well, leaving standard output unaffected:

→ **command** 2> **errorfile**

To redirect both standard output and standard error to files:

→ **command** > **outfile** 2> **errorfile**   *Separate files*
→ **command** &> **outfile**   *Single file (preferred)*
→ **command** >& **outfile**   *Single file (less common)*

Combined Commands

Bash lets you move beyond simple commands by combining multiple programs on a single command line.

Sequences of commands

To invoke several commands in sequence on a single command line, separate them with semicolons:

→ *command1* ; *command2* ; *command3*

To run a sequence of commands as before, but stop execution if any of them fails, separate them with && ("and") symbols:

→ *command1* && *command2* && *command3*

To run a sequence of commands, stopping execution as soon as one succeeds, separate them with || ("or") symbols:

→ *command1* || *command2* || *command3*

Pipes

You can redirect the standard output of one command to be the standard input of another, using the shell's pipe (|) operator.

(On US keyboards, find this symbol just above the Enter key.) For example, this command:

```
→ who | sort
```

sends the output of who into the sort command, printing an alphabetically sorted list of logged-in users. Multiple pipes work too. Let's sort the output of who again, extract the first column of information (using awk), and display the results one page at a time (using less):

```
→ who | sort | awk '{print $1}' | less
```

Command substitution

If you surround a command with backquotes ("backticks"), the shell removes the command and substitutes the command's output.

```
→ date +%Y                    Print the current year
2024
→ echo This year is `date +%Y`
This year is 2024
```

A dollar sign and parentheses are equivalent to backquotes:

```
→ echo This year is $(date +%Y)
This year is 2024
```

but are superior because they can be nested:

```
→ echo Next year is $(expr $(date +%Y) + 1)
Next year is 2025
```

Process substitution

Some programs don't work well with pipes because they don't read from standard input, only from disk files. An example is the diff command that compares two files line by line and prints their differences. *Process substitution* is a way to force a command like *diff* to read from standard input. It runs a command and lets its output "masquerade" as a file, which programs like *diff* will happily accept. With the process

---

substitution operator, `<()`, you can compare the output of two commands instead of two disk files.

Suppose you have a directory full of JPEG and text files in pairs:

```
→ ls jpegexample
file1.jpg   file2.jpg   file3.jpg   ...
file1.txt   file2.txt   file3.txt   ...
```

and you want to confirm that every JPEG file has a corresponding text file and vice versa. Ordinarily, you might create two temporary files, one containing the JPEG filenames and the other containing the text filenames, remove the file extensions with cut, and compare the two temporary files with `diff`:

```
→ cd jpegexample
→ ls *.jpg | cut -d. -f1 > /tmp/jpegs
→ ls *.txt | cut -d. -f1 > /tmp/texts
→ diff /tmp/jpegs /tmp/texts
5a6
> file6          No file6.jpg was found
8d8
< file9          No file9.txt was found
```

Process substitution performs the same task with a single command and no temporary files:

```
→ diff <(ls *.jpg|cut -d. -f1) <(ls *.txt|cut -d. -f1)
```

Each `<()` operator stands in for a filename on the command line, as if that "file" contained the output of ls and cut.

Preventing Evaluation

The shell evaluates every character of a command. To prevent evaluation, use quoting or escaping.

Quoting

Normally, the shell treats whitespace as a separator for strings on the command line. To make a string that *contains* whitespace (e.g., a filename with a space in it), surround it with single or double quotes, and the shell treats it as a unit. Single quotes treat their contents literally, while double quotes permit variables and other shell constructs to be evaluated:

```
→ echo 'The variable HOME has value $HOME'
The variable HOME has value $HOME
→ echo "The variable HOME has value $HOME"
The variable HOME has value /home/smith
```

Escaping

If a character has special meaning to the shell but you want it used literally (e.g., * as a literal asterisk rather than a file pattern), precede the character with the backslash "\" character. This is called *escaping* the special character:

```
→ echo a*                          A file pattern
aardvark  adamantium  apple
→ echo a\*                         A literal asterisk
a*
→ echo "I live in $HOME"           Print a variable value
I live in /home/smith
→ echo "I live in \$HOME"          Print a literal dollar sign
I live in $HOME
```

You can also escape control characters (tabs, newlines, ^D, etc.) to have them used literally on the command line, if you precede them with ^V. This is particularly useful for tab characters, which the shell would otherwise use for filename completion (see "Filename Completion" on page 31).

```
→ echo "There is a tab between here^V    and here"
There is a tab between here        and here
```

Command-line Editing

Bash lets you edit the command line you're working on, using keystrokes inspired by the text editors Emacs and Vim (see "Creating and Editing Files" on page 60). To enable command-line editing with Emacs keys, run this command (and place it in a bash configuration file to make it permanent):

```
→ set -o emacs
```

For vi (or Vim) keys:

```
→ set -o vi
```

Emacs keystroke	Vim keystroke (after ESC)	Meaning
^P or up arrow	k or up arrow	Go to previous command
^N or down arrow	j or down arrow	Go to next command
^R		Search for a previous command interactively
^F or right arrow	l or right arrow	Go forward one character
^B or left arrow	h or left arrow	Go backward one character
^A	0	Go to beginning of line
^E	$	Go to end of line
^D	x	Delete next character
^U	^U	Delete to beginning of line

Command History

A shell can recall previous commands and re-execute them, a feature called *command history*. Try these useful history-related commands and expressions:

Command	Meaning
history	Print your history
history *N*	Print the most recent *N* commands in your history
history -c	Clear (delete) your history
!!	Represents your previous command. To re-run it: → !! <Enter>
!*N*	Represents command number *N* in your history
!-*N*	Represents the command you entered *N* commands ago

Command	Meaning
!$	Represents the last argument from the previous command. Great for checking that files are present before running a destructive command like rm:

```
→ ls z*
zebra.txt  zipfile.zip  zookeeper
→ rm !$        Same as "rm z*"
```

!*	Represents all arguments from the previous command:

```
→ ls myfile emptyfile hugefile
emptyfile  hugefile  myfile
→ wc !*
     18      211     1168 myfile
      0        0        0 emptyfile
 333563  2737540 18577839 hugefile
 333581  2737751 18579007 total
```

Filename Completion

In the middle of typing a filename, press the Tab key and the shell automatically completes the filename for you. If several filenames match what you've entered so far, the shell beeps, indicating the match is ambiguous. Immediately press Tab a second time and the shell presents the alternatives. Try this:

```
→ cd /usr/bin
→ ls un<Tab><Tab>
```

The shell displays all files in */usr/bin* that begin with *un*, such as *uniq* and *unzip*. Enter a few more characters to disambiguate your choice and press Tab again.

Shell Job Control

jobs	List your jobs.
&	Placed after a command, runs it in the background.
^Z	Keystroke to suspend the current (foreground) job.

`suspend`	Suspend a shell.
`fg`	Unsuspend a job: bring it into the foreground.
`bg`	Make a suspended job run in the background.
`disown`	Forget a job.

All Linux shells have *job control*: the ability to run commands in the background (multitasking behind the scenes) and foreground (the active process at your shell prompt). A *job* is simply the shell's unit of work. When you run a command interactively, your current shell tracks it as a job. When the command completes, the associated job disappears. Jobs are at a higher level than Linux processes; the Linux OS knows nothing about them. They are merely constructs of the shell. Here is some important vocabulary about job control:

Foreground job
> In a shell, a running job that occupies the shell prompt so you cannot run another command

Background job
> In a shell, a running job that doesn't occupy the prompt, so you can run other commands in the same shell

Suspend
> To stop a foreground job temporarily

Resume
> To cause a suspended job to start running in the foreground again

Disown
> To tell the shell to stop tracking the job; the underlying processes continue to run

The built-in command jobs lists the jobs running in your current shell by number and name:

```
→ jobs
[1]-  Running        emacs myfile &     A background job
[2]+  Stopped        ssh example.com    A suspended job
```

The integer on the left is the job number, and the plus sign identifies the default job affected by the fg (foreground) and bg (background) commands.

&

Placed at the end of a command line, the ampersand causes the given command to run as a background job:

```
→ emacs myfile &
[2] 28090
```

The shell's response includes the job number (2) and the process ID of the command (28090).

---

^Z

Typing ^Z in a shell, while a job runs in the foreground, suspends that job. It simply stops running, but its state is remembered:

```
→ sleep 10                    Waits for 10 seconds
^Z
[1]+  Stopped    sleep 10
→
```

Now you're ready to run `bg` to put the `sleep` command into the background, or `fg` to resume it in the foreground. You could also leave it suspended and run other commands.

suspend

The built-in `suspend` command pauses the current shell if possible, as if you'd applied `^Z` to the shell itself. For instance, if you create a superuser shell with `sudo` and want to return to your original shell, `suspend` pauses the superuser shell:

```
→ whoami
smith
→ sudo bash                    Run a superuser shell
[sudo] password: xxxxxxxx
# whoami
root
# suspend                      Suspend the superuser shell
[1]+  Stopped      sudo bash
→ whoami                       Back to the original shell
smith
```

bg

bg [%*job*]

The built-in command `bg` sends a suspended job to run in the background. With no arguments, `bg` operates on the most recently suspended job. To specify a particular job (shown by the `jobs` command), supply the job number or name preceded by a percent sign:

```
→ bg %2          Send job 2 to the background
→ bg %cat        Send job beginning with "cat" to the background
```

Some types of interactive jobs cannot remain in the background—for instance, if they are waiting for input. If you try, the shell suspends the job and displays:

```
[2]+  Stopped        command line here
```

Now resume the job (with fg) and continue.

---

fg

```
fg [%job]
```

The built-in command fg brings a suspended or backgrounded job into the foreground. With no arguments, it selects a job, usually the most recently suspended or backgrounded one. To specify a particular job (as shown by the jobs command), supply the job number or name preceded by a percent sign:

→ **fg %2**   *Bring job 2 into the foreground*
→ **fg %cat**   *Bring job beginning with "cat" into the foreground*

---

disown

```
disown [-ar] [-h] [%job]
```

The built-in command disown tells your current shell to "forget" a job. The Linux processes behind the job keep running—you just can't control them anymore with bg, fg, jobs, and other job-related commands. This is useful for long jobs that you don't need to interact with, or jobs that should keep running after your shell exits. See also nohup in "Controlling Processes" on page 151.

→ **disown %2**   *Forget job #2*
→ **disown %cat**   *Forget job beginning with "cat"*
→ **disown -h %2**   *Mark job #2 to keep running after shell exits*
→ **disown -r**   *Forget all running jobs*
→ **disown -a**   *Forget all jobs*

Running Multiple Shells at Once

Job control can manage several commands at once, but only one can run in the foreground at a time. More powerfully, you can run multiple shells at once, each with a foreground command and any number of background commands.

If your Linux computer runs a window system such as KDE or GNOME, you can easily run many shells at the same time by opening multiple shell windows (see "Launching a Shell" on page 3). In addition, certain shell window programs, such as KDE's konsole, can open multiple tabs within a single window, each one running a shell.

Even without a window system—say, over an SSH network connection—you can manage multiple shells at once. The tmux command simulates multiple shell windows in an ordinary ASCII terminal. Using special keystrokes, you can switch from one virtual window to another at will. (Another such program is screen, but tmux is better maintained and easier to configure.) To begin a session with tmux, run:

```
→ tmux
```

A new shell launches with an extra status bar at the bottom of the terminal, indicating that you're running one virtual window. The tmux program provides 10 such windows by default, labeled from 0 to 9, that you may switch between. Each window runs a single shell at first, but you can split a window into multiple "panes" to display multiple shells at once. Try these keystrokes to get the hang of tmux:

1. In the current tmux window, run ls.

2. Press ^Bc (Ctrl-B, then press c). tmux displays a fresh shell prompt in a second virtual window. The status bar changes to show two virtual windows numbered 0 and 1.

3. In this second window, run a different command (say, df).

4. Press ^Bn and you'll switch back to window 0, where your output from ls is now visible again.

5. Press ^Bn a few more times to toggle between the two virtual windows.

6. Press ^B% to split the current window into two panes side by side.

7. Press ^B" to split the current pane into two, vertically. You're now viewing three shells in separate panes.

Most aspects of tmux are configurable in the file *~/.tmux_conf*, even the choice of ^B as the prefix key. Here are common keystroke commands:

Keystroke	Meaning
^B?	Display online help. Press "q" to quit.
^Bc	Create a window.
^B0, ^B1 ... ^B9	Switch to window 0 through 9, respectively.
^Bn	Switch to the next window, numerically.
^Bp	Switch to the previous window, numerically.
^Bl	Switch to the most recently used window.
^B%	Split into two panes side by side.
^B"	Split into two panes top and bottom.
^Bo	Jump to the next pane.
^B left arrow	Jump to the pane to the left.
^B right arrow	Jump to the pane to the right.
^B up arrow	Jump to the pane above.
^B down arrow	Jump to the pane below.
^Bq	Display pane numbers for reference.
^Bx	Kill the current pane.
^B^B	Send a true Ctrl-B to your shell, ignored by tmux.
^B^Z	Suspend tmux.

Keystroke	Meaning
^Bd	"Detach" from a tmux session and return to your original shell. To return to tmux, run tmux attach.
^D	Terminate a shell in a window or pane. This is the ordinary "end of file" keystroke, explained in "Terminating a Shell" on page 40, which closes any shell.
^B:kill-session	Kill all windows and terminate tmux.

A few notes about running tmux:

- If shells within tmux are missing your aliases, variables, or other shell settings, that's because tmux runs a login shell that does not source your *.bashrc* initialization file. It only sources your startup file (*.bash_profile*, *.bash_login*, or *.profile*). To correct this issue, append these lines to your startup file:

  ```
  # Source my .bashrc file
  if [ -f ~/.bashrc ]; then
    . ~/.bashrc
  fi
  ```

- If you run a text editor, tmux captures all Ctrl-B keystrokes, even those intended as editing commands. Press ^B^B to send a true Ctrl-B to your editor.

- Don't run tmux locally on a graphical desktop; run multiple shell windows instead. It's easier and avoids a problem: if you've configured your shell to run commands on logout (for example, in the file *~/.bash_logout*), tmux's shells will run those commands on exit, even though you haven't logged out of the desktop. This may have unwanted effects on your desktop login session.

Killing a Command in Progress

To kill a foreground command immediately, press ^C. Here I kill the cat command as it prints a huge file:

```
→ cat hugefile
Lorem ipsum dolor sit amet, consectetur adipiscing
odio. Praesent libero. Sed cursus ante dapibus diam.
quis sem at nibh elementum blah blah blah ^C
→
```

To kill a background command, bring it into the foreground with fg and then press ^C:

```
→ sleep 50 &
[1] 12752
→ jobs
[1]-  Running          sleep 50 &
→ fg %1
sleep 50
^C
→
```

or run the kill command described in "Controlling Processes" on page 151. The keystroke ^C is a shell feature. It has no effect on programs that "catch" ^C and do not terminate, like text editors and GUI applications. Use kill for those.

Surviving a Kill

Killing a command with ^C may leave your shell in an odd or unresponsive state, because the killed program could not close itself properly. A common symptom is not displaying the keystrokes you type. To fix the shell, follow these steps:

1. Press ^J to get a shell prompt. This keystroke may work even if pressing Enter does not.

2. Type the command reset (even if the letters don't appear while you type) and press ^J to run it. Your shell should return to normal.

Terminating a Shell

To terminate a shell, either run the exit command:

```
→ exit
```

or press ^D on a line by itself. The keystroke ^D sends an "end of file" signal to any program reading from standard input. This includes the shell itself.

Tailoring Shell Behavior

Several files in your home directory control the behavior of bash shells. The startup files *.bash_profile*, *.bash_login*, and *.profile* contain commands that run each time you log in. (Choose just one startup file and stick with it. I recommend *.bash_profile* because some other shells also use *.profile*.) Commands in the initialization file *.bashrc* run every time you launch an interactive shell, and commands in *.bash_logout* run each time you log out. All these files can set variables, run programs, print silly messages, or whatever you like. Other Linux shells use other configuration files as shown in Table 1-1.

Table 1-1. Shell configuration files in $HOME and when they are read

Shell	On login	By other interactive shells	On logout
bash	.bash_profile, .bash_login, .profile	.bashrc	.bash_logout
dash	.profile		
fish	.config/fish/config.fish	.config/fish/config.fish	
ksh[a]	.profile, .kshrc	.kshrc	
tcsh	.tcshrc, .cshrc, .login	.tcshrc, .cshrc	
zsh[a]	.zshenv, .zprofile, .zlogin	.zshenv, .zshrc	.zlogout

[a] To override these file paths with environment variables, see the manpage.

Other shell configuration files live in */etc* for system-wide control; see the respective *manual page*, or manpage, for each shell. All these configuration files are examples of *shell scripts*:

executable files that contain shell commands. I cover this feature in more detail in "Programming with Shell Scripts" on page 293.

Getting Help

If you need more information than this book provides, here are several ways to get more help:

Run the man *command*
> The man command displays documentation for a given program. For example, to learn about counting words in a file with wc, run:
>
> → **man wc**
>
> To search for manual pages (manpages) by keyword for a particular topic, use the -k option followed by the keyword:
>
> → **man -k database**
>
> If the list of manpages is longer than the screen, pipe it to less to display it in pages (press q to quit):
>
> → **man -k database | less**

Run the info *command*
> The info command is an extended, hypertext help system covering many Linux commands.
>
> → **info ls**
>
> While info runs, some useful keystrokes are:
>
> - To get help, press h
> - To quit, press q
> - To page forward and backward, use the space bar and Backspace key, respectively
> - To jump between hyperlinks, press Tab
> - To follow a hyperlink, press Enter

If info has no documentation on a given command, it displays the command's manpage. For a listing of available documentation, type info by itself. To learn how to navigate the info system, run info info.

Use the --help option (if any)
Many Linux commands respond to the option --help or -h by printing a short help message. Try:

→ **wc --help**

If the output is longer than the screen, pipe it into less:

→ **wc --help | less**

Examine the directory /usr/share/doc
This directory contains supporting documents for programs, usually organized by name and version. For example, files for the editor Emacs version 28 are likely found (depending on distro) in */usr/share/doc/emacs28*.

Distro-specific websites
Most Linux distros have an official site with documentation, discussion forums, and other resources. Search the web for your distro name (e.g., "Ubuntu") to find its website. The Arch Linux wiki (*https://oreil.ly/98iAg*) is particularly informative regardless of your distro.

Linux help sites
Ask Linux questions at *cunix.stakexchange.org*, *linuxquestions.org*, *itsfoss.community*, and *nixcraft.com*.

Web search
To decipher a Linux error message, paste it into a search engine, verbatim, optionally surrounded by double quotes.

This concludes my basic overview of Linux and the shell. Now let's turn to the specifics of Linux commands. The rest of the book lists and describes the most useful commands to work with files, processes, users, networking, multimedia, and more.

CHAPTER 2

File Commands

Basic File Operations

ls   List files in a directory.

cp   Copy a file.

mv   Move (rename) a file.

rm   Remove (delete) a file.

ln   Create links (alternative names) to a file.

One of the first things you'll do on a Linux system is manipulate files: copying, renaming, deleting, and so forth.

---

ls   stdin   **stdout**   -file   **-- opt**   **--help**   **--version**

ls [*options*] [*files*]

The ls command (pronounced as it is spelled, *ell ess*) lists attributes of files and directories. You can list files in the current directory:

→ **ls**

---

in given directories:

```
→ ls dir1 dir2 dir3
```

or individually:

```
→ ls myfile myfile2 myfile3
```

TIP

If `ls` behaves differently than you expect, your distro may have defined an alias for `ls` (see "Aliases" on page 24). Check for an alias by running this command:

```
→ alias ls
alias ls='/bin/ls -FHN'        Yes, there's an alias
```

To run the original command rather than the alias, prepend a backslash (`\ls`). To remove the alias, run `unalias ls`. Then look in your shell configuration files for the alias definition (see "Tailoring Shell Behavior" on page 40) and remove it. If you don't see a definition, either add the command `unalias ls` or define a new alias that works the way you want, like `alias ls="/bin/ls"`.

The most important `ls` options are `-a`, `-l`, and `-d`. By default, `ls` hides files whose names begin with a dot, as explained in the sidebar "Dot Files" on page 20. The `-a` option displays all files. Depending on your account settings, `ls` will list dot files at the beginning (sorting based on the dot) or mix them into the listing (sorting based on the character after the dot).

```
→ ls
myfile    myfile2
→ ls -a
.hidden_file    myfile    myfile2
```

The -l option produces a long listing:

```
→ ls -l myfile
-rw-r--r--  1 smith users  1168 Oct 28 2015 myfile
```

that includes, from left to right: the file's permissions (-rw-r--r--), number of hard links (1), owner (smith), group (users), size (1168 bytes), last modification date (Oct 28 2015) and name. See "File Permissions" on page 17 for more information on these attributes.

The -d option lists information about a directory itself, rather than descending into the directory to list its files:

```
→ ls -ld dir1
drwxr-xr-x  1 smith users  4096 Oct 29 2015 dir1
```

Useful options

- -a   List all files, including those whose names begin with a dot.

- -l   Long listing, including file attributes. Add the -h option (human-readable) to print file sizes in KB, MB, and GB, instead of bytes.

- -h   In a long listing, print file sizes in friendly KB, MB, and other human-readable terms, instead of bytes.

- -G   In a long listing, don't print the group ownership of the file.

- -F   Decorate filenames with meaningful symbols, indicating their types. Appends "/" to directories, "*" to executables, "@" to symbolic links, "|" to named pipes, and "=" to sockets. These are just visual indicators, not part of the filenames!

- -S   Sort files by their size.

- -t   Sort files by the time they were last modified.

- -r   Reverse the sorted order.

- -R   If listing a directory, list its contents recursively.

- -d   If listing a directory, do not list its contents, just the directory itself.

cp stdin stdout · file -- opt --help --version

```
cp [options] source_file destination_file
cp [options] (files | directories) directory
```

The cp command copies one file to another:

→ **cp myfile anotherfile**

or copies multiple files into a directory (say *mydir*):

→ **cp myfile myfile2 myfile3 mydir**

Use the -a or -r option to copy directories recursively, including all subdirectories and their contents. For more sophisticated copying, see rsync in "Backups and Remote Storage" on page 223.

Useful options

- -p Copy not only the file contents, but also the file's permissions, timestamps, and, if you have sufficient permission to do so, its owner and group. (Otherwise, you own the copies, the timestamp is now, and permissions are set by applying your umask to the original permissions.)

- -a Copy a directory hierarchy recursively, preserving all file attributes and links.

- -r Copy a directory hierarchy recursively. This option does not preserve the files' attributes such as permissions and timestamps. It does preserve symbolic links.

- -i Interactive mode. Ask before overwriting destination files.

- -f Force the copy. If a destination file exists, overwrite it unconditionally.

---

mv stdin stdout · file -- opt --help --version

```
mv [options] sources target
```

The mv (move) command renames a file:

→ **mv somefile yetanotherfile**

---

or moves files and directories into a destination directory:

→ `mv myfile myfile2 dir1 dir2 destination_directory`

Useful options

-i   Interactive mode. Ask before overwriting destination files.

-f   Force the move. If a destination file exists, overwrite it unconditionally.

---

rm
stdin   stdout   -file   --opt   --help   --version

`rm [options] files | directories`

The rm (remove) command deletes files:

→ `rm deleteme deleteme2`

or recursively deletes directories:

→ `rm -r dir1 dir2`

WARNING

Use rm -r with caution. It can quickly destroy large numbers of files, especially when combined with -f to suppress prompts and ignore errors.

Use **sudo** rm -r with *extreme* caution. It can destroy your whole operating system.

Useful options

-i   Interactive mode. Ask for confirmation before deleting each file.

-f   Force the deletion, ignoring any errors or warnings.

-r   Recursively remove a directory and its contents.

ln [*options*] *source target*

The ln command creates a *link*, which lets a file live at more
than one location in the filesystem at once. There are two kinds
of links, illustrated in Figure 2-1. A *hard link* is a second name
for the same physical file on disk. In tech jargon, both refer to
the same *inode*, a data structure that locates a file's content on
disk. The following command creates a hard link, *myhardlink*,
to the file named *myfile*:

→ **ln myfile myhardlink**

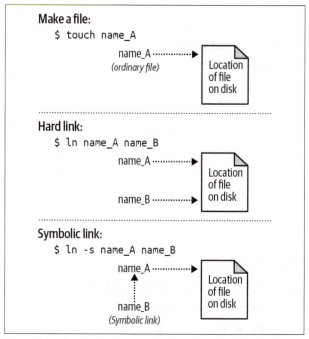

*Figure 2-1. A hard link points to a file's data. A symbolic link points to
a file's path.*

A *symbolic link* (also called a *symlink* or *soft link*) is a pointer to the *path* (not the inode) of another file or directory. If you're familiar with Windows shortcuts or macOS aliases that point to another file or folder, they are much like symbolic links. To create a symbolic link, add the -s option:

```
→ ln -s myfile mysoftlink
```

Hard and symbolic links have important differences:

- If you rename or delete the original file, a hard link is not affected: it still points to the same *data* that the original file did. A symbolic link breaks, however. It still points to the original file's *path*, which no longer exists. The symbolic link is now "dangling," and if you use it in a command, you'll probably receive a "file not found" error.

- Hard links can exist only on the same device as the original file because inodes have meaning only on a single device. Symbolic links can point to files on other devices because they refer to file paths, not file data.

- Symbolic links can point to directories, whereas hard links generally cannot. (On some filesystems, the superuser can create a hard link to a directory with the -d option.)

Useful options

-s   Make a symbolic link instead of a hard link.

-i   Interactive mode. Ask before overwriting target files.

-f   Force the link. If the target already exists, overwrite it unconditionally.

-b   Create a backup. If the target already exists, rename it by appending a tilde, then create the link.

-d   Create a hard link to a directory if possible (superusers only).

To find out where a symbolic link points, run either of the following commands, which show that the link *examplelink* points to the file *myfile*:

```
→ readlink examplelink
myfile
→ ls -l examplelink
lrwxrwxrwx 1 smith    ...    examplelink -> myfile
```

Symbolic links can point to other symbolic links. To follow an entire chain of links to discover where they point in the end, use readlink -f.

Directory Operations

cd	Change your current directory.
pwd	Print the name of your current directory.
basename	Print the final part of a file path, usually the filename.
dirname	Print a file path without its final part.
mkdir	Create (make) a directory.
rmdir	Delete (remove) an empty directory.
rm -r	Delete a nonempty directory and its contents.

I discussed the directory structure of Linux in "The Filesystem" on page 9. Let's cover commands that create, modify, delete, and manipulate directories within that structure.

---

cd   stdin **stdout** - file -- opt **--help** --version

cd [*directory*]

The cd (change directory) command sets the current directory of your shell:

```
→ cd /usr/games
```

With no directory supplied, cd defaults to your home directory:

```
→ cd
```

If the supplied directory is a dash (-), cd returns to the previous directory it visited in the current shell and prints its path.

```
→ cd /etc        Start in /etc
→ cd /bin        Go somewhere else
→ cd -           Return to /etc
/etc
```

---

pwd

pwd

The pwd command ("print working directory") prints the absolute path of your current directory:

```
→ pwd
/users/smith/linuxpocketguide
```

---

basename

basename *path* [*extension*]

The basename command prints the final part of a file path. The path doesn't have to exist in your filesystem.

```
→ basename /users/smith/finances/money.txt
money.txt
→ basename any/string/you/want        Arbitrary string
want
```

If you provide an optional extension, it is stripped from the result:

```
→ basename /users/smith/finances/money.txt .txt
money
```

---

dirname

dirname *path*

The dirname command prints a file path with its final part removed:

```
→ dirname /users/smith/mydir
/users/smith
```

dirname does not change your shell's current directory. It manipulates and prints a string, just like basename does.

---

mkdir

mkdir [*options*] *directories*

mkdir creates one or more directories:

```
→ mkdir directory1 directory2 directory3
```

Useful options

-p   Given a directory path (not just a simple directory name), create any necessary parent directories automatically. The command:

```
→ mkdir -p one/two/three
```

creates directories *one* and *one/two* and *one/two/three* if they don't already exist.

-m *mode*   Create the directory with the given permissions:

```
→ mkdir -m 0755 publicdir
```

By default, your shell's umask controls the permissions. See the chmod command in "Properties of Files" on page 65, and "File Permissions" on page 17.

rmdir

rmdir [*options*] *directories*

The rmdir (remove directory) command deletes one or more empty directories given as arguments:

→ **mkdir /tmp/junk**   *create a directory*
→ **rmdir /tmp/junk**   *delete it*

Useful options

-p   If you supply a directory path (not just a simple directory name), delete not only the given directory, but the specified parent directories automatically, all of which must be empty. So rmdir -p one/two/three deletes not only *one/two/three*, but also *one/two* and *one*.

To delete a nonempty directory and its contents, carefully run rm -r *directory*. Use rm -ri to delete interactively, or rm -rf to annihilate whole trees without error messages or confirmation.

Viewing Files

cat   View files in their entirety.

less   View text files one page at a time.

nl   View text files with their lines numbered.

head   View the first lines of a text file.

tail   View the last lines of a text file.

strings Display text that's embedded in a binary file.

od   View data in octal (base 8) or other formats.

Some files contain readable text, and others contain binary data. Let's see how to display their contents in basic ways.

cat
stdin   stdout   - file   -- opt   --help   --version

cat [options] [files]

The simplest viewer is cat, which just prints its files to standard output, concatenating them (hence the name):

→ **cat myfile**	*Print one file on screen*
→ **cat myfile***	*Print many files*
→ **cat myfile*	wc**	*Concatenate files and pipe the text to wc*

If a file contains more lines than your screen can display, use less to present the output one screenful at a time.

Useful options

- -T Print tabs as ^I.

- -E Print newlines as $.

- -v Print other nonprinting characters in a human-readable format.

- -n Prepend line numbers to every line. (The nl command is more powerful.)

- -b Prepend line numbers to nonblank lines.

- -s Squeeze consecutive blank lines into a single blank line.

less
stdin   stdout   - file   -- opt   --help   --version

less [options] [files]

Use less to view text one "page" at a time (i.e., one window or screenful at a time):

→ **less myfile**

It's great for long text files or as the final command in a shell pipeline with lengthy output:

→ *command1* | *command2* | *command3* | *command4* | **less**

While running `less`, press `h` for a help message describing all its features. Here are some useful keystrokes for paging:

Keystroke	Meaning
h, H	View a help page.
Space bar, f, ^V, ^F	Move forward one screenful.
Enter	Move forward one line.
b, ^B, ESC-v	Move backward one screenful.
/	Search mode. Type a regular expression and press Enter, and `less` locates the first matching line.
?	Same as /, but search backward.
n	Next match: Repeat your most recent search forward.
N	Repeat your most recent search backward.
v	Edit the current file with your default text editor (the value of environment variable VISUAL, or if not defined, EDITOR, or if not defined, the system default editor).
<, g	Jump to beginning of file.
>, G	Jump to end of file.
:n	Jump to next file.
:p	Jump to previous file.

`less` has a mind-boggling number of features; I'm presenting only the most common. (For instance, in many distros, `less` can display the contents of a ZIP file: try `less zipfile.zip`.) The manpage is recommended reading.

Useful options

-c   Clear the screen before displaying the next page. This avoids scrolling and may be more comfortable on the eyes.

-m   Print a verbose prompt showing the percentage of the file displayed so far.

-N   Display line numbers.

- -r Display control characters literally; normally `less` converts them to a human-readable format.

- -s Squeeze multiple, adjacent blank lines into a single blank line.

- -S Truncate long lines to the width of the screen, instead of wrapping.

---

nl   stdin   stdout   - file   -- opt   --help   --version

nl [*options*] [*files*]

nl prints files on standard output with line numbers:

→ **nl poem**
```
    1  Once upon a time, there was
    2  a little operating system named
    3  Linux, which everybody loved.
```

nl provides more control over numbering than cat -n.

Useful options

-b [a|t|n|p*R*]	Number all lines (a), nonblank lines (t), no lines (n), or only lines that contain regular expression *R*. (Default=a)
-v *N*	Begin numbering with integer *N*. (Default=1)
-i *N*	Increment by N for each line. For example, print odd numbers only (-i2) or even numbers only (-v2 -i2). (Default=1)
-n [ln|rn|rz]	Format numbers as left-justified (ln), right-justified (rn), or right-justified with leading zeros (rz). (Default=ln)
-w *N*	Force the width of the number to be *N* columns. (Default=6)
-s *S*	Insert string *S* between the line number and the text. (Default=Tab)

---

head

head [*options*] [*files*]

The head command prints the first 10 lines of a file, which is great to preview the contents:

```
→ head myfile
→ head myfile* | less    Previewing multiple files
```

It's also helpful for previewing output from a pipeline. List the 10 most recently modified files in the current directory:

```
→ ls -lta | head
```

Useful options

- -n *N* Print the first *N* lines instead of 10.

- *-N*   Same as -n *N*.

- -c *N* Print the first *N* bytes of the file.

- -q   Quiet mode: when processing more than one file, don't print a banner (containing the filename) above each file.

---

tail

tail [*options*] [*files*]

The tail command prints the last 10 lines of a file:

```
→ tail myfile
→ nl myfile | tail    See line numbers too
```

The ultra-useful -f option causes tail to watch a file actively while another program writes to it, displaying new lines as they are written. This is invaluable for watching a Linux logfile that's in active use:

```
→ tail -f /var/log/syslog    Or another logfile
```

Useful options

-n *N*   Print the last *N* lines of the file instead of 10.

-*N*   Same as -n *N*.

-n +*N*   Print from line *N* to the end of the file.

+*N*   Same as -n +*N*.

-c *N*   Print the last *N* bytes of the file.

-f   Keep the file open, and whenever lines are appended to the file, print
            them. Add the --retry option if the file doesn't exist yet. ^C to quit.

-q   Quiet mode: when processing more than one file, don't print a banner
            (containing the filename) above each file.

---

strings

stdin   stdout   - file   -- opt   --help   --version

```
strings [options] [files]
```

Binary files, such as compiled programs, usually contain some
readable text, like version information, authors' names, and file
paths. The strings command extracts that text:

```
→ strings /bin/bash
/lib64/ld-linux-x86-64.so.2
@(#)Bash version 5.1.16(1) release GNU
comparison operator expected, found '%s'
⋮
```

Combine strings -n and grep to make your exploring more
efficient. Let's look for email addresses:

```
→ strings -n 10 /bin/bash | grep @
bash-maintainers@gnu.org
```

Useful options

-n *length*   Display only strings with length greater than *length* (default=4).

-f   Prepend the filename to each line of output.

---

od [*options*] [*files*]

To view binary files, consider od (octal dump) for the job. It displays their data in ASCII, octal, decimal, hexadecimal, or floating point, in various sizes (byte, short, long). For example, this command:

```
→ od -w8 /usr/bin/who
0000000 042577 043114 000402 000001
0000010 000000 000000 000000 000000
0000020 000003 000076 000001 000000
⋮
```

displays the bytes in binary file */usr/bin/who* in octal, eight bytes per line. The leftmost column is the file offset of each row, again in octal.

If your binary file also contains text, consider the -tc option, which displays character data. For example, binary executables like who contain the string "ELF" at the beginning:

```
→ od -tc -w8 /usr/bin/who | head -3
0000000 177   E   L   F 002 001 001  \0
0000010  \0  \0  \0  \0  \0  \0  \0  \0
0000020 003  \0   >  \0 001  \0  \0  \0
```

Useful options

-N *B*	Display the first *B* bytes of each file, specified in decimal, hexadecimal (by prepending 0x), 512-byte blocks (append b), KB (append k), or MB (append m).
-j *B*	Begin the output at byte *B* + 1 of each file; acceptable formats are the same as for the -N option. (Default=0)
-w [*B*]	Display *B* bytes per line; acceptable formats are the same as in the -N option. Using -w by itself is equivalent to -w32. (Default=16)

`-s [B]`	Group each row of bytes into sequences of B bytes, separated by whitespace; acceptable formats are the same as in the `-N` option. Using `-s` by itself is equivalent to `-s3`. (Default=2)
`-A (d|o|x|n)`	Display file offsets in the leftmost column, in decimal (d), octal (o), hexadecimal (x), or not at all (n). (Default=o)
`-t(a|c)[z]`	Display output in a character format, with nonalphanumeric characters printed as escape sequences (c) or by name (a).
`-t(d|o|u|x)[z]`	Display output in an integer format: octal (o), signed decimal (d), unsigned decimal (u), hexadecimal (x).

Appending z to the `-t` option displays the printable characters on each line in a column on the right side.

Creating and Editing Files

`nano`	A simple text editor found in virtually all Linux distros.
`emacs`	A powerful text editor from Free Software Foundation.
`vim`	A powerful text editor based on Unix `vi`.

To get far with Linux, you must become proficient with one of its text editors. The three major ones are nano, Emacs, and Vim. Teaching these editors fully is beyond the scope of this book, but they all have online tutorials, and common operations are in Table 2-1. To edit a file, run any of these commands:

```
→ nano myfile
→ emacs myfile
→ vim myfile
```

If *myfile* doesn't exist, the editor creates it.

Linux also has fine programs to edit Microsoft Office documents: LibreOffice (all documents), AbiWord (Word only), and Gnumeric (Excel only). Some are probably included in your distro, or you can find them easily through web search.

Creating a File Quickly

Text editors create files on request, but you can also create an empty file (for later editing) at the command line with the touch command:

→ **touch newfile**   *Create newfile if it doesn't exist*

or use output redirection (see "Input, Output, and Redirection" on page 25) to create a file with or without contents:[1]

→ **echo -n > newfile2**   *Echo the empty string to a file*
→ **> newfile3**   *Redirect nothing to a file*
→ **ls > newfile4**   *Redirect a command's output to a file*

Your Default Editor

Various Linux programs run an editor when necessary. For example, your email program may invoke an editor to compose a new message, and less invokes an editor if you press "v." Usually the default editor is nano or Vim. But what if you want a different default editor? Set the environment variables VISUAL and EDITOR to your choice, for example:

→ **EDITOR=emacs**
→ **VISUAL=emacs**
→ **export EDITOR VISUAL**

Both variables are necessary because different programs check one variable or the other. Set them in a bash configuration file if you want your choices to stick. Any program can be your default editor if it accepts a filename as an argument.

Regardless of how you set these variables, I recommend learning basic commands for all three editors in case another program unexpectedly invokes one on a critical file.

---

1 The -n option of echo suppresses the newline character.

nano

nano [*options*] [*files*]

Nano is a basic text editor included in most Linux distros. To invoke nano to edit a file, run:

→ **nano myfile**

To list all nano keystrokes and commands, press ^G.

Nano commands generally involve holding down the control key and typing a letter, such as ^o to save and ^x to quit. Nano helpfully displays common commands at the bottom of its edit window, though some of the vocabulary is a little obscure. (For example, nano uses the term "WriteOut" to mean "save file.") Other commands involve the *meta* key, which is usually the Escape key or the Alt key. Nano's own documentation notates the meta key as M- (as in M-F to mean "use the meta key and type F"), so this book does the same. For basic keystrokes, see Table 2-1. For more documentation, visit *https://oreil.ly/p_Pvk*.

emacs

emacs [*options*] [*files*]

Emacs is an extremely powerful editing environment with thousands of commands, including a rich programming language to define your own editing features. To invoke Emacs to edit a file, run:

→ **emacs myfile**

On a graphical desktop, Emacs opens a window. To launch Emacs without opening a window, run:

→ **emacs -nw myfile**

Once Emacs is running, invoke its built-in tutorial by pressing ^h t.

Most Emacs keystroke commands involve the control key (like ^F) or the *meta* key, which is usually the Escape key or the Alt key. Emacs's own documentation notates the meta key as M- (as in M-F to mean "use the meta key and type F"), so this book does the same. For basic keystrokes, see Table 2-1.

---

vim

stdin   stdout   - file   -- opt   --help   --version

vim [*options*] [*files*]

Vim is an enhanced version of the old standard Unix editor vi. To invoke Vim to edit a file, run:

→ **vim myfile**

Normally, Vim runs in an existing shell or shell window. To launch Vim on a graphical desktop in a new window, run:

→ **gvim myfile**

To run the Vim tutorial from the shell, run:

→ **vimtutor**

Vim operates in two modes, *insert* and *command*, and you switch between them while editing. *Insert mode* is for entering text in the usual manner, while *command mode* is for deleting text, copy/paste, and other operations. For basic keystrokes in command mode, see Table 2-1.

Table 2-1. Basic keystrokes in text editors

Task	Emacs	Nano	Vim
Type text	Just type	Just type	Switch to insert mode if necessary, by typing i, then type any text
Save and quit	^x^s then ^x^c	^o then ^x	:wq

Task	Emacs	Nano	Vim
Quit without saving	^x^c then respond "no" when asked to save buffers	^x then respond "no" when asked to save	:q!
Save	^x^s	^o	:w
Save As	^x^w	^o, then type a filename	:w *filename*
Undo	^/ or ^x u	M-u	u
Suspend editor (not in X)	^z	^z	^z
Switch to insert mode	*(N/A)*	*(N/A)*	i
Switch to command mode	*(N/A)*	*(N/A)*	ESC
Switch to command-line mode	M-x	*(N/A)*	:
Abort command in progress	^g	^c	ESC
Move forward	^f or right arrow	^f or right arrow	l or right arrow
Move backward	^b or left arrow	^b or left arrow	h or left arrow
Move up	^p or up arrow	^p or up arrow	k or up arrow
Move down	^n or down arrow	^n or down arrow	j or down arrow
Move to next word	M-f	^SPACE	w
Move to previous word	M-b	M-SPACE	b
Move to beginning of line	^a	^a	0
Move to end of line	^e	^e	$
Move down one screen	^v	^v	^f
Move up one screen	M-v	^y	^b

Task	Emacs	Nano	Vim
Move to beginning of document	M-<	M-\	gg
Move to end of document	M->	M-/	G
Delete next character	^d	^d	x
Delete previous character	BACKSPACE	BACKSPACE	X
Delete next word	M-d	(N/A)	de
Delete previous word	M-BACKSPACE	(N/A)	db
Delete current line	^a^k	^k	dd
Delete to end of line	^k	^k[a]	D
Define region (type this keystroke to mark the beginning of the region, then move the cursor to the end of the desired region)	^SPACE	^^ (Ctrl caret)	v
Cut region	^w	^k	d
Copy region	M-w	M-^	y
Paste region	^y	^u	p
Get help	^h	^g	:help
View the manual	^h i	^g	:help

[a] Only if nano's cut-to-end feature is enabled by pressing M-k.

Properties of Files

stat	Display attributes of files and directories.
wc	Count bytes, words, and lines in a file.
du	Measure disk usage of files and directories.
file	Identify (guess) the type of a file.

`mimetype`	Identify (guess) the MIME type of a file.
`touch`	Change timestamps of files and directories.
`chown`	Change owner of files and directories.
`chgrp`	Change group ownership of files and directories.
`chmod`	Change protection mode of files and directories.
`umask`	Set a default mode for new files and directories.
`lsattr`	List extended attributes of files and directories.
`chattr`	Change extended attributes of files and directories.

When examining a Linux file, keep in mind that the contents are only half the story. Every file and directory also has attributes that describe its owner, size, access permissions, and other information. The `ls -l` command (see "Basic File Operations" on page 43) displays some of these attributes. Other commands let you view and change these and other attributes.

---

stat

stdin   **stdout**   - file   **-- opt**   **--help**   **--version**

stat [*options*] *files*

The `stat` command lists the attributes of files (by default) or filesystems (`-f` option):

```
→ stat myfile
  File: 'myfile'
  Size: 1168           Blocks: 8
  IO Block: 4096  regular file
Device: 811h/2065d     Inode: 37224455   Links: 1
Access: (0644/-rw-r--r--)  Uid: ( 600/lisa)
  Gid: ( 620/users)
Access: 2015-11-07 11:15:14.766013415 -0500
Modify: 2015-11-07 11:15:14.722012802 -0500
Change: 2015-11-07 11:15:14.722012802 -0500
 Birth: -
```

Output includes the filename, size in bytes (1168), size in blocks (8), file type (Regular File), permissions in octal (0644), permissions in the format of "ls -l" (-rw-r--r--), owner's user ID (600), owner's name (lisa), owner's group ID (620), owner's group name (users), device type (811 in hexadecimal, 2065 in decimal), inode number (37224455), number of hard links (1), and timestamps of the file's most recent access,[2] modification, status change (of file permissions or other metadata), and file creation ("birth") if available. The output of stat -f for a filesystem is:

```
→ stat -f myfile
  File: "myfile"
    ID: f02ed2bb86590cc6 Namelen: 255
Type: ext2/ext3
Block size: 4096        Fundamental block size: 4096
Blocks: Total: 185788077  Free: 108262724
  Available: 98819461
Inodes: Total: 47202304   Free: 46442864
```

The output includes the filename (*myfile*), filesystem ID (f02ed2bb86590cc6), maximum allowable length of a filename for that filesystem (255 bytes), filesystem type (ext), block size for the filesystem (4096), the counts of total, free, and available blocks in the filesystem (185788077, 108262724, and 98819461, respectively), and the counts of total and free inodes (47202304 and 46442864, respectively).

The -t option presents the same data but on a single line, without headings. This format is handy for parsing the output:

```
→ stat -t myfile
myfile 1168 8 81a4 600 620 811 37224455 1 0 0
  1446912914 1446912914 1446912914 0 4096
→ size=$(stat -t myfile | cut -d' ' -f2)
→ echo $size                          The second value
1168
```

---

2 Most filesystems no longer update access time, or they do so only
  when the file is modified.

Useful options

- -L   Follow symbolic links and report on the file they point to.

- -f   Report on the filesystem containing the file, not the file itself.

- -t   Terse mode: print information on a single line.

---

wc   stdin   stdout   - file   -- opt   --help   --version

wc [*options*] [*files*]

The wc (word count) command prints a count of bytes, words, and lines in (presumably) a text file:

```
→ wc myfile
  18   211 1168 myfile
```

This file has 18 lines, 211 whitespace-delimited words, and 1168 bytes.

Useful options

- -l   Print the line count only.

- -w   Print the word count only.

- -c   Print the byte count only.

- -L   Locate the longest line in each file and print its length in bytes.

---

du   stdin   stdout   - file   -- opt   --help   --version

du [*options*] [*files* | *directories*]

The du (disk usage) command measures the disk space occupied by files or directories. By default, it measures the current directory and all its subdirectories, printing totals in blocks for each, with a grand total at the end:

```
→ du
36    ./Mail
340   ./Files/mine
40    ./Files/bob
416   ./Files
216   ./PC
2404  .                    Grand total, in blocks
```

It can also measure the size of files:

```
→ du myfile emptyfile hugefile
4       myfile
0       emptyfile
18144   hugefile
```

Useful options

- -b   Measure usage in bytes.

- -k   Measure usage in KB.

- -m   Measure usage in MB.

- -B N Display sizes in blocks that you define, where 1 block = *N* bytes. (Default = 1024)

- -h   Print in human-readable units. For example, if two directories are of size
- -H   1 gigabyte or 25 KB, respectively, du -h prints 1G and 25K. The -h option uses powers of 1024, whereas -H uses powers of 1000.

- -L   Follow symbolic links and measure the files they point to.

- -c   Print a total in the last line. This is the default behavior when measuring a directory, but to measure individual files, provide -c if you want a total.

- -s   Print total sizes only, not the sizes of subdirectories.

file

stdin **stdout** - file -- opt --help --version

file [*options*] *files*

The file command reports the type of a file. The output is an educated guess based on the file content and other factors:

```
→ file /etc/hosts /usr/bin/who letter.docx
/etc/hosts:    ASCII text
/usr/bin/who:  ELF 64-bit LSB executable ...
letter.docx:   Microsoft Word 2007+
```

Useful options

-b   Omit filenames (left column of output).

-i   Print MIME types for the file, such as "text/plain" or "audio/mpeg", instead of the usual output.

-f *name_file*   Read filenames, one per line, from the given *name_file*, and report their types. Afterward, process filenames on the command line as usual.

-L   Follow symbolic links, reporting the type of the destination file instead of the link.

-z   If a file is compressed (see "Compressing, Packaging, and Encrypting" on page 108), examine the uncompressed contents to decide the file type, instead of reporting "compressed data."

mimetype

stdin **stdout** - file -- opt --help --version

mimetype [*options*] *files*

The mimetype command, like the file -i command, prints the file's MIME type such as text/plain or application/pdf, but has more options.

```
→ mimetype photo.jpg sample.pdf zipfile.zip
photo.jpg:  image/jpeg
```

```
sample.pdf: application/pdf
zipfile.zip: application/zip
```

Useful options

-b	Omit the leading filenames from the output.
-d	Print longer descriptions like "JPEG image" or "ZIP archive."
-l *language*	When provided with the -d option, print the file types in the given language. Language codes are the standard two-letter ones such as de for German and pt for Portuguese.
-L	For symbolic links, print the type of the linked file instead of the link itself (type inode/symlink).

---

touch

stdin   stdout   - file   -- opt   --help   --version

```
touch [options] files
```

The touch command changes two timestamps associated with a file: its modification time (when the file's data was last changed) and its access time (when the file was last read). To set both timestamps to the present moment, run:

→ **touch myfile**

You can set these timestamps to arbitrary values, for example:

→ **touch -d "November 18 1975" myfile**

If a given file doesn't exist, touch creates an empty file of that name (see "Creating a File Quickly" on page 61).

Useful options

-a	Change the access time only.
-m	Change the modification time only.
-c	If the file doesn't exist, don't create it (normally, touch creates it).

-d *timestamp*	Set the file's timestamp(s). Many formats are acceptable, from "12/28/2001 3pm" to "28-May" (the current year is assumed, and a time of midnight) to "next tuesday 13:59" to "0" (midnight today). Experiment and check your work with stat. Full documentation is available from info touch.
-t *timestamp*	Set a file's timestamp precisely with the format [[*CC*]*YY*]*MMDDhhmm*[.*ss*]. *CC* is the two-digit century, *YY* is the two-digit year, *MM* is the two-digit month, *DD* is the two-digit day, *hh* is the two-digit hour, *mm* is the two-digit minute, and *ss* is the two-digit second. For example, -t 20230812150047 means August 12, 2023 at 15:00:47.

chown

stdin   stdout   - file   -- opt   --help   --version

```
chown [options] user_spec files
```

The chown command changes the owner of files and directories. It requires superuser privileges in most cases. To make user "smith" the owner of several files and a directory, run:

→ **sudo chown smith myfile myfile2 mydir**

The *user_spec* parameter may be any of these possibilities:

user_spec	Meaning
smith	An existing username
1001	A numeric user ID
smith:party	An existing username and group name, separated by a colon
1001:234	Numeric user and group IDs, separated by a colon
:party	An existing group name, preceded by a colon
--reference=*file*	The same user and group values as file *file*

Useful options

--dereference	Follow symbolic links and operate on the files they point to.
-R	Recursively change the owner for a whole directory tree.

---

chgrp

stdin   stdout   -file   **-- opt**   **--help**   **--version**

chgrp [*options*] *group_spec files*

The chgrp (change group) command sets the group ownership of files and directories:

→ **chgrp users myfile myfile2 mydir**

The *group_spec* parameter may be any of these possibilities:

- A group name or numeric group ID
- --reference=*file*, to set the same group ownership as another given file

See "Group Management" on page 174 for more information on groups.

Useful options

--dereference	Follow symbolic links and operate on the files they point to.
-R	Recursively change the group for a whole directory tree.

---

chmod

stdin   stdout   -file   **-- opt**   **--help**   **--version**

chmod [*options*] *permissions files*

The chmod (change mode) command protects files and directories from unauthorized users on the same system, by setting access permissions. Typical permissions are read, write, and execute, and they may be limited to the file owner, the file's group owner, and/or all other users. The permissions argument can take three different forms:

- `--reference=`*file*, to set the same permissions as another given file.
- An octal (base 8) number, up to four digits long, that specifies the file's *absolute* permissions in bits, as in Figure 2-2. The leftmost digit is special (described later) and the second, third, and fourth represent the file's owner, the file's group, and all users, respectively.
- One or more symbolic strings specifying *absolute or relative* permissions (i.e., relative to the file's current permissions). For example, `a+r` makes a file readable by all users.

The most common octal permissions are:

→ `chmod 600 myfile`	*Private file for you*
→ `chmod 644 myfile`	*Everyone can read; you can write*
→ `chmod 700 mydir`	*Private directory for you*
→ `chmod 755 mydir`	*Everyone can read; you can write*

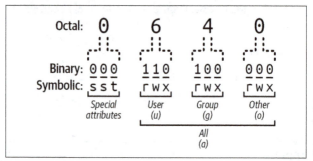

Figure 2-2. File permission bits explained

In the third, symbolic form, each string consists of three parts:

Scope (optional)
    u for user, g for group, o for other users not in the group, a for all users. The default is a.

Command
> + to add permissions; – to remove permissions; or = to set absolute permissions, ignoring existing ones.

Permissions
> r for read, w for write/modify, x for execute (for directories, this is permission to cd into the directory), X for conditional execute (explained later), u to duplicate the user permissions, g to duplicate the group permissions, o to duplicate the "other users" permissions, s for setuid (set user ID) or setgid (set group ID), and t for the sticky bit.

For example, ug+rw would add read and write permission for the user and the group, a-x (or just -x) would remove execute permission for everyone, and o=r would directly set the "other users" permissions to read-only. Combine these strings by separating them with commas, such as ug+rw,a-x,o=r.

Conditional execute permission (X) means the same as x, except that it succeeds only if the file is already executable or is a directory. It's convenient during large-scale chmod operations to change the execute bit on directories but not on files.

Setuid and setgid, when applied to executable files (programs and scripts), have a powerful effect. Suppose you have an executable file *F* owned by user "smith" and the group "friends." If file *F* has setuid enabled, then anyone who runs *F* "becomes" user "smith," with all their rights and privileges, for the duration of the program. Likewise, if *F* has setgid enabled, anyone who executes *F* becomes a member of the "friends" group for the duration of the program. As you might imagine, setuid and setgid can impact system security, so don't use them unless you *really* know what you're doing. One misplaced chmod +s can leave your system vulnerable to attack.

The sticky bit, most commonly used for */tmp* directories, controls removal of files in that directory. Normally, if you have write permission in a directory, you can delete or move files within it, even if you don't have this access to the files themselves. Inside a directory with the sticky bit set, you need write permission on a file to delete or move it.

Useful option

-R   Recursively change permissions for a whole directory tree.

---

umask

stdin   **stdout**   - file   **-- opt**   **--help**   **--version**

umask [*options*] [*mask*]

The umask command sets or displays your shell's default mode for creating files and directories—whether they are readable, writable, and/or executable by yourself, your group, and the world. Print your mask:

```
→ umask                    Octal output
0002
→ umask -S                 Symbolic output
u=rwx,g=rwx,o=rx
```

Running umask is a technical operation that requires binary and octal math, but let's begin with simple recipes. Use mask 0022 to give yourself full privileges on new files and directories, and give all other users read and execute privileges only:

```
→ umask 0022
→ touch newfile && mkdir newdir
→ ls -ldG newfile newdir
-rw-r--r--  1 smith      0 Nov 11 12:25 newfile
drwxr-xr-x  2 smith   4096 Nov 11 12:25 newdir
```

Use mask 0002 to give yourself and your default group full privileges, and read/execute to others:

```
→ umask 0002
→ touch newfile2 && mkdir newdir2
→ ls -ldG newfile2 newdir2
-rw-rw-r--  1 smith      0 Nov 11 12:26 newfile2
drwxrwxr-x  2 smith   4096 Nov 11 12:26 newdir2
```

Use mask 0077 to give yourself full privileges with nothing for anyone else:

```
→ umask 0077
→ touch newfile3 && mkdir newdir3
→ ls -ldG newfile3 newdir3
-rw------- 1 smith    0 Nov 11 12:27 newfile3
drwx------ 2 smith 4096 Nov 11 12:27 newdir3
```

Now, the technical explanation. A umask is a binary (base two) value, though it is commonly presented in octal (base eight). It defines your default protection mode by combining with the octal value 0666 for files and 0777 for directories, using the binary operation NOT AND. For example, the umask 0002 yields a default file mode of 0664:

```
0666 NOT AND 0002
= 000110110110 NOT AND 000000000010
= 000110110110     AND 111111111101
= 000110110100
= 0664
```

Similarly for directories, 0002 NOT AND 0777 yields a default mode of 0775.

---

lsattr

stdin **stdout** · file **-- opt** **--help** --version

```
lsattr [options] [files | directories]
```

Linux files have additional attributes beyond their access permissions. For files on an "ext" filesystem (ext3, ext4, etc.), list these extended attributes with the lsattr (list attribute) command and change them with chattr. For example, this file is immutable (i) and undeletable (u):

```
→ lsattr attrfile
-u--i--- attrfile
```

With no files specified, lsattr prints the attributes of all files in the current directory. Attributes include:

Attribute	Meaning
a	Append-only: appends are permitted to this file, but it cannot otherwise be edited. Root only.
A	Accesses not timestamped: accesses to this file don't update its access timestamp (atime).
c	Compressed: data is transparently compressed on writes and uncompressed on reads.
d	Don't dump: tell the dump program to ignore this file when making backups (see "Backups and Remote Storage" on page 223).
i	Immutable: file cannot be changed or deleted (root only).
j	Journaled data (on filesystems that support journaling).
s	Secure deletion: if deleted, this file's data is overwritten with zeros.
S	Synchronous update: changes are written to disk immediately.
u	Undeletable: file cannot be deleted.

Before using this command seriously, read the manpage for details, especially for filesystem-specific issues.

Useful options

- -R   Recursively process directories.

- -a   List all files, including those whose names begin with a dot.

- -d   If listing a directory, do not list its contents, just the directory itself.

---

chattr   stdin   stdout   -file   **--opt**   **--help**   --version

chattr [*options*] [+|-|=]*attributes* [*files*]

The chattr command changes a file's extended attributes, the same ones that lsattr displays. With syntax similar to the chmod command, chattr adds (+) or removes (-) attributes

---

relatively, or sets attributes absolutely (=). For example, to prevent a file from deletion even by the superuser, run:

```
→ sudo chattr +i attrfile          Set attribute i
→ sudo rm attrfile                 Deletion fails
rm: cannot remove 'attrfile': Operation not permitted
→ sudo chattr -i attrfile          Unset attribute i
→ sudo rm attrfile                 Deletion succeeds
```

Not all attributes are supported by all filesystems. Read the manpage for details, especially for filesystem-specific issues.

Useful option

-R Recursively process directories.

Locating Files

find   Locate files in a directory hierarchy.

xargs   Turn a list of files into a list of commands (and much more).

locate   Create an index of files, and search the index for a string.

which   Locate executables in your search path (command).

type   Locate executables in your search path (bash built-in).

whereis   Locate executables, documentation, and source files.

A typical Linux system has hundreds of thousands of files, so Linux includes commands for locating files of interest. find is a brute-force command that slogs file by file through a directory tree to locate a target. locate is much faster, searching through a prebuilt index that you generate as needed. (Some distros generate the index nightly by default.)

To locate programs in the filesystem, the which and type commands check all directories in your shell search path. type is built into the bash shell, while which is a program (normally */usr/bin/which*); type is faster and can detect shell aliases.[3] In contrast, whereis examines a known set of directories, rather than your search path.

---

find

stdin **stdout** - file -- opt **--help** **--version**

find [*directories*] [*expression*]

The find command searches one or more directories (and their subdirectories recursively) for files matching certain criteria. It is very powerful, with over 50 options, and unfortunately, a rather unusual syntax. Here are some simple examples that search the entire filesystem from the current directory (indicated by a dot):

Find a particular file named *myfile*:

```
→ find . -type f -name myfile -print
./myfile
```

Print filenames beginning with "myfile". Notice that the asterisk is escaped so the shell ignores it for pattern-matching and it's passed literally to the find command:

```
→ find . -type f -name myfile\* -print
./myfile3
./myfile
./myfile2
```

Print all directory names:

```
→ find . -type d -print
.
./jpegexample
./dir2
./mydir
./mydir/dir
⋮
```

---

3 The tcsh shell performs some trickery to make which detect aliases.

Useful options

-name *pattern* -path *pattern* -lname *pattern*	Given a file pattern, find files with names (-name), pathnames (-path), or symbolic link targets (-lname) that match the pattern, which may include shell pattern-matching characters *, ?, and [ ]. (You must escape the patterns, however, so they are ignored by the shell and passed literally to find.) Paths are relative to the directory tree being searched.
-iname *pattern* -ipath *pattern* -ilname *pattern*	These options are the same as -name, -path, and -lname, respectively, but are case-insensitive.
-regex *regexp*	The path (relative to the directory tree being searched) must match the given regular expression.
-type *t*	Locate only files of type *t*. Types include plain files (f), directories (d), symbolic links (l), block devices (b), character devices (c), named pipes (p), and sockets (s).
-atime *N* -ctime *N* -mtime *N*	File was last accessed (-atime), last modified (-mtime), or had a status change (-ctime) exactly *N**24 hours ago. Use +*N* for "greater than *N*," or -*N* for "less than *N*."
-amin *N* -cmin *N* -mmin *N*	File was last accessed (-amin), last modified (-mmin), or had a status change (-cmin) exactly *N* minutes ago. Use +*N* for "greater than *N*," or -*N* for "less than *N*."
-anewer *other_file* -cnewer *other_file* -newer *other_file*	File was accessed (-anewer), modified (-newer), or had a status change (-cnewer) more recently than *other_file*.
-maxdepth *N* -mindepth *N*	Consider files at least (-mindepth) or at most (-maxdepth) *N* levels deep in the directory tree being searched.
-follow	Dereference symbolic links.

-depth	Proceed using depth-first search: completely search a directory's contents (recursively) before operating on the directory itself.
-xdev	Limit the search to a single filesystem (i.e., don't cross device boundaries).
-size N [bckw]	Consider files of size N, which can be given in blocks (b), one-byte characters (c), KB (k), or two-byte words (w). Use +N for "greater than N," or -N for "less than N."
-empty	File has zero size and is a regular file or directory.
-user name	File is owned by the given user.
-group name	File is owned by the given group.
-perm mode	File has permissions equal to mode. Use -mode to check that all of the given bits are set, or +mode to check that any of the given bits are set.

These operators group or negate parts of the expression:

expression1 -a *expression2*

    And. (This is the default if two expressions appear side by side, so the -a is optional.)

expression1 -o *expression2*

    Or.

! *expression*

-not *expression*

    Negate the expression.

(*expression*)

    Precedence markers, just like in algebra class. Evaluate what's in parentheses first. You may need to escape these from the shell with "\".

expression1 , *expression2*

    Comma operator. Evaluate both expressions and return the value of the second one.

Once you've specified the search criteria, tell find to perform the following actions on files that match the criteria:

-print	Print the path to the file, relative to the search directory.
-printf *string*	Print the given string, which may have substitutions applied to it in the manner of the C library function, printf(). See the manpage for the full list of outputs.
-print0	Like -print, but instead of separating each line of output with a newline character, use a null (ASCII 0) character. Use when piping the output of find to another command and your list of filenames may contain space characters. Of course, the receiving command must be capable of reading and parsing these null-separated lines (e.g., xargs -0).
-exec *cmd* ;	Invoke the given shell command, *cmd*. Escape any shell metacharacters, including the required, final semicolon, so they aren't evaluated by the shell. Also, the symbol { } (quoted or escaped) represents the path to the file found. A full example is: find . -exec ls '{}' \;
-ok *cmd* ;	Same as -exec, but also prompts the user before each invocation of the command *cmd*.
-ls	Perform the command ls -dils on each file.
-delete	Perform the command rm on each file. (Careful!!)

---

xargs

stdin   stdout   - file   -- opt   **--help**   **--version**

xargs [*options*] [*command*]

xargs is one of the oddest yet most powerful commands available to the shell. It reads lines of text from standard input, turns them into commands, and executes them. This might not sound exciting, but xargs has some unique uses, particularly for processing a list of files you've located. Suppose you made a file named *important* that lists important files, one per line:

```
→ cat important
/home/jsmith/mail/love-letters
/usr/local/lib/critical_stuff
/etc/passwordfile2
⋮
```

xargs can process each of these files easily with other Linux commands. For instance, the following command runs the ls -l command on all the listed files:

```
→ cat important | xargs ls -l
```

Similarly, view the files with less:

```
→ cat important | xargs less
```

and even delete them with rm:

```
→ cat important | xargs rm -f      Careful! Destroys files!!
```

In each case, xargs reads the file *important* and produces and runs new Linux commands. The power begins when the input list doesn't come from a file, but from another command writing to standard output. In particular, the find command, which prints a list of files, makes a great partner for xargs. For example, to search your current directory hierarchy for files containing the word "tomato":

```
→ find . -type f -print | xargs grep -l tomato
./findfile1
./findfile2
→ cat findfile1 findfile2
This file contains the word tomato.          From findfile1
Another file containing the word tomato.     From findfile2
```

This command has a problem, however: it mishandles file-names that contain whitespace, like *my stuff*. If find prints this filename, then xargs constructs an incorrect grep command:

```
grep -l tomato my stuff
```

which tells grep to process two files named *my* and *stuff*. Oops! Now imagine that the command you passed to xargs was rm instead of grep. Then rm would delete the wrong files! To avoid this problem, tell find and xargs to use a non-whitespace character between lines of text—specifically, a null character (ASCII value zero). The command find -print0 ends lines with nulls, and xargs -0 expects nulls.

```
→ find . -type f -print0 | xargs -0 grep -l tomato
```

I've barely scratched the surface of the xargs command, so I hope you'll continue experimenting. (For safety, tell xargs to invoke harmless commands like grep and ls for your tests, rather than destructive commands like rm.)

Useful options

-n k Feed k lines of input to each executed command. The common -n1 guarantees that each execution processes only one line of input. Otherwise, xargs may pass multiple lines of input to a single command.

-0   Set the end-of-line character for input to be ASCII zero rather than whitespace, and treat all characters literally. Use this when the input comes from find -print0.

---

xargs versus Command Substitution

If you remember "Quoting" on page 28, you might realize that some xargs tricks can be accomplished with command substitution:

```
→ cat file_list | xargs ls -l       With xargs
→ ls -l $(cat file_list)            With $()
→ ls -l `cat file_list`             With backquotes
```

While these commands do similar things, the last two can fail if the output of cat becomes longer than the maximum length of a shell command line. The xargs solution reads unlimited text from standard input rather than the command line, so it's more scalable for large or risky operations.

---

locate

locate [*options*]

The locate command, with its partner updatedb, creates an index (database) of file locations that is quickly searchable.[4] If you plan to search for many files over time in a directory hierarchy that doesn't change much, locate is a good choice. To locate a single file or perform more complex processing of found files, use find.

Some distros automatically index the entire filesystem regularly (e.g., once a day), so you can simply run locate and it works. But if you ever need to create an index yourself of a directory and all its subdirectories (say, ~/*linuxpocketguide*), storing the index in /*tmp/myindex*, run:

→ **updatedb -l0 -U ~/linuxpocketguide -o /tmp/myindex**

(Note that -l0 is a lowercase L followed by a zero, not the number 10.) Then search for a string in the index, such as "myfile":

```
→ locate -d /tmp/myindex myfile
/home/dbarrett/linuxpocketguide/myfile
/home/dbarrett/linuxpocketguide/myfile2
/home/dbarrett/linuxpocketguide/myfile3
```

updatedb has an interesting, optional security feature. If you run it as root, you can create an index that displays only files that the user is permitted to see, based on file permissions. Simply add sudo and omit the -l0 option:

→ **sudo updatedb -U *directory* -o /tmp/myindex**

---

4 My locate command comes from a package called "plocate." Some systems have older packages called "mlocate" or "slocate" with slightly different usage. If you have slocate, simply run slocate instead of updatedb in my examples.

Indexing options for updatedb

-u   Create index from the root directory downward.

-U *directory* Create index from *directory* downward.

-l (0|1) Turn security off (0) or on (1). The default is 1.

-e *paths* Exclude paths from the index, separated by whitespace.

-o *outfile* Write the index to file *outfile*.

Search options for locate

-d *index* Indicate which index to use (in my example, */tmp/myindex*).

-i   Case-insensitive search.

-r *regexp* Search for filenames matching the given regular expression.

---

which   stdin **stdout** - file **-- opt** **--help** **--version**

which *file*

The which command locates an executable file in your shell's search path. To locate the who command, run:

→ **which who**
/usr/bin/who

You can even find the which program itself:

→ **which which**
/usr/bin/which

If several programs in your search path have the same name (e.g., */bin/who* and */usr/bin/who*), which reports only the first.

type

type [*options*] *commands*

The type command, like which, locates an executable file in
your shell's search path:

```
→ type grep who
grep is /bin/grep
who is /usr/bin/who
```

type also identifies shell features, such as aliases and built-in
commands:

```
→ type which type rm if
which is /usr/bin/which
type is a shell builtin
rm is aliased to `/bin/rm -i'
if is a shell keyword
```

As a built-in command, type is faster than which, but it's available only in certain shells such as bash.

---

whereis

whereis [*options*] *files*

The whereis command attempts to locate the given files by
searching a hardcoded list of directories. It can find executables, documentation, and source code. whereis is somewhat
quirky because its internal list of directories might not include
the ones you need.

```
→ whereis nano
nano: /usr/bin/nano /usr/share/nano ...
```

Useful options

-b	List only binary executables (-b), manpages (-m), or source code
-m	files (-s).
-s	

-B dirs... -f	Search for binary executables (-B), manpages (-M), or source
-M dirs... -f	code files (-S) in the given directories. You must follow the
-S dirs... -f	directory list with the -f option before listing the files you seek.

Manipulating Text in Files

grep	Find lines in a file that match a regular expression.
cut	Extract columns from a file.
paste	Append text from multiple files in columns.
column	Organize text into columns.
tr	Translate characters into other characters.
expand	Convert from tabs to spaces.
unexpand	Convert from spaces to tabs.
sort	Sort lines of text by various criteria.
uniq	Locate identical lines in a file.
tac	Reverse a file line by line.
shuf	Randomly shuffle the lines of a file (permutation).
tee	Write to a file *and* print on standard output, simultaneously.

Perhaps Linux's greatest strength is text manipulation: massaging a text file (or standard input) into a desired form by applying transformations, often in a pipeline. Many commands do this, but here I focus on some of the most important tools for transforming text.

grep

grep [*options*] *pattern* [*files*]

The grep command is one of the most consistently useful and powerful in the Linux arsenal. Its premise is simple: given one or more files, print all of their lines that match a regular expression. For example, if a file *randomlines* contains these lines:

```
The quick brown fox jumped over the lazy dogs!
My very eager mother just served us nine pancakes.
Film at eleven.
```

and you print all lines containing "pancake", you get:

```
→ grep pancake randomlines
My very eager mother just served us nine pancakes.
```

Now use a regular expression to print lines ending in an exclamation point:

```
→ grep '!$' randomlines
The quick brown fox jumped over the lazy dogs!
```

grep can use two different types of regular expressions: *basic* and *extended*. They are equally powerful, just different, and their syntax is in Table 2-2. Regular expressions are well worth your time to learn. Other powerful Linux programs use them too, such as sed and perl.

Useful options

-v	Print only lines that *do not* match the regular expression.
-l	Print only the *names* of files that contain matching lines, not the lines themselves.
-L	Print only the names of files that *do not* contain matching lines.
-c	Print only a count of matching lines.
-o	Print only the strings that match, not whole lines.
-n	In front of each line of matching output, print its original line number. (Or print the byte offset with -b.)

`-i`	Case-insensitive match.
`-w`	Match only complete words.
`-x`	Match only complete lines. Overrides `-w`.
`-a`	Treat all files as plain text. Sometimes `grep` mistakenly treats a file as binary and won't print matching lines.
`-A` *N*	After each matching line, print the next *N* lines from its file.
`-B` *N*	Before each matching line, print the previous *N* lines from its file.
`-C` *N*	Same as `-A` *N* `-B` *N*: print *N* lines (from the original file) above *and* below each matching line.
`--color`	Highlight the matched text in color, for better readability.
`-r`	Recursively search all files in a directory and its subdirectories.
`-R`	Same as `-r` but also follow all symbolic links.
`-E`	Use extended regular expressions. See `egrep`.
`-F`	Use lists of fixed strings instead of regular expressions. See `fgrep`.

Table 2-2. Regular expressions for grep (plain) and egrep (extended)

Plain	Extended	Meaning
`.`	`.`	Any single character.
`[...]`	`[...]`	Any single character in this list.
`[^...]`	`[^...]`	Any single character *not* in this list.
`(...)`	`(...)`	Grouping.
`|`	`|`	Or.
`^`	`^`	Beginning of a line.
`$`	`$`	End of a line.
`\<`	`\<`	Beginning of a word.
`\>`	`\>`	End of a word.
`[:alnum:]`	`[:alnum:]`	Any alphanumeric character.

Plain	Extended	Meaning
[:alpha:]	[:alpha:]	Any alphabetic character.
[:cntrl:]	[:cntrl:]	Any control character.
[:digit:]	[:digit:]	Any digit.
[:graph:]	[:graph:]	Any graphic character.
[:lower:]	[:lower:]	Any lowercase letter.
[:print:]	[:print:]	Any printable character.
[:punct:]	[:punct:]	Any punctuation mark.
[:space:]	[:space:]	Any whitespace character.
[:upper:]	[:upper:]	Any uppercase letter.
[:xdigit:]	[:xdigit:]	Any hexadecimal digit.
*	*	Zero or more repetitions of a regular expression.
\+	+	One or more repetitions of a regular expression.
\?	?	Zero or one occurrence of a regular expression.
\{n\}	{n}	Exactly n repetitions of a regular expression.
\{n,\}	{n,}	n or more repetitions of a regular expression.
\{n,m\}	{n,m}	Between n and m (inclusive) repetitions of a regular expression, $n<m$.
\c	\c	The literal character c. For example, use * to match an asterisk or \\ to match a backslash. Alternatively, use square brackets, like [*] or [\].

egrep

egrep [*options*] *pattern* [*files*]

The egrep command runs grep with the option -E pre-applied to use extended regular expressions.[5]

---

fgrep

fgrep [*options*] [*fixed_strings*] [*files*]

The fgrep command runs grep with the option -F pre-applied.[5] Instead of regular expressions, fgrep accepts a list of fixed strings separated by newlines. For example, if you have a dictionary file full of strings, one per line:

```
→ cat my_dictionary_file
aardvark
abbey
abbot
⋮
```

fgrep searches for those strings in one or more input files:

```
→ fgrep -f my_dictionary_file story
a little aardvark who went to
visit the abbot at the abbey.
```

fgrep is convenient when searching for nonalphanumeric characters like * and { because they are treated literally as fixed strings, not as regular expression characters.

It's easiest for fgrep to read the fixed strings from a file, but it can also take them from the command line if you quote them. To search for the strings "one", "two", and "three" in a file, run:

---

5 The commands egrep and fgrep are officially deprecated, but they are so deeply embedded in a million Linux shell scripts that I don't think they'll ever go away.

```
→ fgrep 'one          Note that I am typing newline characters
two
three' myfile
```

grep and End-of-Line Characters

When you match the end of a line ($) with grep, text files created on Microsoft Windows or macOS systems may produce odd results. Each OS has a different standard for ending a line. On Linux, each line in a text file ends with a newline character (ASCII 10). On Windows, text lines end with a carriage return (ASCII 13) followed by a newline character. And on macOS, a text file might end its lines with newlines alone or carriage returns alone. If grep doesn't match the ends of lines properly, check for non-Linux end-of-line characters with `cat -v`, which displays carriage returns as ^M:

```
→ cat -v dosfile.txt
Uh-oh! This file seems to end its lines with^M
carriage returns before the newlines.^M
```

To remove the carriage returns, use the `tr -d` command:

```
→ tr -d '\r' < dosfile.txt > /tmp/linuxfile.txt
→ cat -v /tmp/linuxfile.txt
Uh-oh! This file seems to end its lines with
carriage returns before the newlines.
```

---

cut   stdin stdout -file --opt --help --version

```
cut -(b|c|f)range [options] [files]
```

The cut command extracts columns of text from files. A "column" is defined by character offsets (e.g., the 19th character of each line):

```
→ cut -c19 myfile
```

---

or by byte offsets (which are different from characters if your language has multibyte characters):

```
→ cut -b19 myfile
```

or by delimited fields (e.g., the fifth field in each line of a comma-delimited file, *data.csv*):

```
→ cat data.csv
one,two,three,four,five,six,seven
ONE,TWO,THREE,FOUR,FIVE,SIX,SEVEN
1,2,3,4,5,6,7
→ cut -f5 -d, data.csv
five
FIVE
5
```

You aren't limited to printing a single column: provide a range (3-16), a comma-separated sequence (3,4,5,6,8,16), or both (3,4,8-16). For ranges, if you omit the first number (-16), a 1 is assumed (1-16); if you omit the last number (5-), the final column is assumed.

Useful options

-d *C*	Use character *C* as the *input* delimiter character between fields for the -f option. By default it's a tab character.
--output-delimiter=*S*	Use string *S* as the *output* delimiter character between fields for -f. By default it's a tab character.
-s	Suppress lines that don't contain any delimiter characters at all. Otherwise they're printed unchanged.

paste

stdin   stdout   - file   -- opt   --help   --version

paste [*options*] [*files*]

The paste command is the opposite of cut: it treats several files as vertical columns and combines them on standard output:

```
→ cat letters
A
B
C
→ cat numbers
1
2
3
4
5
→ paste numbers letters
1   A
2   B
3   C
4
5
→ paste letters numbers
A   1
B   2
C   3
    4
    5
```

Useful options

-d *delimiters*   Print the given delimiter characters between columns; the default is a tab character. Provide a single character (-d:) to be used always, or a list of characters (-dxyz) to be applied in sequence on each line (the first delimiter is x, then y, then z, then x, then y, ...).

96 | Chapter 2: File Commands

| -s | Sideways: transpose the rows and columns of output: |

```
→ paste -s letters numbers
A    B    C
1    2    3    4    5
```

column

```
column [options] [files]
```

The column command reads lines of text and prints them in columns. By default, it creates as many columns as will fit in the width of your terminal, so the output may vary.

```
→ seq 1 18                          Print 18 numbers
1
2
3
⋮
18
→ seq 1 18 | column              Create columns vertically
1    4    7    10    13    16
2    5    8    11    14    17
3    6    9    12    15    18
→ seq 1 18 | column -x           Create columns horizontally
1    2    3    4    5    6
7    8    9    10    11    12
13    14    15    16    17    18
```

column can also convert existing columns into a nicely formatted table:

```
→ cat threes                    Original file
one two three                   Ragged columns
Do Re Mi
you and me
→ column -t threes              Format as a table with -t
one   two   three               Neat columns
Do    Re    Mi
you   and   me
```

```
→ column -t -N A,B,C threes          Add headings with -N
A     B     C
one   two   three
Do    Re    Mi
you   and   me
```

Useful options

-s C	Use character C as the input separator between columns.
-o C	Use character C as the output separator between columns.
-t	Format the output as a table.
-N headings	Add headings to a table (requires -t). Provide a comma-separated list.
--json	Print the output in JSON format (requires -t and -N).

---

tr   stdin stdout -file --opt **--help** **--version**

tr [options] charset1 [charset2]

The tr command performs some simple translations of one set of characters into another. For example, to capitalize everything in a file:

```
→ cat wonderfulfile
This is a very wonderful file.
→ cat wonderfulfile | tr a-z A-Z
THIS IS A VERY WONDERFUL FILE.
```

or to change all vowels into asterisks:

```
→ cat wonderfulfile | tr aeiouAEIOU '*'
Th*s *s * v*ry w*nd*rf*l f*l*.
```

or to delete all vowels:

```
→ cat wonderfulfile | tr -d aeiouAEIOU
Ths s  vry wndrfl fl.
```

Delete all carriage returns from a DOS text file so it's more compatible with Linux text utilities like grep:

→ **tr -d '\r' < dosfile.txt > linuxfile.txt**

tr translates the first character in *charset1* into the first character in *charset2*, the second into the second, the third into the third, and so on. If the length of *charset1* is N, only the first N characters in *charset2* are used. (If *charset1* is longer than *charset2*, see the -t option.)

Character sets can have the following forms:

Form	Meaning
ABDG	The sequence of characters A, B, D, G.
A-Z	The range of characters from A to Z.
[x*y]	y repetitions of the character x.
[:class:]	The character classes accepted by grep, such as [:alnum:] and [:digit:]. See Table 2-2.

tr also understands the escape characters "\a" (^G = alert by ringing bell), "\b" (^H = backspace), "\f" (^L = formfeed), "\n" (^J = newline), "\r" (^M = return), "\t" (^I = tab), and "\v" (^K = vertical tab) accepted by printf (see "Screen Output" on page 257), as well as the notation \nnn to mean the character with octal value nnn.

tr is great for quick and simple translations, but for more powerful jobs consider sed, awk, or a programming language such as perl.

Useful options

-d Delete the characters in *charset1* from the input.

-s Eliminate adjacent duplicates (found in *charset1*) from the input. For example, tr -s aeiouAEIOU would squeeze adjacent, duplicate vowels to be single vowels (*reeeeeeally* would become *really*).

-c Complement: operate on all characters *not* found in *charset1*.

-t If *charset1* is longer than *charset2*, make them the same length by truncating *charset1*. If -t is not present, the last character of *charset2* is (invisibly) repeated until *charset2* is the same length as *charset1*.

---

expand
stdin   stdout   - file   -- opt   --help   --version

expand [*options*] [*files*]

unexpand [*options*] [*files*]

The expand command converts tab characters to an equivalent-looking number of space characters, and unexpand does the opposite. By default, a tab stop occurs every eight spaces, but you can change this with options.

```
→ expand tabfile > spacefile
→ unexpand spacefile > tabfile
```

To check whether a file contains spaces or tabs, use the cat -T command, which displays tabs as ^I, or the od -c command, which displays tabs as \t.

Useful option

-t *N* Specify that one tab stop occurs every *N* spaces.

---

sort
stdin   stdout   - file   -- opt   --help   --version

sort [*options*] [*files*]

The sort command prints lines of text in alphabetical order, or sorted by some other rule you specify. All provided files are concatenated, and the result is sorted and printed:

```
→ cat threeletters
def
xyz
abc
```

```
→ sort threeletters
abc
def
xyz
```

Useful options

-f	Case-insensitive sorting.
-n	Sort numerically (i.e., 9 comes before 10) instead of alphabetically (10 comes before 9 because it begins with a "1" character).
-g	Another numerical sorting method with a different algorithm that, among other things, recognizes scientific notation (7.4e3 means "7.4 times ten to the third power," or 7400). Run info sort for full technical details.
-u	Unique sort: discard duplicate lines. (If used with -c to check sorted files, fail if any consecutive lines are identical.)
-c	Don't sort, just check if the input is already sorted. If it is, print nothing; otherwise, print an error message.
-b	Ignore leading whitespace in lines.
-r	Reverse the output: sort from greatest to least.
-k key	Choose sorting keys, described next. (Combine with -t to choose a separator character between keys.)
-t X	Use X as the field separator for the -k option.

A sorting key indicates a portion of a line to consider when sorting, instead of the entire line. Consider this file of names and addresses:

```
→ cat people
George Washington,123 Main Street,New York
Abraham Lincoln,54 First Avenue,San Francisco
John Adams,39 Tremont Street,Boston
```

An ordinary sort displays the "Abraham Lincoln" line first. But you can sort on the second value (-k2), the address, if you consider each line as three comma-separated values (-t,). The first address alphabetically is "123 Main Street":

```
→ sort -k2 -t, people
George Washington,123 Main Street,New York
John Adams,39 Tremont Street,Boston
Abraham Lincoln,54 First Avenue,San Francisco
```

Likewise, sort on the third value (-k3), the city, where "Boston" is first alphabetically:

```
→ sort -k3 -t, people
John Adams,39 Tremont Street,Boston
George Washington,123 Main Street,New York
Abraham Lincoln,54 First Avenue,San Francisco
```

The general syntax is -k *F1*[.*C1*][,*F2*[.*C2*]] which means:

Item	Meaning	Default value
F1	Starting field	Required
C1	Starting position within field 1	1
F2	Ending field	Last field
C2	Starting position within ending field	1

So sort -k1.5 sorts by the first field beginning at its fifth character; and sort -k2.8,5 means "from the eighth character of the second field, up to the first character of the fifth field." The -t option changes the behavior of -k so it considers delimiter characters such as commas rather than spaces.

Repeat the -k option to define multiple keys. sort applies them from first to last as found on the command line.

uniq   stdin   stdout   - file   -- opt   --help   --version

uniq [*options*] [*files*]

The uniq command operates on consecutive, duplicate lines of text. For example, if you have a file *letters2*:

```
→ cat letters2
a
b
b
c
b
```

then uniq would detect and process (in whatever way you specify) the two consecutive b's, but not the third b. By default, uniq
deletes the consecutive duplicates:

```
→ uniq letters2
a
b                         Deleted one "b" character
c
b
```

uniq is often used after sorting a file:

```
→ sort letters2 | uniq
a
b
c
```

In this case, only a single b remains because sort placed all
three adjacently, and then uniq collapsed them to one. To count
duplicate lines instead of eliminating them, use the -c option:

```
→ sort letters2 | uniq -c
      1 a
      3 b
      1 c
```

Useful options

-c   Count adjacent duplicate lines.

-i   Case-insensitive operation.

-u   Print unique lines only.

-d   Print duplicate lines only.

-s *N*   Skip the first *N* characters on each line when detecting duplicates.

-f *N*	Ignore the first *N* whitespace-separated fields on each line when detecting duplicates.
-W *N*	Consider only the first *N* characters on each line when detecting duplicates. If used with -s or -f, uniq ignores the specified number of characters or fields first, then considers the next *N* characters.

---

tac

```
tac [options] [files]
```

The tac command, which is "cat" spelled backwards, prints the lines of a file in reverse order.

```
→ cat lines
one
two
three
→ tac lines
three
two
one
```

It's great for reversing lines that are in chronological order, such as the contents of a logfile for a Linux service.

Given multiple filenames as arguments, tac reverses each file in turn. To reverse all lines in all files together, combine them first with cat and pipe the output to tac:

```
→ cat myfile myfile2 myfile3 | tac
```

---

shuf

```
shuf [options] [files]
```

The shuf command shuffles (permutes) lines of text randomly, from a file or other sources.

```
→ cat lines            Original file
one
two
three
→ shuf lines           Run it once
two
three
one
→ shuf lines           Run it again with different output
one
three
two
```

Or, provide strings on the command line with shuf -e:

```
→ shuf -e apple banana guava
guava
apple
banana
```

Or, randomize the numbers in a range with shuf -i:

```
→ shuf -i 0-3
3
1
0
2
```

The shuf command is great for extracting random subsets of lines from a file. For example, given a file of people's first names, shuf can randomize the file and can print a set number of lines with the -n option:

```
→ cat names
Aaron
Ahmed
Ali
Ana
⋮
→ shuf -n3 names
Ying
Robert
Patricia
```

```
→ shuf -n1 names
Fatima
```

Useful options

-e   Shuffle strings provided on the command line.

-i *range*   Shuffle a range of whole numbers, such as 1 - 10.

-n *K*   Print at most *K* lines.

-r   Repeatedly shuffle and print, producing unlimited output. Combine
           with - n to limit the output.

---

tee   stdin   stdout   - file   -- opt   --help   --version

```
tee [options] files
```

Like the cat command, the tee command copies standard
input to standard output unaltered. Simultaneously, it copies
the input to one or more files. tee is most often found in the
middle of pipelines, writing some intermediate data to a file
while passing it to the next command in the pipeline:

```
→ who | tee original_who | sort
barrett    pts/1     Sep 22 21:15
byrnes     pts/0     Sep 15 13:51
silver     :0        Sep 23 20:44
silver     pts/2     Sep 22 21:18
```

The preceding command line writes the unsorted output of who
to the file *original_who* and also passes the same text to sort,
which produces sorted output on screen:

```
→ cat original_who
silver     :0        Sep 23 20:44
byrnes     pts/0     Sep 15 13:51
barrett    pts/1     Sep 22 21:15
silver     pts/2     Sep 22 21:18
```

Useful options

- `-a` Append instead of overwriting files.

- `-i` Ignore interrupt signals.

More powerful manipulations

Linux has hundreds of other filters that produce ever more complex manipulations of the data. But with great power comes a great learning curve, too much for a short book. Here are a few of the most capable filters to get you started.

awk

AWK is a pattern-matching language. It matches data by regular expression and then performs actions based on the data. Here are a few simple examples to process a text file, *myfile*.

Print the second and fourth word on each line:

```
→ awk '{print $2, $4}' myfile
```

Print all lines that are shorter than 60 characters:

```
→ awk 'length < 60 {print}' myfile
```

sed

Like AWK, sed is a pattern-matching engine that manipulates lines of text. Its syntax is shared by several other Linux programs, such as Vim. For example, print a file with all occurrences of the string "me" changed to "YOU":

```
→ sed 's/me/YOU/g' myfile
```

Print lines 3 through 5, inclusive, from a file:

```
→ sed -n '3,5p' myfile
```

m4

m4 is a macro processor. It locates keywords within a file and substitutes values for them. For example, given this file:

```
→ cat substitutions
My name is NAME and I am AGE years old.
ifelse(QUOTE,yes,Learn Linux today!)
```

see m4 perform substitutions (-D) for NAME, AGE, and QUOTE:

```
→ m4 -D NAME=Sandy substitutions
My name is Sandy and I am AGE years old.
```

```
→ m4 -D NAME=Sandy -D AGE=25 substitutions
My name is Sandy and I am 25 years old.
```

```
→ m4 -D NAME=Sandy -D AGE=25 -D QUOTE=yes substitutions
My name is Sandy and I am 25 years old.
Learn Linux today!
```

Perl, PHP, Python, Ruby

If you need even more powerful text processing, Linux includes
interpreters for Perl, PHP, Python, Ruby, and other full-fledged
programming languages. See "Beyond Shell Scripting" on page
309 for references.

Compressing, Packaging, and Encrypting

tar	Package multiple files into a single file.
gzip	Compress files with GNU Zip.
gunzip	Uncompress GNU Zip files.
bzip2	Compress files in BZip format.
bunzip2	Uncompress BZip files.
bzcat	Uncompress BZip data to standard output.
compress	Compress files with traditional Unix compression.
uncompress	Uncompress files with traditional Unix compression.
zcat	Uncompress to standard output (gzip or compress).
zip	Package and compress files in Windows Zip format.
unzip	Uncompress and unpack Windows Zip files.

`7z`	Package and compress/uncompress 7-Zip files.
`munpack`	Extract MIME data to files.
`mpack`	Convert a file to MIME format.
`gpg`	Encrypt a file with the GNU Privacy Guard (GnuPG).

Linux can pack and compress files in a variety of formats. The most popular formats are GNU Zip (`gzip`), whose compressed files are named with the *.gz* extension, and BZip, which uses the *.bz2* extension. Other common formats include ZIP files from Windows systems (*.zip* extension), 7-Zip files (*.7z* and *.lzma* extensions), and occasionally, classic Unix compression (*.Z* extension). If you come across a format I don't cover, such as macOS sit files, ARC, Zoo, RAR, and others, learn more at *https://oreil.ly/vO7l8*.

TIP

Several popular commands have been adapted to work directly on compressed files. Check out `zgrep`, `zless`, `zcmp`, and `zdiff`, which work just like `grep`, `less`, `cmp`, and `diff`, respectively, but accept compressed files as arguments. Compare compressed and uncompressed files:

→ `zdiff sample1.gz sample2`

An operation related to compression is the encoding of binary files as text for email attachments. Nowadays, most email clients do this automatically, but I cover the commands `munpack` and `mpack`, which decode and encode on the command line, respectively. Finally, I cover the most popular file encryption command for Linux, `gpg`, the GNU Privacy Guard.

tar

`tar [options] [files]`

The `tar` command packs many files and directories into a single file for easy transport, optionally compressed. (It was originally for backing up files onto a tape drive; its name is short for "tape archiver.") TAR files are the most common file-packaging format for Linux.

```
→ tar -czf myarchive.tar.gz mydir          Create archive
→ ls -lG myarchive.tar.gz
-rw-r--r-- 1 smith 350 Nov  7 14:09 myarchive.tar.gz
→ tar -tf myarchive.tar.gz                 List contents
mydir/
mydir/dir/
mydir/dir/file10
mydir/file1
mydir/file2
⋮
→ tar -xf myarchive.tar.gz                 Extract
```

If you specify files on the command line, only those files are processed:

```
→ tar -xvf myarchive.tar.gz mydir/file3 mydir/file7
```

Otherwise, the entire archive is processed.

Useful options

- `-c` Create an archive from files and directories listed as arguments.

- `-r` Append files to an existing archive.

- `-u` Append new/changed files to an existing archive.

- `-A` Append one archive to the end of another: for example, `tar -A -f first.tar second.tar` appends the contents of *second.tar* to *first.tar*. Does not work for compressed archives.

- `-t` List (test) the archive.

- `-x` Extract files from the archive.

-C *dir*	Extract the files into directory *dir*.
-f *file*	Read the archive from, or write the archive to, the given file. This is usually a TAR file on disk (such as *myarchive.tar*) but can also be a tape device (such as */dev/tape*).
-d	Diff (compare) the archive against the filesystem.
-z	Use gzip compression.
-j	Use bzip2 compression.
-Z	Use classic Unix compression.
-v	Verbose mode: print extra information.
-h	Follow symbolic links rather than merely copying them.
-p	When extracting files, restore their original permissions and ownership.

---

gzip

stdin stdout -file --opt --help --version

```
gzip [options] [files]
gunzip [options] [files]
zcat [options] [files]
```

gzip and gunzip compress and uncompress files in GNU Zip format. Compressed files have the extension *.gz*.

Sample commands

gzip *file*	Compress *file* to create *file.gz*. Original *file* is deleted.
gunzip *file.gz*	Uncompress *file.gz* to create *file*. Original *file.gz* is deleted.
gunzip -c *file.gz*	Uncompress a file to standard output.
zcat *file.gz*	Uncompress a file to standard output.
cat *file* | gzip | …	Compress data in a pipeline.

| `cat file.gz | gunzip` | Uncompress data from a pipeline. |
| `tar -czf tarfile dir` | Pack directory *dir* into a gzipped TAR file. Add `-v` to print filenames as they are processed. |

---

bzip2

stdin   stdout   - file   -- opt   --help   --version

```
bzip2 [options] [files]
bunzip2 [options] [files]
bzcat [options] [files]
```

`bzip2` and `bunzip2` compress and uncompress files in Burrows–Wheeler format. Compressed files have the extension *.bz2*.

Sample commands

`bzip2 file`	Compress *file* to create *file.bz2*. Original *file* is deleted.
`bunzip2 file.bz2`	Uncompress *file.bz2* to create *file*. Original *file.bz2* is deleted.
`bunzip2 -c file.bz2`	Uncompress a file to standard output.
`cat file	bunzip2	...`	Compress data in a pipeline.
`cat file.bz2	bunzip2`	Uncompress data from a pipeline.
`bzcat file.bz2`	Uncompress a file to standard output.
`tar -cjf tarfile dir`	Pack directory *dir* into a BZipped TAR file. Add `-v` to print filenames as they are processed.

compress

stdin   stdout   - file   -- opt   --help   --version

```
compress [options] [files]
uncompress [options] [files]
zcat [options] [files]
```

compress and uncompress compress and uncompress files in classic Unix compression format (Lempel-Ziv). Compressed files have the extension *.Z*.

Sample commands

compress *file*	Compress *file* to create *file*.Z. Original *file* is deleted.
uncompress *file.Z*	Uncompress *file*.Z to create *file*. Original *file.Z* is deleted.
uncompress -c *file.Z*	Uncompress a file to standard output.
zcat *file.Z*	Uncompress a file to standard output.
cat *file* | compress | …	Compress data in a pipeline.
cat *file.Z* | uncompress	Uncompress data from a pipeline.
tar -cZf *tarfile dir*	Pack directory *dir* into a compressed TAR file. Use -cvZf to print filenames as they are processed.

zip

stdin   stdout   - file   -- opt   --help   --version

```
zip archive.zip [options] [files]
unzip [options] archive.zip [files]
```

zip packs and compresses files in Windows Zip format, and unzip extracts them. Compressed files have the extension *.zip*.

zip archive.zip *file1 file2*...	Pack.

```
zip -r archive.zip dir          Pack a directory recursively.

unzip -l archive.zip            List contents.

unzip archive.zip               Unpack.
```

7z

```
7z [command] [options] archive_file [(files | dirs)]
```

The 7z command, also known as 7-Zip, packs and compresses files and directories. By default, it produces archive files in LZMA format with the filename extension *.7z*. It also supports other compression methods, such as ZIP, gzip, and BZip2, but you might as well use the original Linux commands (zip, gzip, and bzip2, respectively), which are more commonly found on Linux machines. 7z also extracts from a variety of archive files, even Microsoft CAB files. See the manpage for a full list.

```
7z a archive.7z file1 file2...  Pack.

7z a archive.7z dir             Pack a directory (same as for files).

7z l archive.7z                 List contents.

7z x archive.7z                 Unpack.
```

---

munpack

```
munpack [options] mail_file
mpack [options] files
```

Modern email programs handle attachments so seamlessly that we rarely think about the process behind the scenes. The commands munpack and mpack work directly with attachments on the command line. For example, if you have an email message in a file, *messagefile*, and it contains a JPEG image and a PDF

---

file as attachments, munpack can extract both attachments into files:

```
→ munpack messagefile
beautiful.jpg (image/jpeg)
researchpaper.pdf (application/pdf)
```

Its partner program, mpack, does the opposite: it inserts files as attachments into a MIME-format file. Create the file *attachment.mime* containing a MIME-encoded image, *photo.jpg*:

```
→ mpack -o attachment.mime photo.jpg
Subject: My example photo
```

---

gpg
stdin stdout -file --opt --help --version

gpg [*options*] [*args*]

The gpg command encrypts and decrypts files, manipulates digital signatures, maintains encryption keys, and more. It's part of the encryption application GNU Privacy Guard (GnuPG).

The simplest approach, symmetric encryption, uses the same password to encrypt and decrypt a file (so don't lose it!):

```
→ ls secret*
secret
→ gpg -c secret
Passphrase: xxxxxxxx          Invent a password on the spot
Repeat: xxxxxxxx
→ ls secret*
secret  secret.gpg            Creates the encrypted file
```

More common is public key encryption, which requires a pair of keys (public and private), encrypting with the public key, and decrypting with the private. Get started by creating a key pair, assuming your email address is *smith@example.com*:

```
→ gpg --quick-generate-key smith@example.com \
  default default never
```

Encrypt a file with public key encryption, creating *secret.gpg*:

```
→ gpg -e secret            Use your default public key
→ gpg -e -r key secret     Use a specific public key
```

Encrypt and digitally sign a file, creating *secret.gpg*:

```
→ gpg -es secret
Passphrase: xxxxxxxx
```

Decrypt the file *secret.gpg* and verify any signature. (If you're not reprompted for a passphrase, gpg has cached it for now.)

```
→ rm secret                Delete the original file
→ gpg secret.gpg           Decrypt
Passphrase: xxxxxxxx
gpg: encrypted with 4096-bit ELG key, ID 3EE49F4396C9,
 created 2023-02-26 "John Smith <smith@example.com>"
⋮
Good signature from "John Smith <smith@example.com>"
→ ls secret*
secret  secret.gpg         See the original file, decrypted
```

List the keys on your GnuPG keyring:

```
→ gpg --list-public-keys
→ gpg --list-secret-keys
```

Useful options

gpg has about 100 options. Here are some common ones.

-r *name*   Encrypt for a recipient on your public keyring. The *name* may be the key ID, email address, or various other parts of the key name.

-u *name*   Sign as the user with this name from your keyring.

-o *file*   Write output to the given file.

-a   Create output in ASCII armor format instead of OpenPGP format. ASCII armor is plain text and suitable for inserting into email messages. Output files have the extension *.asc* rather than *.gpg*.

-q   Be quiet—don't print messages while running.

-v   Print more verbose messages while running.

Comparing Files

diff	Line-by-line comparison of two files or directories.
comm	Line-by-line comparison of two sorted files.
cmp	Byte-by-byte comparison of two files.
shasum	Compute checksums of the given files.
md5sum	Compute checksums of the given files (insecure).

You can compare Linux files in at least three ways:

- Line by line (diff, comm), best suited to text files.

- Byte by byte (cmp), often used for binary files.

- By comparing checksums (shasum). Avoid older, weaker commands such as sum, cksum, and md5sum, which use insecure algorithms.

---

diff
stdin   **stdout**   **- file**   **-- opt**   **--help**   **--version**

```
diff [options] file1 file2
```

The diff command compares two files line by line, or two directories file by file. If there are no differences, diff produces no output. For text files, diff produces detailed reports of their differences. For binary files, diff merely reports whether they differ or not.

The traditional output format looks like this:

```
Affected line numbers, and the type of change
< Corresponding section of file1, if any
---
> Corresponding section of file2, if any
```

For example, start with a file *fileA*:

```
Hello, this is a wonderful file.
The quick brown fox jumped over
the lazy dogs.
Goodbye for now.
```

Suppose you delete the first line, change "brown" to "blue" on the second line, and add a final line, creating a file *fileB*:

```
The quick blue fox jumped over
the lazy dogs.
Goodbye for now.
Linux r00lz!
```

The diff command reports two differences labeled 1,2c1 and 4a4:

```
→ diff fileA fileB
1,2c1                                    fileA lines 1-2 became fileB line 1
< Hello, this is a wonderful file.              Lines 1-2 of fileA
< The quick brown fox jumped over
---                                             diff separator
> The quick blue fox jumped over                Line 1 of fileB
4a4                                       Line 4 was added in fileB
> Linux r00lz!                                  The added line
```

The leading symbols < and > are arrows indicating *fileA* and *fileB*, respectively. This output format is the default: many others are available, some of which can be fed directly to other tools. Try them out to see what they look like.

Option	Output format
-c	Context diff format, as used by the patch command (man patch).
-D *macro*	C preprocessor format, using #ifdef *macro* ... #else ... #endif.
-u	Unified format, which merges the files and prepends "-" for deletion and "+" for addition. Used by git.
-y	Side-by-side format; use -W to adjust the width of the output.
-q	Don't report changes, just say whether the files differ.

`diff` can also compare directories. By default, it compares any same-named files in those directories and also lists files that appear in one directory but not the other:

→ **`diff dir1 dir2`**

To compare entire directory trees recursively, run `diff -r` which produces a (potentially massive) report of all differences.

→ **`diff -r dir1 dir2`**

Useful options

- `-b` Don't consider whitespace.

- `-B` Don't consider blank lines.

- `-i` Ignore case.

- `-r` When comparing directories, recurse into subdirectories.

`diff` is one member of a family of commands that operate on file differences. Some others are `diff3`, which compares three files at a time, and `sdiff`, which merges the differences between two files to create a third file according to your instructions.

---

comm

stdin   **stdout** **- file**   **-- opt**   **--help**   **--version**

`comm [options] file1 file2`

The `comm` command compares two sorted files and produces three columns of output, separated by tabs:

1. All lines that appear in *file1* but not in *file2*.

2. All lines that appear in *file2* but not in *file1*.

3. All lines that appear in both files.

For example, if *commfile1* and *commfile2* contain these lines:

```
commfile1:          commfile2:
apple               baker
baker               charlie
charlie             dark
```

then comm produces this three-column output:

```
→ comm commfile1 commfile2
apple
                baker
                charlie
        dark
```

Useful options

-1   Suppress column 1.

-2   Suppress column 2.

-3   Suppress column 3.

-23 Show lines that appear only in the first file.

-13 Show lines that appear only in the second file.

-12 Show only common lines.

---

cmp   stdin   stdout - file -- opt --help --version

```
cmp [options] file1 file2 [offset1 [offset2]]
```

The cmp command compares two files. If their contents are the same, cmp reports nothing; otherwise, it lists the location of the first difference:

```
→ cmp myfile yourfile
myfile yourfile differ: byte 225, line 4
```

By default, cmp does not tell you what the difference is, only where it is. It also is perfectly suitable for comparing binary files, as opposed to diff, which operates best on text files.

Normally, cmp starts its comparison at the beginning of each file, but if you provide offsets, it starts elsewhere:

```
→ cmp myfile yourfile 10 20
```

This comparison begins at the 10th character of *myfile* and the 20th of *yourfile*.

Useful options

-l Long output: print all differences, byte by byte:

```
→ cmp -l myfile yourfile
225 167 127
```

The output says that at offset 225 (in decimal), *myfile* has a small "w" (octal 167) but *yourfile* has a capital "W" (octal 127).

-s Silent output: don't print anything, just exit with an appropriate return code; 0 if the files match, 1 if they don't. (Or other codes if the comparison fails.)

---

shasum   stdin   stdout   - file   -- opt   --help   --version

```
shasum -a (256|384|512|512224|512256) [options] files
shasum --check file
```

The shasum command calculates and validates checksums to verify that files are unchanged. By default, shasum uses an *insecure* algorithm called SHA-1. Add the option -a 256 (or a higher value) for cryptographically secure results. Here I produce a 256-bit checksum of the given files (64 hexadecimal digits) using the secure SHA-256 algorithm:

```
→ shasum -a 256 myfile          SHA-256 algorithm
e8183aaa23aa9b74c7033cbc843041fcf1d1e9e937... myfile
```

The second form of the command tests whether a checksum matches the original file, using --check:

```
→ shasum -a 256 myfile myfile2 myfile3 > /tmp/mysum
→ cat /tmp/mysum
e8183aaa23aa9b74c7033cbc843041fcf1d1e9e937... myfile
```

```
2254f6879ae5fdf174b3a2ebbdc7fb4fa41e0ddf4a...  myfile2
0bfa73d888300e3d4f5bc9ac302c1eb38e37499b5e...  myfile3
→ shasum --check /tmp/mysum
myfile: OK
myfile2: OK
myfile3: OK
→ echo "new data" > myfile2               Change myfile2
→ shasum --check /tmp/mysum
myfile: OK
myfile2: FAILED
myfile3: OK
shasum: WARNING: 1 computed checksum did NOT match
```

Two different files are unlikely to have the same SHA-256 checksum, so comparing their checksums is a reliable way to detect if two files differ.

```
→ shasum -a 256 myfile | cut -c1-64 > /tmp/sum1
→ shasum -a 256 myfile2 | cut -c1-64 > /tmp/sum2
→ diff -q /tmp/sum1 /tmp/sum2
Files /tmp/sum1 and /tmp/sum2 differ
```

---

md5sum   stdin   stdout · file -- opt   --help   --version

md5sum *files* | --check *file*

The md5sum command computes checksums using an *insecure* algorithm called MD5. Do not use it for production work. Run it much like shasum:

```
→ md5sum myfile myfile2 myfile3 > /tmp/mysum    Generate
→ md5sum --check /tmp/mysum                      Check
```

Converting Files to Other Formats

pandoc   Convert from one markup language to another.

hxselect Extract information from an HTML file.

jq   Extract information from a JSON file.

`xmllint`	Validate and extract information from an XML file.
`csvtool`	Extract information from a comma-separated values (CSV) file.
`split`	Split up a file simply into multiple files.
`csplit`	Split up a file into multiple files using complex criteria.

Have you ever tediously converted a text file from one format to another by hand, or manually extracted values from CSV, JSON, or XML files? Never again! Linux has an arsenal of file-conversion commands that make this kind of work disappear.

---

pandoc

stdin   stdout   - file   -- opt   --help   --version

`pandoc [options] [files]`

The amazing `pandoc` command converts files of many formats into many other formats. It handles HTML, JSON, CSV, LaTeX, Microsoft DOCX and PPTX, DocBook XML, manpages, numerous flavors of markdown and wiki text, and dozens of other formats. The results aren't perfect and may require a bit of manual cleanup, but they're surprisingly good.[6]

Running `pandoc` couldn't be simpler: just provide an input file and pick an output format with the `-t` option, and `pandoc` prints the converted results. Look how easy it is to convert a CSV file to HTML, GitHub markdown, LaTeX, and JSON:

```
→ cat data.csv                          Original file
one,two,three,four,five,six,seven
ONE,TWO,THREE,FOUR,FIVE,SIX,SEVEN
1,2,3,4,5,6,7
→ pandoc -t html data.csv               CSV to HTML
<table>
<thead>
```

---

6 I ran `pandoc` to convert material from the third edition of this book, written in DocBook XML, to AsciiDoc for the fourth edition.

```
<tr class="header">
<th>one</th>
<th>two</th>
⋮
→ pandoc -t gfm data.csv                       CSV to markdown
| one | two | three | four | five | six | seven |
|-----|-----|-------|------|------|-----|-------|
| ONE | TWO | THREE | FOUR | FIVE | SIX | SEVEN |
| 1   | 2   | 3     | 4    | 5    | 6   | 7     |
→ pandoc -t latex data.csv                      CSV to LaTeX
\begin{longtable}[]{@{}lllllll@{}}
\toprule
one & two & three & four & five & six & seven ...
⋮
→ pandoc -t json data.csv                       CSV to JSON
{"blocks":[{"t":"Table","c":[[], ...
```

Redirect the results to a file, or better yet, add the -o option
to write the results to an output file, particularly if they're in a
binary format. If pandoc can guess the output format from the
output filename, you can omit the -t option:

```
→ pandoc -o page.pdf page.html           HTML to PDF
```

If pandoc can't guess the format of the input file, add the option
-f ("from"):

```
→ pandoc -o page.pdf -f html page.html
```

Useful options

pandoc has many more options than I list here, and it supports
configuration files for setting multiple options conveniently.
See the manpage for details.

--list-input-formats	List all supported input formats (34 so far).
--list-output-formats	List all supported output formats (57 so far).
-f *input_format*	Explicitly convert *from* this format.
-t *output_format*	Explicitly convert *to* this format.
-o *file*	Write the output to this file.

--wrap=*type*	Determine whether text should be wrapped in the output. Values are none for no wrapping, auto to wrap at 72 columns, or preserve to keep the same wrapping as the original file.
--columns=*N*	Wrap the next at column *N* (default=72).

---

hxselect

```
hxselect [options] CSS_selectors
```

The hxselect command extracts strings from HTML data based on CSS selectors. For example, extract all div tags from a file *page.html*:

```
→ cat page.html                     Original file
<html>
  <head>
  </head>
  <body>
    <div>
      This is the first div.
    </div>
    <div class="secondary">
      This is the second div.
    </div>
  </body>
</html>
→ hxselect 'div' < page.html        Print one div
<div>
      This is the first div
    </div><div class="secondary">
      This is the second div
    </div>
→ hxselect -c 'div' < page.html              Contents
      This is the first div
      This is the second div
→ hxselect -c 'div.secondary' < page.html    By selector
      This is the second div
```

For best results, pass the content first through `hxnormalize -x` to clean up the HTML code.

→ **hxnormalize -x page.html | hxselect ...**

Pipe the source of a web page to `hxselect` using `curl`:

→ **curl** *url* **| hxnormalize -x | hxselect ...**

Useful options

-c   Just print the content within tags, not the tags themselves.

-i   Match strings case-insensitively.

---

jq   stdin   stdout - file -- opt --help   --version

jq [*options*] *filter* [*JSON_files*]

The jq command extracts and manipulates JSON data, according to a filter that you provide, and pretty-prints the results. I present a few examples of using this powerful tool (see the manpage for more).

```
→ cat book.json                    Original file
{
  "title": "Linux Pocket Guide",
  "author": "Daniel J. Barrett",
  "publisher": {
    "name": "O'Reilly Media",
    "url": "https://oreilly.com"
  },
  "editions": [1, 2, 3, 4]
}
→ jq .title book.json              Simple value
"Linux Pocket Guide"
→ jq .title,.author book.json      Multiple values
"Linux Pocket Guide"
"Daniel J. Barrett"
→ jq .publisher book.json          Object
{
```

```
  "name": "O'Reilly Media",
  "url": "https://oreilly.com"
}
→ jq .publisher.url book.json          Nested value
"https://oreilly.com"
→ jq .editions book.json               Array
[
  1,
  2,
  3,
  4
]
→ jq .editions[0] book.json            One array value
1
→ jq '.editions|length' book.json      Array length
4
→ jq '.editions|add' book.json         Sum 1+2+3+4
10
→ cat oneline.json                     A one-line JSON file
{"title":"Linux Pocket Guide","author": ...
→ jq < oneline.json                    Pretty-print the file
{
  "title": "Linux Pocket Guide",
  "author": ...
  ⋮
```

Useful options

-f *file*   Read the filter from a file instead of the command line.

-S   Sort the output by its JSON keys.

---

xmllint   stdin   stdout   - file   -- opt   --help   --version

xmllint [*options*] [*XML_files*]

The xmllint command validates and extracts XML data. Validating a valid XML file just prints the contents. Add the option --noout to suppress the output.

```
→ xmllint good.xml
<?xml version="1.0"?>
<hello> </hello>
→ xmllint --noout good.xml
→ echo $?
0                                    Success code
```

An invalid XML file prints an error:

```
→ cat bad.xml
<?xml version="1.0"?>
<hello> </helo>                      Mismatched tags
→ xmllint bad.xml
bad.xml:2: parser error : Opening and ending tag
mismatch: hello line 2 and helo
⋮
→ echo $?
1                                    Error code
```

Provide an XPath expression (*https://oreil.ly/WZdhL*) to extract
data:

```
→ cat book.xml                       Original file
<?xml version="1.0"?>
<book>
  <title>Linux Pocket Guide</title>
  <author>Daniel J. Barrett</author>
  <pub>
    <name>O'Reilly Media</name>
    <url>https://oreilly.com</url>
  </pub>
  <eds>
    <ed id="1">First edition</ed>
    <ed id="2">Second edition</ed>
    <ed id="3">Third edition</ed>
    <ed id="4">Fourth edition</ed>
  </eds>
</book>
→ xmllint --xpath '//book/title' book.xml
<title>Linux Pocket Guide</title>
→ xmllint --xpath '//book/title/text()' book.xml
Linux Pocket Guide
→ xmllint --xpath '//book/pub/url/text()' book.xml
```

```
https://oreilly.com
→ xmllint --xpath '//book/eds/ed[@id][4]' book.xml
<ed id="4">Fourth edition</ed>
→ xmllint --xpath '//book/eds/ed[@id][4]/text()' \
  book.xml
Fourth edition
```

Useful options

--xpath *path*	Query the given XPath expression in the XML data.
--format	Print the output nicely formatted.
--noout	Don't print output.

---

csvtool   stdin stdout - file -- opt --help --version

csvtool [*options*] *command* [*command_args*] *CSV_files*

The csvtool command extracts data from CSV files. It can extract columns:

```
→ cat data.csv                    Original file
one,two,three,four,five,six,seven
ONE,TWO,THREE,FOUR,FIVE,SIX,SEVEN
1,2,3,4,5,6,7
→ csvtool col 3 data.csv          One column
three
THREE
3
→ csvtool col 2,5-7 data.csv      Multiple columns
two,five,six,seven
TWO,FIVE,SIX,SEVEN
2,5,6,7
```

It can count the number of rows and columns:

```
→ csvtool height data.csv    Number of rows
3
→ csvtool width data.csv     Number of columns (max)
7
```

It can insert values from each row into longer strings:

```
→ csvtool format 'Third column is "%3"\n' data.csv
Third column is "three"
Third column is "THREE"
Third column is "3"
```

It can remove the first row, which often contains headings:

```
→ csvtool drop 1 data.csv
ONE,TWO,THREE,FOUR,FIVE,SIX,SEVEN
1,2,3,4,5,6,7
```

It can isolate a single value, say, row 2, column 6:

```
→ csvtool drop 1 data.csv \      Delete the first row
  | csvtool head 1 - \           Print the first remaining row
  | csvtool col 6 -              Extract column 6
SIX
```

and much more. The csvtool manpage is sparse, so run csvtool --help for more information.

Useful options

-c *char*   Change the input separator character from a comma to *char*. For tab characters, use -c TAB.

-o   Same as -c but for the output separator character.

---

split   stdin   stdout   - file   -- opt   --help   --version

split [*options*] [*file* [*prefix*]]

The split command divides a file into equal-sized pieces (for various definitions of "equal-sized") and stores them in separate files. The output files are named sequentially, such as *Xaa*, *Xab*, *Xac*, and so on, by default. *X* is called the *prefix* and the endings *aa*, *ab*, and so on, are the *suffix*.

Divide the input file by number of lines:

→ **split hugefile**   *1000 lines each*
→ **split -l 2000 hugefile**   *2000 lines each*

or by bytes:

→ **split -b 1024 hugefile**   *1024 bytes each*

or split it at a given character, called the separator:

→ **split -t@ -l1 hugefile**   *Separator character is @*

Optionally change the prefix with a final argument:

→ **split hugefile part-**   *Set the prefix to "part-"*
→ **ls**
hugefile part-aa part-ab part-ac part-ad ...

split can help you work with files that are too large to load into other programs, or too large to store on offline media. Reassemble the parts afterward with *cat*:

→ **cat part-* > /tmp/outfile**   *Join part-aa, part-ab, etc.*

Useful options

-l *lines*	Split into files of this many lines or records.
-b *bytes*	Split into files of this many bytes.
-t *separator*	Set the separator character, if any, between records.
-a *length*	Set the length of the suffix, in characters.
-d	Use numeric suffixes instead of letters, starting from zero. Change the starting value to *N* with - -numeric-suffixes *N*.

---

csplit   stdin **stdout** **-file** -- opt **--help** **--version**

csplit [*options*] file patterns

The csplit command divides one file into many based on regular expressions. The output files are named sequentially, such as *xx01*, *xx02*, *xx03*, and so on, by default. *xx* is called the *prefix* and the endings *01*, *02*, and so on, are the *suffix*. By default, csplit prints the size of each file it creates.

The syntax is a bit unusual. After the input filename, provide one or more patterns that represent dividing lines in the file. Patterns have two types:

Regular expressions
> An expression (see Table 2-2) enclosed in forward slashes, such as /^[A-Z]*$/ for a line of all uppercase letters. Each expression is matched just once by default.

Repeaters
> A repeater has the form '{*N*}' which means "match the preceding pattern up to *N* times." An example is '{2}' which matches its preceding pattern twice. The special repeater '{*}' matches its preceding pattern as many times as possible until the input ends.

csplit is great for splitting up structured text such as HTML, XML, or programming source code.

```
→ cat page.html          Original file
<html>
  <head>
  </head>
  <body>
    <div>
      This is the first div.
    </div>
    <div class="secondary">
      This is the second div.
    </div>
  </body>
</html>
```

Use four patterns (in quotes below) to split a file at the first <head>, then at the next <body>, and then every <div> tag:

```
→ csplit page.html '/<head>/' '/<body>/' '/<div/' '{*}'
7
```

```
19
9                          Sizes of the output files, in bytes
49
86
```

View the five output files:

```
→ ls xx*
xx00  xx01  xx02  xx03  xx04
→ cat xx00
<html>
→ cat xx01
  <head>
  </head>
→ cat xx02
  <body>
→ cat xx03
    <div>
      This is the first div
    </div>
→ cat xx04
    <div class="secondary">
      This is the second div
    </div>
  </body>
</html>
```

Useful options

-f *prefix*   Set the prefix for output filenames.

-n *length*   Set the suffix for output filenames to be *length* digits long.

-s   Silent operation: don't print the sizes of the generated files.

PDF and PostScript File Handling

pdftotext	Extract text from PDF files.
ps2ascii	Extract text from PostScript or PDF files.
pdfseparate	Extract individual pages from a PDF file.
pdftk	Split, join, rotate, and otherwise manipulate PDF files.

| `pdf2ps, ps2pdf` | Convert between PDF and PostScript file formats. |
| `ocrmypdf` | Perform optical character recognition (OCR) on a PDF. |

To view PDF files and PostScript files on Linux, you'll need a graphical desktop and a document viewer like these:[7]

→ `okular sample.pdf`   *KDE's document viewer*
→ `evince sample.pdf`   *GNOME's document viewer*
→ `gv sample.pdf`   *Ghostscript viewer*

In addition, Linux has a rich set of command-line tools to work with PDF and Postscript files without displaying them. They are well worth learning, especially the amazing `pdftk`.

---

pdftotext

stdin   stdout   -**file**   -- **opt**   --**help**   --version

`pdftotext [options] [file.pdf [outfile.txt]]`

The `pdftotext` command extracts text from a PDF file and writes it to a file. This works if the PDF contains actual text, not images that look like text (in which case, run `ocrmypdf` first).

→ `pdftotext sample.pdf`   *Creates sample.txt*

Useful options

`-f N`	Begin with page *N* of the PDF file. You must have a space between the option and the number.
`-l N`	End with page *N* of the PDF file. You must have a space between the option and the number.
`-htmlmeta`	Generate HTML rather than plain text (creates *sample.html*).
`-eol OS`	Write end-of-line characters for the given operating system, *OS*, which can be dos, mac, or unix.

---

7 To edit PDF files, the best Linux program I've used is Master PDF Editor by Code Industry (*https://oreil.ly/l5Hto*), a commercial product.

ps2ascii

stdin   stdout   - file   -- opt   --help   **--version**

ps2ascii *file*.(ps|pdf) [*outfile*.txt]

The ps2ascii command extracts text from a PostScript file. It's a simple command with no options.[8] To extract text from *sample.ps* and place it into */tmp/extracted.txt*:

→ **ps2ascii sample.ps /tmp/extracted.txt**

ps2ascii can also extract text from a PDF file, though you wouldn't guess that from the command name.

→ **ps2ascii sample.pdf /tmp/extracted2.txt**

pdfseparate

stdin   stdout   - file   **-- opt**   **--help**   version

pdfseparate [*options*] [*file*.pdf] [*pattern*.txt]

The pdfseparate command splits a PDF file into separate PDF files, one per page. For example, if *one.pdf* has 10 pages, then the following command creates 10 PDF files in */tmp* named *split1.pdf* through *split10.pdf*, each containing one page:

→ **pdfseparate one.pdf /tmp/split%d.pdf**

The final argument is a pattern to form the names of the individual page files. The special notation %d stands for the extracted page number.

---

8 Actually, ps2ascii --help describes command-line options, but they don't work. They are the options of a related command, gs, invoked by ps2ascii.

Useful options

- `-f N` Begin with page *N* of the PDF file. You must have a space between the option and the number.

- `-l N` End with page *N* of the PDF file. You must have a space between the option and the number.

---

pdftk
stdin   stdout - file -- opt --help --version

pdftk [*arguments*]

pdftk is the Swiss Army knife of PDF commands. This versatile program can extract pages from a PDF file, join several PDFs into one, rotate pages, add watermarks, encrypt and decrypt files, and much more, all from the command line. This power comes with quirky syntax, unfortunately, but with a little effort you can learn a few useful tricks.

To join the files *one.pdf* and *two.pdf* into a single PDF file, *combined.pdf*:

→ **pdftk one.pdf two.pdf cat output combined.pdf**

To extract pages 3, 5, and 8–10 from the file *one.pdf* and write them to *new.pdf*:

→ **pdftk one.pdf cat 3 5 8-10 output new.pdf**

Extract the first five pages from *one.pdf* and the odd-numbered pages from *two.pdf* and combine them as *combined.pdf*:

→ **pdftk A=one.pdf B=two.pdf cat A1-5 Bodd output **
combined.pdf

Copy the file *one.pdf* to *new.pdf*, but with page 7 rotated by 90 degrees clockwise ("east"):

→ **pdftk one.pdf cat 1-6 7east 8-end output new.pdf**

Interleave the pages of *one.pdf* and *two.pdf*, creating *mixed.pdf*:

```
→ pdftk one.pdf two.pdf shuffle output mixed.pdf
```

The criteria for page selection are very powerful and typically appear before the output keyword. They consist of one or more page ranges with qualifiers. A page range can be a single page like 5, a range like 5-10, or a reverse range like 10-5 (which reverses the pages in the output). Qualifiers can remove pages from a range, like 1-100~20-25, which means "all pages from 1 to 100 except for pages 20 to 25." They can also specify only odd pages or even pages, using the keywords odd or even, and rotations using the compass directions north, south, east, and west. I've only scratched the surface of pdftk's abilities. The manpage has more details and examples.

---

pdf2ps

<small>stdin stdout **-file** -- opt **--help** --version</small>

```
pdf2ps [options] file.pdf [file.ps]
ps2pdf [options] file.ps [file.pdf]
```

The pdf2ps command converts an Adobe PDF file into a Post-Script file. If you don't provide an output filename, the default is to use the input filename, with *.pdf* replaced by *.ps*.

```
→ pdf2ps sample.pdf converted.ps
```

To go in the opposite direction, converting a PostScript file to PDF format, use ps2pdf:

```
→ ps2pdf sample.ps converted.pdf
```

---

ocrmypdf

<small>stdin stdout **-file** -- opt **--help** --version</small>

```
ocrmypdf [options] input_file output_file
```

The ocrmypdf command performs optical character recognition (OCR) to create a searchable PDF file. The input file can be an image file or a PDF file that contains images.

```
→ ocrmypdf imageoftext.png outfile.pdf        Convert
→ okular outfile.pdf                          Display
```

Useful options

`-l` *language*   Use *language* rather than English. For a list of languages, run
                  `tesseract --list-langs`.

`-r`   Attempt to rotate pages into their correct orientation.

Printing

`lpr`   Print a file.

`lpq`   View the print queue.

`lprm` Remove a print job from the queue.

Linux has two popular printing systems, CUPS and LPRng. Both systems use commands named `lpr`, `lpq`, and `lprm`, but their options are different on CUPS and LPRng. I'll present common options that work with both systems.

To install and maintain printers, GNOME and KDE have printer configuration tools in their system settings. To troubleshoot a CUPS printer, visit *http://localhost:631* to access your computer's CUPS management system.

---

lpr
stdin stdout - file -- opt **--help** --version

`lpr [options] [files]`

The `lpr` (line printer) command sends a file to a printer:

```
→ lpr myfile                    Print on default printer
→ lpr -P myprinter myfile       Print on a named printer
```

Useful options

-P *printername*	Send the file to printer *printername*, which you have previously set up.
-# *N*	Print *N* copies of the file. (The option is a literal hash mark.)
-J *name*	Set the job *name* that prints on the cover page (if your system is set up to print cover pages).

---

lpq

stdin **stdout** - file -- opt **--help** --version

lpq [*options*]

The lpq (line printer queue) command lists print jobs that are waiting to be printed.

Useful options

-P *printername*	List the queue for printer *printername*.
-a	List the queue for all printers.
-l	Be verbose: display information in a longer format.

---

lprm

stdin **stdout** - file -- opt --help --version

lprm [*options*] [*job_IDs*]

The lprm (line printer remove) command cancels one or more print jobs. Use lpq to learn the ID of the desired print jobs (say, 61 and 78), then run:

→ **lprm -P** *printer_name* **61 78**

If you don't supply any job IDs, your current print job is canceled. (The superuser can cancel other users' jobs.) The -P option specifies which print queue contains the job.

Spellchecking

look   Look up the spelling of a word quickly.

aspell   Interactive spelling checker.

spell   Batch spelling checker.

Linux has several spellcheckers built in. If you're accustomed to graphical spellcheckers, you might find Linux's text-based ones fairly primitive, but they're useful in a pinch (or a pipeline).

---

look

stdin   **stdout**   - file   **-- opt**   **--help**   **--version**

look [*options*] *prefix* [*dictionary_file*]

The look command prints words that begin with a given string *prefix*. The words are located in a dictionary file (default */usr/share/dict/words*):

```
→ look bigg
bigger
biggest
Biggs
```

If you supply your own dictionary file—any text file with alphabetically sorted lines—look prints all lines in the dictionary that begin with the given *prefix*.

Useful options

-f   Ignore case. Needed only if you supply a dictionary file.

---

aspell

aspell [*options*] *file*

aspell is an interactive spellchecker. It identifies words that it doesn't recognize and presents alternatives. A few useful commands are:

aspell -c *file*
> Interactively check, and optionally correct, the spelling of all words in *file*.

aspell dump master
> Print aspell's master dictionary on standard output.

aspell help
> Print a concise help message. See *http://aspell.net* for more information.

---

spell

spell [*files*]

The spell command prints all words in the given files that are misspelled, according to its dictionary. It is not interactive.

```
→ cat badwords
This Linux file has some spelling errors.
You may naturaly wonder if a spelling checker
will pick them up. Careful Linuxx users should
run thier favorite spelling checker on this file.
→ spell badwords
naturaly
Linuxx
thier
```

System Administration Basics

Becoming the Superuser

Normal users, for the most part, can modify only the files they own. One special user, called the *superuser* or *root*, has full access to the machine and can do anything on it. Superuser privileges are mainly for system administration tasks; use them only when absolutely necessary so you don't accidentally harm your Linux system. And don't log in as root unless you must (e.g., when rescuing a broken boot process).

WARNING

Superuser commands can destroy a Linux system if you're not careful.

You can become the superuser in several ways. One is to use the sudo command to gain superuser abilities for the duration of a single command. Simply type "sudo" followed by the command. You may be prompted for your password, depending on how sudo is configured on your machine:

```
→ sudo rm some_protected_file
[sudo] password: xxxxxxxx          Your own password
```

To maintain your superuser powers without constantly running sudo, launch a superuser shell with either of the following commands:

```
→ sudo -s
→ sudo bash
```

A superuser shell is convenient, say, for browsing through many protected directories with cd. When finished executing commands as the superuser, press ^D or run exit to end the superuser shell and become yourself again. If you forget whether your shell is a superuser shell or just a normal one, check your identity with the whoami command. If you're the superuser, it displays root.

Another way to become the superuser is the su command, which also creates a superuser shell, but you'll need a different password, called the root password, to use it. (Whoever installed Linux chose the root password during installation.)

```
→ su
Password: xxxxxxxx                 root password
#
```

Your shell prompt may change, often to a hash mark (#), to indicate you are the superuser. Add the option -l to run a login shell that includes root's full environment, such as root's shell aliases.

```
→ su -l                            Run a login shell
Password: xxxxxxxx                 root password
#
```

If you provide a username to sudo or su, you become that user, provided you have the prerequisites:

```
→ sudo -u sophia command           Become user sophia with sudo
[sudo] password: xxxxxxxx          You must have sudo permission
→ su sophia                        Become user sophia with su
Password: xxxxxxxx                 You must know sophia's password
```

Use sudo rather than su whenever possible, especially if your system has multiple users. su relies on a shared password, which is a security concern. sudo uses your own password, but it must be configured to do so (and many distros come with sudo preconfigured). sudo also provides precise control over privileges in the file */etc/sudoers*, and it even logs the commands that users run. A full discussion is beyond the scope of this book: see man sudo for details.

Viewing Processes

ps	List processes.
pgrep	List the IDs of processes that match a regular expression.
uptime	View the system load.
w	List active processes for all users.
top	Monitor resource-intensive processes interactively.
free	Display free memory.

A *process* is a unit of work on a Linux system. Each program you run represents one or more processes, and Linux provides commands for viewing and manipulating them. Every process is identified by a numeric *process ID*, or PID, and can be examined in the directory */proc* (see "Kernel-Related Directories" on page 15).

Processes are different from jobs (see "Shell Job Control" on page 31). Processes are part of the OS. Jobs are higher-level constructs known only to the shell in which they're running. A running program comprises one or more processes; a shell job consists of one or more programs executed as a shell command.

ps

ps [*options*]

The ps command displays information about your running processes, and optionally the processes of other users:

```
→ ps
  PID TTY          TIME CMD
 4706 pts/2    00:00:01 bash
15007 pts/2    00:00:00 emacs
16729 pts/2    00:00:00 ps
```

ps has at least 80 options; I cover just a few useful combinations. If the options seem arbitrary or inconsistent, it's because the supplied ps command (GNU ps) incorporates the features of several other, competing ps commands, attempting to be compatible with all of them.

View your processes:

```
→ ps -ux
```

View all processes owned by user "smith":

```
→ ps -U smith
```

View all occurrences of a running program:

```
→ ps -C python
```

View processes on terminal *N*:

```
→ ps -t*N*
```

View particular processes 1, 2, and 3505:

```
→ ps -p1,2,3505
```

View all processes with their command lines truncated to the width of the screen:

```
→ ps -ef
```

View all processes with full command lines:

```
→ ps -efww
```

View all processes in a threaded view that indents child processes below their parents:

→ `ps -efH`

Use grep and other filter commands to extract information more finely from the output of ps:

→ `ps -ux | grep python`

---

pgrep

`pgrep [options] regex`

The pgrep command prints the process IDs (PIDs) of processes that match certain criteria, given by a regular expression. (A similar command, pidof, matches only fixed strings.) For example, print the PIDs of all running python processes:

→ `pgrep python`
```
4675
79493
82866
83114
```

or count the processes by adding the option -c:

→ `pgrep -c python`
```
4
```

Limit the results to processes owned by a particular user:

→ `pgrep -u smith`
```
79493
```

pgrep is most useful for passing a list of related PIDs to another command. For example, locate processes that match a string, using ps and command substitution (see "Command substitution" on page 27).

→ `ps -fwp $(pgrep python)`

See more examples of `pgrep` with the `kill` command in "Controlling Processes" on page 151.

Useful options

`-d` *string*	Use *string* as the delimiter character between PIDs (newline by default).
`-u` *user*	Print only processes running as the given username or user ID (UID). This is the effective user ID. For real user ID, use `-U`.
`-f`	Match against the process's full command line, not just its name.
`-x`	Exact match, rather than a substring match.
`-v`	Print PIDs of processes that *don't* match.

---

uptime

stdin **stdout** -file --opt **--help** **--version**

```
uptime
```

The `uptime` command tells you how long the system has been running since the last boot:

```
→ uptime
  10:54pm up 8 days, 3:44, 3 users,
  load average: 0.89, 1.00, 2.15
```

This information is, from beginning to end: the current time (10:54 p.m.), system uptime (8 days, 3 hours, 44 minutes), number of users logged in (3), and system load average for three time periods: 1 minute (0.89), 5 minutes (1.00), and 15 minutes (2.15). The load average is the average number of processes ready to run in that time interval.

w stdin **stdout** -file -- **opt** --**help** --**version**

w [*username*]

The w command displays the current process running in each shell for all logged-in users:

```
→ w
 10:51pm  up 8 days,  3:42,  8 users,
 load average: 2.02, 3.79, 5.44
USER    TTY   FROM LOGIN@  IDLE   JCPU   PCPU  WHAT
barrett pts/0 :0   Sat 2pm 27:13m 0.07s  0.07s emacs
jones   pts/1 host1 6Sep03 2:33m 0.74s  0.21s bash
smith   pts/2 host2 6Sep03 0.00s 13.35s 0.04s w
```

The top line is the same one printed by uptime. The columns indicate the user's terminal, originating host or X display (if applicable), login time, idle time, two measures of the CPU time (run man w for details), and the current process. Provide a username to see only that user's information.

For the briefest output, try w -hfs.

Useful options

- -h Don't print the header line.

- -f Don't print the FROM column.

- -s Don't print the JCPU and PCPU columns.

top stdin **stdout** -file -- opt --**help** --**version**

top [*options*]

The top command monitors the most active processes, updating the display at regular intervals (every 3 seconds, by default):

```
→ top
top - 13:02:14 up 1 day, 32 min, 9 users, ...
Tasks: 719 total, 2 running, 717 sleeping, 0 stopped...
%Cpu(s): 0.3 us, 0.2 sy, 0.0 ni, 99.6 id, 0.0 wa, ...
MiB Mem : 31950.5 total, 3040.6 free, 5267.4 used ...
MiB Swap: 32000.0 total, 31991.7 free, 8.2 used ...

PID   USER  PR NI VIRT SHR S  %CPU %MEM TIME CMD
26265 smith 20  0 1092 840 R   4.7  0.2 0:00 top
    1 root  20  0  540 472 S   0.0  0.1 0:07 systemd
  914 www    0  0    0   0 SW  0.0  0.0 0:00 httpd
⋮
```

While top runs, change its behavior interactively by pressing keys, such as setting the update speed (s key), hiding idle processes (i), or killing processes (k). Press h to list the keystrokes and q to quit. For similar commands to monitor your system's I/O and network bandwidth, try iotop and iftop. Also check out the all-in-one command btop, which displays stats for your CPUs, disks, processes, and network interfaces together.

Useful options

- -nN Perform N updates, then quit.

- -dN Update the display every N seconds.

- -pN Display the process with PID N. You may repeat this option for up to 20 PIDs.

- -c   Display the command-line arguments of processes.

- -b   Print on standard output instead of behaving like an interactive application. Suitable for piping or redirecting the output to a file. To save a single iteration of top to a file, run top -b -n1 > outfile.

---

free

stdin **stdout** - file -- opt **--help** **--version**

```
free [options]
```

The free command displays total memory use in KB:

```
        total      used      free  shared buf/cache available
Mem:    523812    491944    31868       0    224812    299000
Swap:   530104         0   530104
```

The Linux kernel reserves memory for caching purposes (buf/cache column), so your best estimate of free RAM in the preceding output is in the available column (i.e., 299,000 KB) rather than the free column (31,868 KB).

Useful options

- `-s` N   Run continuously and update the display every N seconds.

- `-m`   Display amounts in MB.

- `-h`   Display amounts in human-readable units like "Gi" for GB.

- `-t`   Add a totals row at the bottom.

Controlling Processes

`kill`   Terminate a process (or send it a signal).

`pkill`   Terminate processes by name (or send them a signal).

`timeout` Kill a command that runs for too long.

`nice`   Invoke a program at a particular priority.

`renice`   Change a process's priority as it runs.

`nohup`   Run a process that continues after you log out.

`flock`   Ensure that only one instance of a command runs at a time.

Once processes are started, they can be stopped, restarted, killed, and prioritized. I discussed some of these operations as handled by the shell in "Shell Job Control" on page 31. Let's continue to killing and prioritizing processes.

```
kill [options] [process_ids]
```

The `kill` command sends a signal to a process. This can terminate a process (the default action), interrupt it, suspend it, crash it, and so on. You must own the process, or be the superuser, to affect it. To terminate process 13243, run:

```
→ kill 13243
```

If this does not work—some programs catch this signal without terminating—add the `-KILL` or (equivalently) `-9` option:

```
→ kill -KILL 13243
```

which is virtually guaranteed to work. However, this is not a clean exit for the program, which may leave resources allocated (or cause other inconsistencies) upon its death.

To learn the PID of a process, run `ps` and examine the output, or better yet, run `pgrep` to produce the PID directly:

```
→ ps -uax | grep emacs
smith 8374  ...  emacs myfile.txt      Actual emacs process
smith 9051  ...  grep emacs            Spurious result to ignore
→ pgrep emacs                          More accurate output
8374
```

Now kill this process by PID, or kill it by name using command substitution (see "Command substitution" on page 27):

```
→ kill 8374                            Kill by PID
→ kill $(pgrep emacs)                  Kill by name
```

Or use the `pkill` command to kill all processes for a given program:

```
→ pkill emacs
```

In addition to the `kill` program in the filesystem (usually */bin/ kill*), most shells have built-in `kill` commands. Their syntax and behavior differ, but they all support the following usage:

```
kill -N PID
kill -NAME PID
```

where *N* is a signal number, *NAME* is a signal name without its leading "SIG" (e.g., to send the SIGHUP signal, use `-HUP`), and *PID* is the ID of the process to kill. To see a complete list of signals transmitted by `kill`, run `kill -l`, though its output differs depending on which `kill` you're running. For descriptions of the signals, run `man 7 signal`.

---

timeout   stdin stdout -file --opt **--help** **--version**

timeout [*options*] *seconds command...*

The `timeout` command sets a time limit for running a program, in seconds. If the program runs longer than the limit, `timeout` kills it. As a demonstration, here is a `sleep` command that should run for one minute but is killed after 3 seconds:

→ **timeout 3 sleep 60**   *Killed after 3 seconds*

As a more practical example, play music from your MP3 collection for an hour (3,600 seconds), then stop:

→ **timeout 3600 mplayer *.mp3**

Useful options

-s *signal*   Send a signal other than the default (TERM). The choices are the same ones listed by `kill -l`.

-k *seconds*   If the program doesn't die after the first signal, wait this many seconds longer and send a deadly KILL signal.

nice [-n *level*] *command_line*

When invoking a system-intensive program, be nice to the other processes (and users) by lowering its priority. That's what the nice command is for: it sets a *nice level* (an amount of "niceness") for a process so it receives less attention from the Linux process scheduler.[1] Here's an example of setting a big job to run at nice level 7:

→ **nice -n 7 sort hugefile > outfile**

Normal processes (run without nice) run at level zero, which you can see by running nice with no arguments:

→ **nice**
0

If you omit the -n option, the default nice level is 10. The superuser can also lower the nice level, increasing a process's priority:

→ **sudo nice -n -10** *some_program*

The nice levels of processes appear in the output of ps (the NI column) and top (the N column).

→ **ps -o pid,user,args,nice**

For programs with a lot of disk accesses, also check out the command ionice, which is like nice for input/output.

---

1 This is called "nicing" the process. You'll hear the term used as a verb: "I niced the process to 12."

renice

renice [-n *N*] [*options*] *PID*

While the nice command invokes a program at a given nice level, renice changes the nice level of an already-running process. As a quick (though trivial) test, create a process that just sleeps for 2 minutes, run it in the background, and raise its nice level by 5:

```
→ sleep 120 &
[1] 2673                       The PID of "sleep" is 2673
→ renice -n 5 -p 2673
2673 (process ID) old priority 0, new priority 5
```

Ordinary users can increase the nice level of their own processes, while the superuser can also decrease the level (increasing the priority) and can operate on any process. The valid range is −20 to +20, but avoid large negative values or you might interfere with vital system processes.

Useful options

-p *pid*   Affect the process with the given ID, *pid*. You can omit the -p
                  and just provide a PID (renice -n 5 28734).

-u *username*   Affect all processes owned by the given user.

nohup

nohup *command*

Use nohup to keep a command running after you terminate the shell that launched it. Ordinarily, when a shell or other process terminates, its child processes are sent a termination signal, called a hangup signal. The command nohup, which stands for "no hangup," causes the named command to ignore hangup signals.

```
→ nohup some_long_running_command &
```

If the supplied command writes to stdout or stderr, nohup redirects output to a file *nohup.out* in the current directory (if you have permission) or in your home directory (if you don't).

---

flock   stdin   stdout   - file   -- opt   **--help**   **--version**

```
flock [options] lockfile command…
```

Do you ever need to ensure that only one instance of a program runs at a time on your computer? For example, if you run automatic backups every hour using a command like rsync, there's a slight chance that a previous backup might still be running when the next backup launches. The flock command solves this sort of problem. It creates a lock file that prevents a command, such as a backup script, from running concurrently with itself. If you try to run two copies of the command at once with the same lock file, the second fails. For example, this rsync command, when run with flock and the lock file */tmp/mylock*, instantly fails if another instance of the same command is already running:

```
→ flock -n /tmp/mylock rsync -av dir1 dir2
```

To see flock in action, open two shell windows and run the following command in each shell, one at a time (I use the sleep command as a demonstration, which does nothing but wait for a given number of seconds):

```
→ flock -n /tmp/mylock sleep 60
```

The first command runs and the second instantly terminates because they have the same *lockfile*. This can be any file or directory name, which flock treats as a unique marker to prevent other commands from running. For example, if you run the preceding sleep command in one shell and a different command such as ls in another, with the same lock file:

```
→ flock -n /tmp/mylock ls
```

then flock prevents the second command (ls) from running.

Useful options

-n   Instantly fail if another command is already running.

-w *N*   Fail after waiting *N* seconds, if another command is already running.

-s   Use a shared lock instead of an exclusive lock. You can run multiple commands simultaneously with this option, but flock fails if you omit the option. This is useful to limit the number of commands that can run simultaneously.

Scheduling Jobs

sleep   Wait a set number of seconds, doing nothing.

watch   Run a command at set intervals.

at   Schedule a job for a single, future time.

crontab   Schedule jobs for many future times.

If you need to launch programs at particular times or at regular intervals, Linux provides several scheduling tools with various degrees of complexity.

---

sleep
stdin   stdout - file -- opt --help --version

```
sleep time_specification
```

The sleep command simply waits a set amount of time. The given time specification can be an integer (meaning seconds) or an integer followed by the letter s (also seconds), m (minutes), h (hours), or d (days). For example:

```
→ sleep 5m
```
                  Do nothing for 5 minutes

---

sleep is useful to delay a command for a set amount of time:

```
→ sleep 3 && echo 'Three seconds have passed.'
(3 seconds pass)
Three seconds have passed.
```

---

watch

watch [*options*] *command*

watch executes a supplied command at regular intervals; the default is every two seconds. The command is passed to the shell (so be sure to quote or escape any special characters), and the results are displayed in a full-screen mode, so you can observe the output conveniently and see what has changed. For example, watch -n 1 date executes the date command once per second, sort of a poor man's clock. Press ^C to exit.

Useful options

-n *seconds*	Set the time between executions, in seconds.
-d	Highlight differences in the output, to emphasize what has changed from one execution to the next.
-g	Exit when the command produces output that is different from the previous execution.

---

at

at [*options*] *time_specification*

The at command schedules one or more shell commands to run later:

```
→ at 7am next sunday
at> echo Remember to go shopping | mail smith
at> lpr $HOME/shopping-list
at> ^D
```

```
<EOT>
job 559 at 2024-09-08 21:30
```

If the host is sleeping or off at the scheduled time, the job will run immediately when the host comes up again. The time specifications understood by at are enormously flexible, such as:

- A time followed by a date (not a date followed by a time)
- Only a date (assumes the current clock time)
- Only a time (assumes the very next occurrence, whether today or tomorrow)
- A special word like now, midnight, or teatime (16:00)
- Any of the preceding followed by an offset, like "+ 3 days"

Dates may take many forms: december 25 2030, 25 december 2030, december 25, 25 december, 12/25/2030, 25.12.2030, 20301225, today, thursday, next thursday, next month, next year, and more. Month names can be abbreviated to three letters (jan, feb, mar, ...). Times are also flexible: 8pm, 8 pm, 8:00pm, 8:00 pm, 20:00, and 2000 are equivalent. Offsets are a plus or minus sign followed by whitespace and an amount of time: + 3 days, + 2 weeks, - 1 hour, and so on.[2]

If you omit part of the date or time, at copies the missing information from the system date and time. So next year alone means one year from right now, thursday alone means the upcoming Thursday at the current clock time, december 25 alone means the next December 25, and 4:30pm alone means the very next occurrence of 4:30 p.m. in the future.

The command you supply to at is not evaluated by the shell until execution time, so file patterns, variables, and other shell constructs are not expanded until then. Also, your current environment (see printenv) is preserved within each job so

---

2 See the formal syntax in the file */usr/share/doc/at/timespec*.

it executes as if you were logged in. Aliases, however, aren't available to at jobs, so don't include them.

To list your at jobs, use atq ("at queue"):

```
→ atq
559  2024-09-08 21:30 a smith
```

To delete a job, run atrm ("at remove") with the job number:

```
→ atrm 559
```

Useful options

-f *filename* Read commands from the given file instead of standard input.

-c *job_number* Print a job's commands to standard output.

---

crontab stdin **stdout** **- file** **-- opt** --help --version

crontab [*options*] [*file*]

The crontab command, like the at command, schedules jobs for specific times. However, crontab is for recurring jobs, such as "Run this command at midnight every Tuesday." To make this work, you edit and save a file, called your *crontab file*, which automatically gets installed in a system directory (*/var/spool/cron*). Once a minute, a Linux process called cron wakes up, checks all crontab files, and executes any jobs that are due.

crontab -e
  Edit your crontab file in your default editor ($VISUAL).

crontab -l
  Print your crontab file on standard output.

crontab -r
  With *no confirmation*, delete your crontab file immediately and permanently.

```
crontab myfile
```
Install the file *myfile* as your crontab file.

The superuser can add the option `-u` *username* to work with other users' crontab files.

Crontab files contain one job per line. (Blank lines and comment lines beginning with "#" are ignored.) Each line has six fields, separated by whitespace. The first five fields specify the time to run the job, and the last is the job command itself.

Minutes of the hour
> Integers between 0 and 59. This can be a single number (`30`), a sequence of numbers separated by commas (`0,15,30,45`), a range (`20-30`), a sequence of ranges (`0-15,50-59`), or an asterisk to mean "all." You can also specify "every *n*th time" with the suffix `/n`; for instance, both `*/12` and `0-59/12` mean `0,12,24,36,48` (i.e., every 12 minutes).

Hours of the day
> Same syntax as for minutes.

Days of the month
> Integers between 1 and 31; again, you may use sequences, ranges, sequences of ranges, or an asterisk.

Months of the year
> Integers between 1 and 12; again, you may use sequences, ranges, sequences of ranges, or an asterisk. Additionally, you may use three-letter abbreviations (`jan`, `feb`, `mar`, ...), but not in ranges or sequences.

Days of the week
> Integers between 0 (Sunday) and 6 (Saturday); again, you may use sequences, ranges, sequences of ranges, or an asterisk. Additionally, you may use three-letter abbreviations (`sun`, `mon`, `tue`, ...), but not in ranges or sequences.

Command to execute

Any shell command. It's executed in your login environment, so you can include environment variables like $HOME and they'll work. Use only absolute paths to your commands (e.g., */usr/bin/who* instead of *who*) to ensure that cron runs the right programs, since a Linux system may have several programs with the same name.

Here are some example time specifications:

*	*	*	*	*	Every minute
45	*	*	*	*	45 minutes after each hour (1:45, 2:45, etc.)
45	9	*	*	*	Every day at 9:45 a.m.
45	9	8	*	*	The eighth day of every month at 9:45 a.m.
45	9	8	12	*	Every December 8 at 9:45 a.m.
45	9	8	dec	*	Every December 8 at 9:45 a.m.
45	9	*	*	6	Every Saturday at 9:45 a.m.
45	9	*	*	sat	Every Saturday at 9:45 a.m.
45	9	*	12	6	Every Saturday in December, at 9:45 a.m.
45	9	8	12	6	Every Saturday in December, plus December 8, all at 9:45 a.m.

Here's a complete crontab entry to run a script every Saturday at 9:45 a.m.:

```
45  9  *  *  sat  /usr/local/bin/myscript
```

If a job prints any output, cron emails a copy to the owner of the crontab file.

Avoid long, messy shell commands in the *crontab* file. Instead, store them in shell scripts to run from *crontab*.

Logins, Logouts, and Shutdowns

systemctl   Control the state of your machine and its services.

shutdown   Shut down your local machine.

reboot   Reboot your local machine.

Logging in and out from GNOME, KDE, or other graphical desktops is easy. To log out from a remote shell, just close the shell (run exit or logout or press ^D on a line by itself). Linux also provides commands for rebooting and shutting down the computer or individual services. Never simply turn off the power to a Linux system: it needs a more graceful shutdown to preserve its filesystem.

systemctl stdin **stdout** -file --opt **--help** **--version**

systemctl [*options*] *command* [*arguments*]

The systemctl command controls system services. It's part of a service manager called systemd. A full treatment of systemd is beyond the scope of this book, but I cover a few basic uses. (See man systemd for more details.)

systemctl can control the system as a whole:

sudo systemctl poweroff   Shut down the system.

sudo systemctl reboot   Reboot the system.

sudo systemctl suspend   Suspend the system.

It also manages individual services, such as web servers and databases, with the following basic commands (among others):

`systemctl`	List all services and their statuses.
`sudo systemctl enable` *service_name*	Make a service runnable, but do not launch it.
`sudo systemctl start` *service_name*	Launch an enabled service.
`sudo systemctl restart` *service_name*	Same as `stop` followed by `start`.
`sudo systemctl reload` *service_name*	Force a running service to reread its configuration.
`sudo systemctl status` *service_name*	Print the service's current status. For more detailed status information, see `man journalctl`.
`sudo systemctl stop` *service_name*	Shut down a running service.
`sudo systemctl disable` *service_name*	Prevent a service from being started.

Service names have the suffix ".service", which you may omit. For example, to restart the mySQL database server, either of the following commands works:

→ **sudo systemctl restart mysqld.service** *With suffix*
→ **sudo systemctl restart mysqld** *No suffix*

---

shutdown

stdin **stdout** -file --opt **--help** --version

shutdown [*options*] *time* [*message*]

The shutdown command halts or reboots a Linux machine; only the superuser may run it. (In many Linux distros, the shutdown command is a symbolic link to systemctl.) Here's a command

---

to halt the system in 10 minutes, broadcasting the message "scheduled maintenance" to all users logged in:

```
→ sudo shutdown -h +10 "scheduled maintenance"
```

The *time* may be a number of minutes preceded by a plus sign, like +10; an absolute time in hours and minutes, like 16:25; or the word now to mean immediately.

With no options, shutdown puts the system into single-user mode, a special maintenance mode in which only root is logged in (at the system console), and all nonessential services are off. To exit single-user mode, either perform another shutdown to halt or reboot, or exit the shell with exit or ^D to boot the system in normal, multiuser mode.

Useful options

- -r   Reboot the system.

- -h   Halt the system.

- -k   Kidding: don't really perform a shutdown, just broadcast warning messages to all users as if the system were going down.

- -c   Cancel a shutdown in progress (omit the *time* argument).

- -f   On reboot, skip the usual filesystem check performed by the fsck command (described in "Using Disks and Filesystems" on page 195).

- -F   On reboot, require the usual filesystem check.

For technical information about shutdowns, single-user mode, and various system states, see man systemd or man init.

---

reboot   stdin **stdout** -file --opt **--help** --version

```
reboot [options]
```

The reboot command does exactly what it sounds like. It immediately reboots the computer. You might assume that

---

reboot requires root privileges, but on some distros, any user can run it.

reboot has options (see the manpage) but I rarely use them. In some Linux distros, the reboot command is just a symbolic link to systemctl.

Users and Their Environment

logname	Print your login name.
whoami	Print your current, effective username.
id	Print the user ID and group membership of a user.
who	List logged-in users, long output.
users	List logged-in users, short output.
tty	Print your terminal device name.
last	Determine when someone last logged in.
printenv	Print your environment.

Who are you? Only the system knows for sure. This grab-bag of programs tells you all about *users*: their names, login times, and properties of their environment.

---

logname
stdin **stdout** -file --opt **--help** **--version**

logname

The logname command prints your login name:

```
→ logname
smith
```

If this command does not work on your system, try instead:

```
→ echo $LOGNAME
```

---

whoami

stdin **stdout** - file -- opt **--help** **--version**

whoami

The whoami command prints the name of the current, effective user. This may differ from your login name (the output of logname) when using the sudo command. This example distinguishes whoami from logname:

```
→ logname              Login name
smith
→ sudo logname         The value does not change
smith
→ whoami               Effective username
smith
→ sudo whoami          The value changes
root
```

id

stdin **stdout** - file -- opt **--help** **--version**

id [options] [username]

Every user has a unique, numeric *user ID*, and a default group with a unique, numeric *group ID*. The id command prints these values along with their associated user and group names:

```
→ id
uid=500(smith) gid=500(smith) groups=500(smith),6(disk)
```

Useful options

- -u   Print the effective user ID and exit.

- -g   Print the effective group ID and exit.

- -G   Print the IDs of all groups to which the user belongs.

With any of the preceding options, add -n to print user and group names instead of IDs, and add -r to print real IDs/names rather than effective ones.

who

who [*options*] [*filename*]

The who command lists all logged-in users. Users with multiple interactive shells appear multiple times:

```
→ who
smith    pts/0    Sep  6 17:09 (:0)
barrett  pts/1    Sep  6 17:10 (10.24.19.240)
jones    pts/2    Sep  8 20:58 (192.168.13.7)
jones    pts/4    Sep  3 05:11 (192.168.13.7)
```

Normally, who reads its data from the file */var/run/utmp*. The *filename* argument selects a different file, such as */var/log/wtmp* for past logins or */var/log/btmp* for failed logins.[3]

Useful options

-H	Print a row of headings as the first line.
--lookup	For remotely logged-in users, print the hostnames of origin.
-u	Also print each user's idle time at their terminal.
-m	Display information only about yourself, the user associated with the current terminal.
-q	Quick display of usernames only and a count of users. Much like the users command, but it adds a count.

users

users [*filename*]

The users command prints a quick listing of users who are logged in. Users with multiple interactive shells appear multiple times:

---

3 If your system is configured to log this information.

```
→ users
barrett jones smith smith smith
```

Like the who command, users reads */var/log/utmp* by default but can read from another supplied file instead.

---

tty
stdin **stdout** ·file --opt **--help** **--version**

```
tty
```

The tty command prints the name of the terminal device associated with the current shell:

```
→ tty
/dev/pts/4
```

---

last
stdin **stdout** ·file --opt **--help** **--version**

```
last [options] [users] [ttys]
```

The last command displays a history of logins in reverse chronological order:

```
→ last
bob pts/3 localhost Mon Sep 8 21:07 - 21:08 (00:01)
sue pts/6 :0        Mon Sep 8 20:25 - 20:56 (00:31)
bob pts/4 myhost    Sun Sep 7 22:19 still logged in
⋮
```

You may provide usernames or tty names to limit the output.

Useful options

-N	Print only the latest N lines of output, where N is a positive integer.
-p time	Print only users who were logged in at the given time. For current logins, run last -p now.
-i	Display IP addresses instead of hostnames.

-R	Don't display hostnames.
-x	Also display system shutdowns and changes in system runlevel (e.g., from single-user mode into multiuser mode).
-f *filename*	Read from some data file other than */var/run/wtmp*; see the who command for more details.

---

printenv

```
printenv [environment_variables]
```

The printenv command prints all environment variables known to your shell and their values:

```
→ printenv
HOME=/home/smith
MAIL=/var/spool/mail/smith
NAME=Sandy Smith
SHELL=/bin/bash
⋮
```

or only specified variables:

```
→ printenv HOME SHELL
/home/smith
/bin/bash
```

User Account Management

useradd	Create an account.
usermod	Delete an account.
usermod	Modify an account.
passwd	Change a password.
chsh	Change a user's shell.

Linux installation software automatically creates the root account and usually an ordinary user account (presumably for

---

yourself). You can also create other accounts. Just remember that every account is a potential avenue for an intruder to enter your system, so give them all strong, hard-to-guess passwords.

useradd

useradd [*options*] *username*

The useradd command lets the superuser create a user account. (Don't confuse it with the similarly named adduser command.)

→ **sudo useradd -m smith**

Its defaults are not very useful (run useradd -D to see them), so be sure to supply all desired options. For example:

→ **sudo useradd -d /home/smith -s /bin/bash **
  -G games,video smith

Useful options

-m	Create the user's home directory, and copy some standard files into it from your system skeleton directory, */etc/skel*. The skeleton directory traditionally contains minimal (skeletal) versions of initialization files, like *~/.bashrc*, to get new users started. If you prefer to copy from a different directory, add the -k option (-k *dirname*).
-d *dir*	Set the user's home directory to be *dir*.
-s *shell*	Set the user's login shell to be *shell*.
-u *uid*	Set the user's ID to be *uid*. Unless you know what you're doing, omit this option and accept the default.
-c *string*	Set the user's comment field (historically called the GECOS field). This is usually the user's full name, but it can be any string.

-g *group*	Set the user's initial (default) group to *group*, which can either be a numeric group ID or a group name, and which must already exist.
-G *group1*,*group2*,…	Make the user a member of the additional, existing groups *group1*, *group2*, and so on.

userdel

stdin **stdout** file **-- opt** **--help** --version

userdel [-r] *username*

The userdel command deletes an existing user.

→ **sudo userdel smith**

It does not delete the user's files (home directory, mailbox, etc.) unless you supply the -r option. Think carefully before deleting a user; consider deactivating the account instead (with usermod -L). And make sure you have backups of all the user's files before deleting them—you might need them someday.

usermod

stdin **stdout** file **-- opt** **--help** --version

usermod [*options*] *username*

The usermod command modifies the given user's account in various ways, such as changing a home directory:

→ **sudo usermod -d /home/another smith**

Useful options

-a	When adding the user to a group (- G), preserve the user's existing group memberships.
-c *string*	Set the user's comment field (historically called the GECOS field). This is usually the user's full name, but it can be any string.

-d *dir*	Change the user's home directory to *dir*.
-l *username*	Change the user's login name to *username*. Think carefully before doing this, in case anything on your system depends on the original name. And don't change system accounts (root, daemon, etc.) unless you really know what you're doing!
-s *shell*	Change the user's login shell to *shell*.
-g *group*	Change the user's initial (default) group to *group*, which can either be a numeric group ID or a group name, and which must already exist.
-G *group1,group2,...*	Make the user a member *only* of the existing groups *group1*, *group2*, and so on. **WARNING:** if the user currently belongs to other groups and you don't list them here, usermod removes the user from the other groups. To prevent this behavior and preserve the user's existing groups, add the -a option.
-L	Disable (lock) the account so the user cannot log in.
-U	Unlock the account after a lock (-L) operation.

---

passwd

stdin **stdout** file **--opt** **--help** --version

passwd [*options*] [*username*]

The passwd command changes a login password, yours by default:

→ **passwd**

or another user's password if run by the superuser:

→ **sudo passwd smith**

passwd does have options, most of them related to password expiration. Use them only in the context of a well thought-out security policy.

---

chsh [*options*] [*username*]

The chsh (change shell) command sets your login shell program. Invoked without a username, chsh affects your account; invoked with a username (by root), it affects that user. With no options, chsh prompts you for the desired information:

```
→ chsh
Password: xxxxxxxx
New shell [/bin/bash]: /bin/tcsh
```

The new shell must be listed in the file */etc/shells*.

Useful options

-s *shell*   Specify the new shell.

-l   List all permissible shells installed on your system.

Group Management

groups   Print the group membership of a user.

groupadd   Create a group.

newgrp   Use a new group membership immediately.

groupdel   Delete a group.

groupmod   Modify a group.

A *group* is a set of accounts treated as a single entity. If you give permission for a group to take some action (such as modify a file), then all members of that group can take it. For example, give full permissions for the group "friends" to read, write, and execute the file */tmp/sample*:

```
→ groups
users smith friends
→ chgrp friends /tmp/sample
→ chmod 770 /tmp/sample
```

```
→ ls -l /tmp/sample
-rwxrwx--- 1 smith friends 2874 ... /tmp/sample
```

To add users to a group, run usermod -aG or edit */etc/group* as root. To change the group ownership of a file, recall the chgrp command from "Properties of Files" on page 65.

---

groups
stdin **stdout** - file -- opt **--help** **--version**

groups [*usernames*]

The groups command prints the Linux groups to which you belong, or to which other users belong:

```
→ whoami
smith
→ groups
smith users
→ groups jones root
jones : jones users
root : root bin daemon sys adm disk wheel src
```

---

groupadd
stdin stdout - file -- opt **--help** --version

groupadd [*options*] *group*

The groupadd command creates a group. (Don't confuse it with the similarly named addgroup command.) In most cases, add the -f option to prevent duplicate groups from being created:

```
→ sudo groupadd -f friends
```

Useful options

-g *gid* Specify a numeric group ID, *gid*. Normally, groupadd chooses it.

-f   If the named group exists already, complain and exit.

---

newgrp

stdin   stdout - file -- opt **--help** --version

```
newgrp [-] [group]
```

When you're added to a new group (e.g., with usermod -aG), normally the change isn't effective until your next login. The newgrp command avoids this hassle. Run newgrp with the new group name as an argument, and it launches a fresh shell with your current group ID set to that group. In this way, you can immediately use newly granted group privileges. The effect lasts only while the new shell runs, but it beats logging out and back in. Exit the shell to restore your default group ID.

For example, suppose you've just been added to the group video. If you haven't logged out yet, you won't see video among your groups.

```
→ groups                    View your active groups
smith sudo docker
```

Run newgrp to set your group ID to video:

```
→ newgrp video              Launch a shell with group ID = video
→ groups                    Now "video" is your default group
video sudo docker smith
→ exit                      Set group ID back to default
```

The only option, a single dash, causes newgrp to set up your environment as if you'd just logged in, like su -l does.

groupdel

stdin   stdout - file **-- opt** **--help** --version

```
groupdel group
```

The groupdel command deletes an existing group:

```
→ sudo groupdel friends
```

Before removing a group, identify all files owned by that group so you can clean them up later:

```
→ sudo find / -group friends -print > /tmp/friend.files
```

because groupdel does not change the group ownership of any files. It simply removes the group name from */etc/group*. Any files owned by the deleted group will retain the now-obsolete group ID.

---

groupmod

groupmod [*options*] *group*

The groupmod command modifies the given group, changing its name or group ID:

```
→ sudo groupmod -n newname friends
```

groupmod does not affect any files owned by this group: it simply changes the ID or name in the system's records.

Useful options

-n *name*   Change the group's name to *name* (safe).

-g *gid*   Change the group's ID to *gid* (risky). Any files with the original group ID will now have invalid group ownership and need cleanup.

Installing Software Packages

dnf   Standard package manager for RPM files (CentOS, Fedora, Red Hat, Rocky, etc.).

yum   Older package manager for RPM files.

rpm   Manipulate RPM packages locally.

apt   Standard package manager for DEB files (Debian, Deepin, elementary OS, Kodachi, Linux Lite, MX, Mint, Nitrux, POP!_OS, Rescatux, Ubuntu, Zorin OS, etc.).

aptitude   Alternative package manager for DEB files.

dpkg   Manipulate DEB packages locally.

`emerge`	Portage package manager for Gentoo Linux.
`pacman`	Package manager for Arch Linux (plus Garuda, EndeavourOS, Manjaro, etc.).
`zypper`	Package manager for openSUSE Linux.
`flatpak`	Container-based package manager.
`snap`	Container-based package manager.

Your Linux distro comes with a *package manager* application to install software packages via the command line, GUI tools, or both. Confusingly, every package manager has unique commands and may use a different file format for packages. So, one of your first tasks as a Linux user is to learn which package manager is standard for your distro. If you aren't sure which Linux distro you're running, one of the following commands should give you a clue:

```
→ cat /etc/issue
Ubuntu 22.04.2 LTS \n \l          Running Ubuntu Linux
→ more /etc/*-release
DISTRIB_ID=Ubuntu
DISTRIB_RELEASE=22.04
DISTRIB_CODENAME=jammy
⋮
```

Then search for your distro's package manager on the web, or just run each package management command in my list to see which ones are installed. The most common package types and managers are:

Debian, dpkg, or .deb packages
> Used by Debian, Ubuntu, and other distros. I cover the package management commands apt, aptitude, and dpkg.

RPM packages
> Used by Red Hat, Fedora, CentOS, and other distros. I cover dnf, yum, rpm, and zypper.

These package types and others (some of which I cover) install software into system directories like */usr/bin*. Another kind of package manager takes a different approach and runs its software in a restricted mini-environment called a container. Examples are Snap and Flatpak.

dnf

stdin   **stdout**   - file   -- opt   **--help**   **--version**

```
dnf [options] [packages]
```

dnf is the latest package manager for RPM packages (.rpm files). The following table lists common operations:

Action	dnf command
Search for a package that meets your needs (supports wildcards * and ?).	dnf search *string*
Check if a package is installed.	dnf list installed *package*
Download but don't install a package.	dnf download *package*
Download and install a package.	sudo dnf install *package*
Install a package file.	sudo dnf install *file*.rpm
Learn about a package.	dnf info *package*
List the contents of a package.	rpm -ql *package*
Discover which package an installed file belongs to.	dnf provides */path/to/file*
Update an installed package.	sudo dnf upgrade *package*
Remove an installed package.	sudo dnf remove *package*
List all packages installed on the system (tip: pipe through less).	dnf list installed
Check for updates for all installed packages.	dnf check-update
Update all packages on the system.	sudo dnf upgrade
Update the distro to the next version.	sudo dnf system-upgrade

yum

yum [options] [packages]

yum is an older package manager for RPM packages (.rpm files), which has been largely replaced by dnf. The following table lists common operations with yum. For operations on local files, which yum does not provide, use the rpm command directly.

Action	yum command
Search for a package that meets your needs (supports wildcards * and ?).	yum search string
Check if a package is installed.	yum list installed package
Download a package but don't install it.[a]	sudo yum --downloadonly install package
Download and install a package.	sudo yum install package
Install a package file.	rpm -ivh file.rpm
Learn about a package.	yum info package
List the contents of a package.	rpm -ql package
Discover which package an installed file belongs to.	yum provides /path/to/file
Update an installed package.	sudo yum update package
Remove an installed package.	sudo yum remove package
List all packages installed on the system (tip: pipe through less).	yum list installed
Check for updates for all installed packages.	yum check-update
Update all packages on the system.	sudo yum update

[a] May require the downloadonly plug-in. To install it, run sudo yum install yum-downloadonly

rpm

rpm [*options*] [*files*]

If you prefer to download and install RPM packages by hand, use the rpm command. Unlike dnf or yum, rpm works locally on your computer: it does not search software archives on the internet for new packages.

RPM filenames typically take the following form *<name>-<version>.<architecture>.rpm*. For example, the filename *emacs-29.1-2.x86_64.rpm* indicates the emacs package, version 29.1-2, for 64-bit x86 processors. Be aware that rpm sometimes requires a filename argument (like *emacs-29.1-2.x86_64.rpm*) and other times just the package name (like *emacs*). The following table lists common operations:

Action	rpm command
Check if a package is installed.	rpm -q *package*
Install a package file.	sudo rpm -ivh *file*.rpm
Learn about a package.	rpm -qi *package*
List the contents of a package.	rpm -ql *package*
Discover which package an installed file belongs to.	rpm -qf */path/to/file*
Update an installed package.	sudo rpm -Uvh *package_file*.rpm
Remove an installed package.	sudo rpm -e *package*
List all packages installed on the system (tip: pipe through less).	rpm -qa

```
apt subcommand [options] packages
```

```
dpkg [options] packages
```

The APT (Advanced Packaging Tool) suite of commands can install, remove, and manipulate Debian Linux (*.deb*) packages. The following table lists common operations:

Action	APT command
Retrieve the latest information about available packages before running other commands.	sudo apt update
Search for a package that meets your needs.	apt search *string*
Check if a package is installed.	apt policy *package*
Download but don't install a package.	sudo apt install -d *package*
Download and install a package.	sudo apt install *package*
Install a package file.	sudo apt install *file*.deb
Learn about a package.	apt show *package*
List the contents of a package.	dpkg -L *package*
Discover which package an installed file belongs to.	dpkg -S */path/to/file*
Update an installed package.	sudo apt upgrade *package*
Remove an installed package.	sudo apt remove *package*
Remove an installed package and associated files.	sudo apt purge *package*
List all packages installed on the system (tip: pipe through less).	apt list --installed
Check for updates for all installed packages (run sudo apt update first).	sudo apt list --upgradable

Action	APT command
Update all packages on the system.	`sudo apt upgrade`
Update the distro to the next version.	`sudo apt dist-upgrade`

aptitude

`aptitude [options] [packages]`

aptitude is another package manager for the command line that manipulates Debian (*.deb*) packages. When run with no arguments, it provides a full-terminal interactive interface to the APT system:

→ **sudo aptitude**

aptitude can also run some, but not all, APT operations from the command line. The following table lists common operations, including a few that aptitude does not support and the appropriate apt or dpkg commands to run instead.

Action	aptitude command
Retrieve the latest information about available packages before running other commands.	`sudo aptitude update`
Search for a package that meets your needs.	`aptitude search string`
Check if a package is installed (see "State" in the output).	`aptitude show package`
Download but don't install a package.	`aptitude download package`
Download and install a package.	`sudo aptitude install package`

Action	aptitude command
Install a package file.	`sudo apt install file.deb`
Learn about a package.	`aptitude show package`
List the contents of a package.	`dpkg -L package`
Discover which package an installed file belongs to.	`dpkg -S /path/to/file`
Update an installed package.	`sudo aptitude safe-upgrade package`
Remove an installed package.	`sudo aptitude remove package`
List all packages installed on the system (tip: pipe through `less`).	`aptitude search ~i`
Check for updates for all installed packages.	`aptitude --simulate full-upgrade`
Update all packages on the system.	`sudo aptitude full-upgrade`

emerge

stdin **stdout** - file -- opt **--help** **--version**

```
emerge [options] [arguments]
emaint [options] subcommand
equery [options] subcommand [arguments]
```

The `emerge` command controls the package manager in Gentoo Linux, called Portage. Before working with Portage packages for the first time, run the following command:

→ **sudo emerge gentoolkit**   *Install additional Portage commands*

Action	emerge command
Retrieve the latest information about available packages before running other commands.	`sudo emaint -a sync`
Search for a package that meets your needs, by name.	`emerge -s string`
Search for a package that meets your needs, by description.	`emerge -S string`
Check if a package is installed.	`equery list "*"	grep package`
Download but don't install a package.	`sudo emerge -f package`
Download and install a package.	`sudo emerge package`
Learn about a package.	`sudo equery meta [--description] package`
List the contents of a package.	`equery files package`
Discover which package an installed file belongs to.	`equery belongs /path/to/file`
Update an installed package.	`sudo emerge -u package`
Remove an installed package.	`sudo emerge -cav package`
List all packages installed on the system (tip: pipe through less).	`equery list "*"`
Check for updates for all installed packages.	`emerge -puD world`
Update all packages on the system.	`sudo emerge -uD world`

If emerge won't remove a package because of dependencies, try including the dependencies on the command line:

```
→ sudo emerge -cav my/package                    fails
Calculating dependencies... done!
  my/package-29.3 pulled in by:
    other/pack-16.1 requires ...               dependency!
>>> No packages selected for removal by depclean
→ sudo emerge -cav my/package other/pack      succeeds
Would you like to unmerge these packages? [Yes/No] Yes
```

---

pacman

stdin **stdout** - file -- opt **--help** **--version**

pacman *subcommand* [*options*] [*arguments*]

The pacman command is a package manager for Arch Linux. Arch packages are typically tar files compressed with the command zstd. The following table lists common operations:

Action	pacman command
Retrieve the latest information about available packages before running other commands.	sudo pacman -Sy
Search for a package that meets your needs (by regular expression).	pacman -Ss *string*
Check if a package is installed.	pacman -Q *package*
Download but don't install a package.	sudo pacman -Sw *package*
Download and install a package.	sudo pacman -S *package*
Install a package file.	sudo pacman -U *file*.pkg.tar.zst
Learn about a package.	pacman -Qi *package*
List the contents of a package.	pacman -Ql *package*

Action	pacman command
Discover which package an installed file belongs to.	`pacman -Qo /path/to/file`
Update an installed package.	`sudo pacman -S package`
Remove an installed package.	`sudo pacman -R package`
List all packages installed on the system (tip: pipe through `less`).	`pacman -Qe`
Check for updates for all installed packages.	`sudo pacman -Syup`
Update all packages on the system.	`sudo pacman -Syu`

zypper

stdin · **stdout** · -file · --opt · **--help** · **--version**

```
zypper [options] subcommand [subcommand_opts] [arguments]
```

The zypper command is a package manager for openSUSE Linux. It uses RPM packages under the hood. The following table lists common operations:

Action	zypper command
Retrieve the latest information about available packages before running other commands.	`sudo zypper refresh`
Search for a package that meets your needs.	`zypper search string`
Check if a package is installed.	`zypper search -i package`
Download but don't install a package.	`sudo zypper install -d package`
Download and install a package.	`sudo zypper install package`
Install a package file.	`sudo rpm -ivh file.rpm`

Action	zypper command
Learn about a package.	`zypper info package`
List the contents of a package.	`rpm -ql package`
Discover which package an installed file belongs to.	`rpm -qf /path/to/file`
Update an installed package.	`sudo zypper update package`
Remove an installed package.	`sudo zypper remove package`
List all packages installed on the system (tip: pipe through `less`).	`zypper search -i`
Check for updates for all installed packages.	`sudo zypper update --dry-run`
Update all packages on the system.	`sudo zypper update`
Update the distro to the next version.	`sudo zypper dist-upgrade`

flatpak

stdin **stdout** - file -- opt **--help** **--version**

`flatpak subcommand [options] [arguments]`

Flatpak is a system for installing software packages, called "Flatpaks," that run in a restricted environment, called a container or sandbox. A container includes all the package's dependencies. Use the `flatpak` command to install, update, and remove packages. You may need to add a remote repository first:

→ **sudo flatpak remote-add --if-not-exists flathub \
  https://flathub.org/repo/flathub.flatpakrepo**

Flatpaks have limited access to the host filesystem, but for the most part, they operate like ordinary applications...except when you run them at the command line. Flatpaks must be run with the `flatpak` command. So if you've installed GNU Emacs, for example, find out its Flatpak ID, which is a three-part string containing dots, such as `org.gnu.emacs`. Then run the program by its ID:

```
→ flatpak list | grep emacs
ID              ...
org.gnu.emacs ...            The flatpak ID
→ flatpak run org.gnu.emacs
```

If typing the ID is annoying, define an alias:

```
alias emacs='flatpak run org.gnu.emacs'
```

The following table lists common operations for working with Flatpaks system-wide, which often requires superuser privileges. To install Flatpaks just for yourself, run `flatpak --user` instead of `sudo flatpak`.

Action	Flatpak command
Add a remote repository for downloading Flatpaks.	`sudo flatpak remote-add --if-not-exists name url`
List the remotes installed on your system.	`flatpak remotes`
Search for a package that meets your needs.	`flatpak search string`
Check if a package is installed.	`flatpak list	grep package`
Download and install a package.	`sudo flatpak install package`
Install a package file.	`sudo flatpak install /path/to/file`
Run a package.	`flatpak run package_id`
Learn about a package.	`flatpak info package_id`
Update an installed package.	`sudo flatpak update package_id`
Remove an installed package.	`sudo flatpak uninstall package_id`

Action	Flatpak command
List all packages installed on the system (tip: pipe through `less`).	`flatpak list`
Update all packages on the system.	`sudo flatpak update`

snap

`snap [options] subcommand [subcommand_options]`

Snap is a system for installing software packages, called "snaps," that run in a restricted environment, called a container or sandbox. A container includes all the package's dependencies. Snaps have limited access to the host filesystem, but for the most part, they operate like ordinary applications. Use the `snap` command to install, update, and remove packages. The following table lists common operations:

Action	snap command
Search for a package that meets your needs.	`snap find string`
Check if a package is installed.	`snap list	grep package`
Download but don't install a package.	`sudo snap download package`
Download and install a package.	`sudo snap install package`
Learn about a package.	`snap info package`
List the contents of a package.	`ls /snap/package/current`
Update an installed package.	`sudo snap refresh package`
Remove an installed package.	`sudo snap remove package`
List all packages installed on the system (tip: pipe through `less`).	`snap list`

Action	snap command
Check for updates for all installed packages.	`snap refresh --list`
Update all packages on the system.	`sudo snap refresh`

Installing Software from Source Code

`configure` Prepare to build software manually with `make`.

`make` Build software from source code.

Package managers, described in "Installing Software Packages" on page 177, generally require superuser privileges to install software. As an ordinary user, you can also install software within your home directory. The process requires more steps and more understanding than using a package manager.

Downloading the Source Code

Plenty of Linux software is distributed as source code to be downloaded and built on your local system. The two most common forms of distribution are:

- Compressed TAR or ZIP files found on websites
- Git repositories, cloned from servers like GitHub

I briefly explain each and then show how to build the source code with the commands `configure` and `make`.

Method 1: Download and unpack a TAR or ZIP file

A compressed TAR file, or "tarball," is just a collection of files packed up by `tar`. The file is usually compressed with `gzip` and has the filename extension *.tar.gz* or *.tgz*, or bzip2 with the extension *.tar.bz2* or *.tbz*. Similarly, a *.zip* file is a collection of files packed by `zip`. To unpack files:

1. List the package contents. Assure yourself that each file, when extracted, won't overwrite something precious on your system, either accidentally or maliciously:[4]
   - → `tar -tvf package.tar.gz | less`   *gzip*
   - → `tar -tvf package.tar.bz2 | less`   *bzip2*
   - → `unzip -l package.zip | less`   *zip*

2. If satisfied, extract the files into a new directory:
   - → `mkdir newdir`
   - → `tar -xvf package.tar.gz -C newdir`   *gzip*
   - → `tar -xvf package.tar.bz2 -C newdir`   *bzip2*
   - → `unzip -d newdir package.zip | less`   *zip*

If this worked, continue to "Building and Installing the Code" on page 192.

Method 2: Clone a Git repository

To obtain software from GitHub or a similar repository, copy the URL of the desired repository and pass it to the git clone command, which should look something like this:

→ `git clone git@github.com:username/repository.git`

git clone downloads a copy of the repository to your local system. Now you're ready to build the software.

Building and Installing the Code

Once you've downloaded and/or extracted the source code, build the software. Briefly, the usual sequence of commands is:

→ `./configure PREFIX=any_writable_directory`
→ `make`
→ `make install`

---

4 A malicious archive could include an absolute file path like */etc/passwd* which, if extracted, could overwrite your system password file. Nasty.

In more detail, the sequence is as follows:

1. In the source code directory, read the extracted file named
   INSTALL or *README*. For example:
   ```
   → less INSTALL
   ```

2. Usually, you're instructed to run a provided script called
   configure, then run make, then run make install. To view
   the options for the configure script, run this command
   (the output is usually long):
   ```
   → ./configure --help | less
   ```

   The most important option for our purposes is --prefix,
   which sets the installation directory. For example, to
   install the software in your home directory, in a subdirectory named *packages*, you'd run:
   ```
   → ./configure --prefix=$HOME/packages
   ```

   If you omit the --prefix option, then configure arranges
   to install the software system-wide, and you'll need superuser privileges later to complete the installation.
   ```
   → ./configure
   ```

   If configure fails, it usually means your local system is
   missing some prerequisite software. Read the output of
   configure carefully, install what is missing, and try again.

3. Once configure succeeds, build (compile) the software by
   running make. It performs all necessary steps to prepare
   the software for installation, without installing it.
   ```
   → make
   ```

   If make fails, read the error output carefully, search the
   web for solutions, and if appropriate, file a bug with the
   maintainers of the software you're building.

4. If make completed successfully, and you ran configure
   with the --prefix option, complete the installation:
   ```
   → make install
   ```

Or, if you omitted --prefix to install the software system-wide, use sudo:

```
→ sudo make install
```

If you originally ran configure with the --prefix option, the installed software will be in the directory you specified, usually in a subdirectory named *bin*. Optionally, add this *bin* directory to your search path (see "Search Path" on page 23). If you installed the software in *$HOME/packages* as in my example, append its *bin* subdirectory to your PATH with this command:

```
→ PATH=$PATH:$HOME/packages/bin
```

Add this line to your shell configuration file (see "Tailoring Shell Behavior" on page 40) to make the new software available to your future shells.

Filesystem Maintenance

Using Disks and Filesystems

df   Display available space on mounted filesystems.

lsblk   List disks and other block devices.

mount   Make a disk partition accessible.

umount Unmount a disk partition (make it inaccessible).

fsck   Check a disk partition for errors.

Linux systems can have multiple disks or partitions. In casual conversation, these are variously called devices, filesystems, volumes, even directories. I'll try to be more precise.

A *disk* is a mass storage device, which may be divided into *partitions* that act as independent devices. Disks and partitions are represented on Linux systems as special files in the directory */dev*. For example, */dev/sda7* could be a partition on your hard drive. Some common devices in */dev* are:

sda   First block device, such as SCSI, SATA, or USB hard drives; partitions are *sda1*, *sda2*, ...

sdb   Second block device; partitions are *sdb1*, *sdb2*, ... Likewise for *sdc*, *sdd*, etc.

md0	First RAID device; partitions are *md0p1*, *md0p2*, ... Likewise for *md1*, *md2*, etc.
nvme0n1	First NVMe SSD device; partitions are *nvme0n1p1*, *nvme0n1p2*, ... Likewise for *nvme1n1*, *nvme2n1*, etc. The second integer, like the 1 in *nvme0n1p2*, is called the namespace ID, and most users can ignore it.

Before a partition can hold files, it is formatted by a program that creates a *filesystem* on it (see "Creating and Modifying Filesystems" on page 201). A filesystem defines how files are represented; examples are ext4 (a Linux journaling filesystem) and NTFS (a Microsoft Windows filesystem). Formatting is generally done for you when you install Linux.

After creating a filesystem, make it available by *mounting* its partition on an empty directory.[1] For example, if you mount a Windows filesystem on a directory */mnt/win*, it becomes part of your system's directory tree, and you can create and edit files like */mnt/win/myfile.txt*. Mounting generally happens automatically at boot time. You can also unmount partitions to make them inaccessible via the filesystem for maintenance.

---

df

stdin · **stdout** · -file · **--opt** · **--help** · **--version**

```
df [options] [disk devices | files | directories]
```

The df (disk free) command shows you the size, used space, and free space on a given disk partition. If you supply a file or directory, df describes the disk device on which that file or directory resides. With no arguments, df reports on all mounted filesystems:

---

[1] You can mount a filesystem on a nonempty directory, but the directory's contents become inaccessible until you unmount.

```
→ df
Filesystem 1k-blocks     Used     Avail Use% Mounted on
/dev/sda    1011928    225464    735060  24% /
/dev/sda9    521748    249148    246096  51% /var
/dev/sda8   8064272   4088636   3565984  54% /usr
/dev/sda10  8064272   4586576   3068044  60% /home
```

The df command may list all sorts of devices besides disks. To
limit the display to disks, try these options (and create an alias
if it's helpful):

```
→ df -h -x tmpfs -x devtmpfs -x squashfs
```

Useful options

-k	List sizes in KB (the default).
-m	List sizes in MB.
-B *N*	Display sizes in blocks of *N* bytes. (Default = 1024)
-h -H	Print human-readable output and choose the most appropriate unit for each size. For example, if your two disks have 1 gigabyte and 25 KB free, respectively, df -h prints 1G and 25K. The -h option uses powers of 1024, whereas -H uses powers of 1000.
-l	Display only local filesystems, not networked filesystems.
-T	Include the filesystem type (ext3, vfat, etc.) in the output.
-t *type*	Display only filesystems of the given type.
-x *type*	Don't display filesystems of the given type.
-i	Inode mode. Display total, used, and free inodes for each filesystem, instead of disk blocks. When all inodes on a filesystem are used, the filesystem is "full" even if free disk space remains.

lsblk

lsblk [*options*] [*devices*]

The lsblk command lists the mass storage devices, known as block devices, available on a Linux system, such as hard disks, SSDs, and RAM disks.

```
→ lsblk
NAME          MAJ:MIN RM   SIZE RO TYPE  MOUNTPOINTS
sda              8:0   0    20G  0 disk
├─sda1           8:1   0     1M  0 part
├─sda2           8:2   0   513M  0 part  /boot/efi
├─sda3           8:3   0  19.5G  0 part  /
sdb              8:80  0   7.6G  0 disk
└─sdb1           8:81  1   7.6G  0 part  /mnt/usb-key
```

The output shows a hard drive at */dev/sda* with three partitions, and a USB thumb drive at */dev/sdb* with a single partition. lsblk has a ton of formatting options and can limit itself to particular devices.

```
→ lsblk -o NAME,SIZE /dev/sda
NAME     SIZE
sda       20G
├─sda1     1M
├─sda2   513M
└─sda3  19.5G
```

Useful options

-l   Display a simple list instead of a tree.

-a   Show all block devices, including those normally hidden.

-f   Add information about the filesystems on each device.

-o *columns* Print only the given columns, which you provide as a comma-separated list. View the available columns with lsblk --help.

-J   Print the list in JSON format for easy processing by programs.

mount [*options*] [*device* | *directory*]

The mount command makes a partition accessible. Most commonly it handles disk drives (say, */dev/sda1*) and removable media (e.g., USB keys), making them accessible via an existing directory (say, */mnt/mydir*):

```
→ sudo mkdir /mnt/mydir
→ ls /mnt/mydir                        Notice it's empty
→ sudo mount /dev/sda1 /mnt/mydir
→ ls /mnt/mydir
file1  file2  file3              Files on the mounted partition
→ df /mnt/mydir
Filesystem 1K-blocks   Used  Avail Use% Mounted on
/dev/sda1   1011928 285744 674780  30% /mnt/mydir
```

mount has many uses; I discuss only the most basic. In most common cases, mount reads the file */etc/fstab* (filesystem table, pronounced "F S tab") to learn how to mount a desired disk. For example, if you run mount /usr, the mount command looks up "/usr" in */etc/fstab*, whose line might look like this:

```
/dev/sda8    /usr    ext4    defaults    1    2
```

Here mount learns that device */dev/sda8* should be mounted on */usr* as a Linux ext4-formatted filesystem with default options. Mount it with either of these commands:

```
→ sudo mount /dev/sda8        By device
→ sudo mount /usr             By directory
```

mount is run typically by the superuser, but common removable devices like USB keys and DVDs often can be mounted and unmounted by any user.

Useful options

-t *type*   Specify the type of filesystem, such as ext4 or ntfs.

-l   List all mounted filesystems; works with -t too.

-a	Mount all filesystems listed in */etc/fstab*. Ignores entries that include the noauto option. Works well with -t too.
-r	Mount the filesystem read-only (see the manpage for disclaimers).

umount

umount [*options*] [*device* | *directory*]

umount does the opposite of mount: it makes a disk partition unavailable via the filesystem.[2] For instance, if you've mounted a USB thumb drive, umount it before you unplug it:

→ **umount "/media/smith/My Vacation Photos"**

Always unmount any removable medium before ejecting it, particularly if it's writable, or you risk damage to its filesystem. To unmount all mounted devices:

→ **sudo umount -a**

Don't unmount a filesystem that's in use; in fact, the umount command refuses to do so for safety reasons.

fsck

fsck [*options*] [*devices*]

The fsck (filesystem check) command validates a Linux disk filesystem and, if requested, repairs errors found on it. fsck runs automatically when your system boots, or manually. In general, unmount a device before checking it, so no other programs are operating on it at the same time:

---

2 Notice the spelling is "umount," not "unmount."

```
→ sudo umount /dev/sda10
→ sudo fsck -f /dev/sda10
Pass 1: Checking inodes, blocks, and sizes
Pass 2: Checking directory structure
Pass 3: Checking directory connectivity
Pass 4: Checking reference counts
Pass 5: Checking group summary information
/home: 172/1281696 files (11.6% non-contiguous), ...
```

You cannot use fsck to fix your root filesystem while your system is running normally. Boot first on a Linux USB thumb drive or other rescue media, then run fsck.

fsck is a frontend for a set of filesystem-checking commands found in */sbin*, with names beginning "fsck". Only certain types of filesystems are supported; list them with the command:

```
→ ls /sbin/fsck.* | cut -d. -f2 | column
cramfs    ext3    fat    hfsplus    msdos
ext2      ext4    hfs    minix      vfat
```

Useful options

- -A Check all disks listed in */etc/fstab*, in order.

- -f Force fsck to run even if no errors are apparent.

- -N Print a description of the checking that would be done, but exit without performing any checking.

- -r Fix errors interactively, prompting before each fix.

- -a Fix errors automatically (use only if you *really* know what you're doing; if not, you can seriously mess up a filesystem).

Creating and Modifying Filesystems

mkfs   Format (create a filesystem on) a disk partition.

resize2fs   Grow or shrink a disk partition.

e2label   Change the volume label on a disk partition.

Disk-related operations like partitioning and formatting can be complex at the command line. In general, for anything more complicated than formatting a single partition, I recommend using a graphical application such as gparted. Honestly, it's easier and less error-prone.

Nevertheless, I still run a few operations at the command line that are quick and easy. One is listing the partitions of a storage device like */dev/sda* with fdisk:

```
→ sudo fdisk -l /dev/sda
Disk /dev/sda: 20 GiB, 21474836480 bytes, ...
⋮
Device       Start       End   Sectors  Size Type
/dev/sda1     2048      4095      2048   1M BIOS boot
/dev/sda2     4096   1054719   1050624  513M EFI System
/dev/sda3  1054720  41940991  40886272 19.5G Linux
```

or similarly with parted:

```
→ sudo parted /dev/sda -- print
```

Another is exporting the partition table of a storage device for safekeeping. (Store it on a USB thumb drive or other device, not the disk you're working on!)

```
→ sudo sfdisk -d /dev/sda > /mnt/thumb/sda.txt
```

Later, if you mess up a risky partitioning operation, you can restore the partition table (but *be careful* to specify the correct disk device or you'll overwrite the wrong partition table):

```
→ sudo sfdisk /dev/device < /mnt/thumb/sda.txt
```

The commands that follow are also relatively basic operations on disks and filesystems without graphical tools.

mkfs stdin **stdout** - file -- opt **--help** **--version**

mke2fs [*options*] *device*

mkfs.ext3 [*options*] *device*

mkfs.ext4 [*options*] *device*

mkntfs [*options*] *device*

mkfs.ntfs [*options*] *device* *...and many other variations...*

The mkfs family of commands formats a Linux storage device for a variety of filesystems. The storage device is usually a partition, such as */dev/sdb1*.

WARNING

mkfs erases a storage device. Make sure the device name you provide is the correct one!

Examples:

→ **sudo mkfs.ext4 /dev/***device*   *Standard Linux filesystem*
→ **sudo mke2fs /dev/***device*   *Standard Linux filesystem*
→ **sudo mkfs.ntfs /dev/***device*   *Microsoft Windows filesystem*
→ **sudo mkntfs /dev/***device*   *Microsoft Windows filesystem*

As you can see, most of the command names are "mkfs" followed by a dot and a filesystem type, like mkfs.ext4. They may also have alternate names (links) with the filesystem type embedded in the middle of "mkfs", such as mke2fs for an "ext" filesystem. To list all such commands installed on your system, run:

→ **ls /usr/*bin/mkfs.***
```
/usr/sbin/mkfs.ext2    /usr/sbin/mkfs.hfs
/usr/sbin/mkfs.ext3    /usr/sbin/mkfs.minix
/usr/sbin/mkfs.ext4    /usr/sbin/mkfs.msdos
/usr/sbin/mkfs.fat     /usr/sbin/mkfs.ntfs
```

Useful options

-n   Dry-run mode: don't format anything. Just display what *would* be done.

-L *name*   Label the formatted volume with the given *name*, which can be up to 16 bytes long.

-b *N*   Set the block size to *N* bytes.

resize2fs

```
resize2fs [options] device [size]
```

The resize2fs command grows or shrinks a standard Linux filesystem of type ext2, ext3, or ext4. To enlarge a filesystem:

1. Confirm that the device has enough free space immediately following the current partition.

2. Unmount the filesystem.

3. Enlarge its disk partition with gparted or similar program. (This requires free space just after the current partition.)

4. Check the filesystem with fsck.

5. Run resize2fs with appropriate arguments. In modern kernels, the filesystem may be mounted during resizing.

To shrink a filesystem:

1. Confirm with df that the data in the filesystem (the "Used" column) will fit within the proposed new size.

2. Unmount the filesystem.

3. Run resize2fs with appropriate arguments.

4. Shrink its disk partition with `gparted` or a similar program.

5. Check the filesystem with `fsck`.

To resize a filesystem on */dev/sda1*, assuming you've already completed any checking and partitioning, run `resize2fs` either with or without a size:

→ **sudo resize2fs /dev/sda1 100G**   *Resize to 100 GB*
→ **sudo resize2fs /dev/sda1**   *Resize to the partition size*

Sizes can be an absolute number of blocks, like 12345690, or a size followed by K (KB), M (MB), G (GB), T (terabytes), or s (512-byte sectors). The values are powers of two, so 1K means 1024, not 1000, and so on.

If you resize filesystems often, make your life easier with logical volume management (LVM), as explained in "Logical Volumes for Flexible Storage" on page 211, or a more modern filesystem, as in "ZFS: A Modern, Do-It-All Filesystem" on page 217.

Useful options

- -f Force the resizing operation, even if `resize2fs` complains.

- -p Display the progress of the operation as it runs.

e2label   stdin stdout -file --opt --help --version

e2label *device* [*label*]

A label is a nickname for a filesystem. The e2label command sets or prints the label of a standard Linux filesystem of type ext2, ext3, or ext4. Filesystems don't require labels, but they're convenient for referring to filesystems in */etc/fstab*.

→ **sudo e2label /dev/sdb1 backups**   *Assign a label*
→ **sudo e2label /dev/sdb1**   *Print a label*
backups

RAID Arrays for Redundancy

mdadm   Manage RAID arrays.

RAID (Redundant Array of Independent Disks) is a technique that distributes a computer's data across multiple disks, transparently, while acting like a single disk. Usually, RAID is for redundancy—if one disk dies, your files are still intact. Other types of RAID increase the performance of storage.

A bunch of disks in a RAID arrangement is called a RAID *array*. The type of RAID, called the RAID *level*, determines how many drive failures the array can tolerate and still guarantee the data's safety. Some standard RAID levels are RAID-0, RAID-1, RAID-5, RAID-10, and others you can explore on the web.

Let's create a minimal RAID-1 array using the most common RAID software for Linux, mdadm. RAID-1 adds redundancy simply by mirroring data from one drive to the others in the array. As long as one drive is still operating, the data is safe. For this example, I start with two disks, */dev/sdf* and */dev/sdg*, each of which has a 10 GB partition, */dev/sdf1* and */dev/sdg1*. The steps I show are largely the same for other RAID levels and additional devices. For full details, visit the Linux Raid Wiki (*https://oreil.ly/ibL7l*).

WARNING

RAID operations can wipe out filesystems without confirmation. Practice the commands on spare drives or a virtual machine for safety.

Create a RAID Array

First, show that no RAID setup exists yet:

```
→ cat /proc/mdstat
Personalities :                    No RAID types listed
```

Create the RAID-1 array */dev/md1*, from the two partitions:

```
→ sudo mdadm --create /dev/md1 --level 1 \
  --raid-devices 2 /dev/sdf1 /dev/sdg1
```

View */proc/mdstat* again. The Personalities line now shows that RAID-1 is in use, and the next line shows the new array, *md1*, which is being built:

```
→ cat /proc/mdstat
Personalities : [raid1]
md1 : active raid1 sdg1[1] sdf1[0]
      10474496 blocks super 1.2 [2/2] [UU]
      [=========>..........] resync = 45.8% ...
                            finish=0.4min ...
```

Optionally, wait for the build ("resync") to complete:

```
→ cat /proc/mdstat
Personalities : [raid1]
md1 : active raid1 sdg1[1] sdf1[0]
      10474496 blocks super 1.2 [2/2] [UU]
```

However, you don't have to wait. The array is usable immediately. Format and mount it like any other storage device:

```
→ sudo mke2fs /dev/md1            Format the array
→ sudo mkdir /mnt/raid            Mount it
→ sudo mount /dev/md1 /mnt/raid
→ df -h /mnt/raid                 View it
Filesystem    Size  Used Avail Use% Mounted on
/dev/md1      9.9G   24K  9.4G   1% /mnt/raid
```

Run lsblk to illustrate the RAID configuration:

```
→ lsblk
⋮
sdf          8:80    0    10G  0 disk
└─sdf1       8:81    0    10G  0 part
  └─md1      9:1     0    10G  0 raid1 /mnt/raid
sdg          8:96    0    10G  0 disk
└─sdg1       8:97    0    10G  0 part
  └─md1      9:1     0    10G  0 raid1 /mnt/raid
```

Run mdadm to see more details about the array:

```
→ sudo mdadm --detail /dev/md1
dev/md1:
  ⋮
  Creation Time : Thu Jul 20 13:15:08 2023
     Raid Level : raid1
     Array Size : 10474496 (9.99 GiB 10.73 GB)
   Raid Devices : 2
          State : clean
Working Devices : 2
  ⋮
Number   Major   Minor   RaidDevice State
   0       8       81        0      active sync /dev/sdf1
   1       8       97        1      active sync /dev/sdg1
```

When you're satisfied with the array, save its configuration so it will survive reboots and mount itself. **Don't skip any steps.**

1. Save the RAID configuration to a file:

   ```
   → sudo mdadm --detail --scan --verbose > /tmp/raid
   → cat /tmp/raid
   ARRAY /dev/md1 level=raid1 num-devices=2 ...
   ```

2. Use a text editor to append the contents of *tmp/raid* to the configuration file */etc/mdadm/mdadm.conf*, replacing any previous RAID configuration.

3. Run this command to update the Linux kernel:

   ```
   → sudo update-initramfs -u
   ```

4. Reboot. Check that your RAID array survived by mounting it by hand:[3]

   ```
   → sudo mount /dev/md1 /mnt/raid
   ```

5. If everything worked, add this line to */etc/fstab* so your RAID array mounts at boot time:

   ```
   /dev/md1  /mnt/raid  ext4  defaults  0  2
   ```

---

3 If your RAID array mysteriously renames itself */dev/md127*, you forgot to run update-initramfs in the previous step.

Replace a Device in a RAID Array

So, your RAID array is up and running. What happens when a device dies and needs replacement? First, the failure is visible in */proc/mdstat*. The failed device, */dev/sdf1*, is marked with (F), and the uptime indicator, which should read [UU] (two devices up), reads [U_] (first device up, second device down).

```
→ cat /proc/mdstat
Personalities : [raid1]
md1 : active raid1 sdf1[1](F) sdg1[0]
      10474496 blocks super 1.2 [2/1] [U_]
```

mdadm also shows the array as "degraded" and the device as "faulty":

```
→ sudo mdadm --detail /dev/md1
/dev/md1:
    ⋮
    Raid Devices : 2
           State : clean, degraded
 Working Devices : 1
  Failed Devices : 1
    ⋮
 Number  Major  Minor  RaidDevice State
     1      8     97        -      faulty /dev/sdf1
```

To replace device */dev/sdf1*, mark it as failed (if it isn't already) and remove it from the RAID array:

```
→ sudo mdadm --manage /dev/md1 --fail /dev/sdf1
→ sudo mdadm --manage /dev/md1 --remove /dev/sdf1
```

Shut down the computer, unplug the power cable, and physically swap the failed storage device for a new one of the same size or larger. I'll call it by a nonexistent name */dev/NEW* to clearly distinguish it in my instructions because the following commands are destructive, and you don't want to mix up your drives. Substitute the correct device name on your system.

Boot the computer, identify a good drive in the RAID array (in our case, */dev/sdg*), and copy its partition table onto the new device with the sgdisk command.

```
→ sudo sgdisk -R /dev/NEW /dev/sdg        Copy from sdg to NEW
→ sudo sgdisk -G /dev/NEW                 Randomize GUIDs
```

The device */dev/NEW* now has a 10 GB partition, */dev/NEW1*. Add it to the array:

```
→ sudo mdadm --manage /dev/md1 --add /dev/NEW1
mdadm: added /dev/NEW1
```

The array immediately begins rebuilding itself, mirroring data onto the new device:

```
→ cat /proc/mdstat
⋮
[==========>..........]  recovery = 51.5% ...
                         finish=0.4min ...
```

When mirroring is complete, the new device */dev/NEW1* has replaced the faulty device */dev/sdf1*:

```
→ cat /proc/mdstat
Personalities : [raid1]
md1 : active raid1 NEW1[1] sdg1[0]
      10474496 blocks super 1.2 [2/2] [UU]
```

Destroy a RAID Array

Should you ever want to destroy the RAID array and use the partitions for other purposes, run these commands, assuming your device names are */dev/sdg1* and */dev/sdh1*:

```
→ sudo umount /mnt/raid
→ sudo mdadm --stop /dev/md1
```

```
mdadm: stopped /dev/md1
→ sudo mdadm --zero-superblock /dev/sdg1 /dev/sdh1
```

Finally, update */etc/fstab* and */etc/mdadm/mdadm.conf* to remove the RAID array */dev/md1*, and inform the kernel that the array is gone:

```
→ sudo update-initramfs -u
```

Logical Volumes for Flexible Storage

pvcreate	Create a physical volume.
pvdisplay	View details of physical volumes.
pvremove	Delete a physical volume.
pvs	View other details of physical volumes.
vgcreate	Create a volume group.
vgdisplay	View details of volume groups.
vgextend	Add physical volumes to a volume group.
vgreduce	Remove physical volumes from a volume group.
vgremove	Delete a volume group.
lvcreate	Create a logical volume.
lvdisplay	View details of logical volumes.
lvresize	Resize a logical volume.
lvremove	Delete a logical volume.

Logical volume management (LVM) solves two annoying problems with disk storage:

- **Limited size**. When a disk fills up, you have to delete files or replace it with a larger disk.
- **Fixed partitions**. When you partition a disk, you guess how much space each partition will require, and if you're wrong, it's time-consuming to change.

LVM solves these problems by wrapping a layer of abstraction around physical storage. It collects together a bunch of physical disks of any sizes, called *physical volumes*, to simulate one big disk, which it calls a *volume group*. The volume group becomes a playground for creating simulated partitions, called *logical volumes*, that can grow and shrink on demand. Figure 4-1 shows the relationship between physical volumes (PVs), the volume group (VG) that contains them, and logical volumes (LVs) that you carve out of the total space. If the VG runs out of space, simply add another physical volume and the VG grows. If a partition (LV) is the wrong size, just change it. Existing files are preserved. Any mass storage devices can be part of a volume group, even RAID arrays created with mdadm (see "RAID Arrays for Redundancy" on page 206).

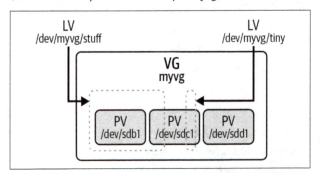

Figure 4-1. LVM concepts. Physical volumes (PV) are collected into a volume group (VG). Logical volumes (LV) are carved out of the VG.

The most popular LVM software for Linux is called lvm2. It includes over 50 commands, which might seem like a lot, but their names follow a simple pattern: pv, vg, or lv, followed by a verb like create, remove, or display. So vgcreate creates a volume group, and pvdisplay prints information about a physical volume.

I now present examples of using the most common lvm2 commands, using three empty 10 GB disk partitions, */dev/sdb1*, */dev/sdc1*, and */dev/sdd1*.[4] lvm2 has dozens more commands, however. For a full list, view the manpage of any lvm2 command and jump to the end or visit sourceware.org/lvm2 (*https://oreil.ly/yLLli*).

Create a First Logical Volume

This sequence of steps sets up two physical volumes, groups them into a 20 GB volume group, *myvg*, and creates a 15 GB logical volume, *stuff*:

```
→ sudo pvcreate /dev/sdb1 /dev/sdc1          Create two PVs
  Physical volume "/dev/sdb1" successfully created.
  Physical volume "/dev/sdc1" successfully created.
→ sudo vgcreate myvg /dev/sdb1 /dev/sdc1     Create a VG
  Volume group "myvg" successfully created
→ sudo lvcreate -L 15G -n stuff myvg         Create the LV
  Logical volume "stuff" created.
→ sudo pvs                                   View the PVs
  PV          VG    Fmt  Attr PSize    PFree
  /dev/sdb1   myvg  lvm2 a--  <10.00g      0
  /dev/sdc1   myvg  lvm2 a--  <10.00g  5.34g
```

---

4 Operate on partitions rather than whole disks (*https://oreil.ly/Gl2AZ*).

The logical volume *stuff* is usable like any other storage device. Format and mount it:

```
→ sudo mke2fs /dev/myvg/stuff            Format the LV
→ sudo mkdir /mnt/stuff                  Mount it
→ sudo mount /dev/myvg/stuff /mnt/stuff
→ df -h /mnt/stuff                       View it
Filesystem                 Size Used Avail Use% Mounted on
/dev/mapper/myvg-stuff     15G  24K  1.4G   1% /mnt/stuff
```

When your LV is ready, add this line to */etc/fstab* to mount it at boot time:

```
/dev/mapper/myvg-stuff  /mnt/stuff  ext4  defaults  0 2
```

View LVM Details

The pvdisplay, vgdisplay, and lvdisplay commands print details about physical volumes, volume groups, and logical volumes, respectively. The commands pvs, vgs, and lvs print helpful summaries of that information.

```
→ sudo pvdisplay                 Show all PVs
→ sudo pvdisplay /dev/sdb1       Show selected PVs
→ sudo pvs                       Summarize PVs
→ sudo vgdisplay                 Show all VGs
→ sudo vgdisplay myvg            Show selected VGs
→ sudo vgs                       Summarize VGs
→ sudo lvdisplay                 Show all LVs
→ sudo lvdisplay myvg/stuff      Show selected LVs
→ sudo lvs                       Summarize LVs
```

Add a Logical Volume

Let's run lvcreate again to add a 2 GB logical volume called *tiny* to our volume group:

```
→ sudo lvcreate -L 2G -n tiny myvg
  Logical volume "tiny" created.
→ sudo mke2fs /dev/myvg/tiny                 Format
→ sudo mkdir /mnt/tiny                       Mount
→ sudo mount /dev/myvg/tiny /mnt/tiny
```

```
→ df -h /mnt/tiny                                    View
Filesystem              Size Used Avail Use% Mounted on
/dev/mapper/myvg-tiny   2.0G  24K  1.9G   1% /mnt/tiny
```

Add Disks to a Volume Group

The vgextend command adds physical volumes to a volume
group. Suppose you want to increase the size of *stuff* by 10
GB (to 25 GB), but there's only 3 GB of space left in volume
group *myvg*. Enlarge your VG by adding a third physical volume, */dev/sdd1*, increasing the VG's total size to 30 GB:

```
→ sudo pvcreate /dev/sdd1            Create another PV
→ sudo vgextend myvg /dev/sdd1       Grow the VG
```

At this point, the LVM setup looks like Figure 4-1. Run lsblk
to illustrate the LVM configuration:

```
→ lsblk /dev/sdb /dev/sdc /dev/sdd
NAME           MAJ:MIN RM SIZE RO TYPE MOUNTPOINTS
sdb              8:16   0  10G  0 disk
└─sdb1           8:17   0  10G  0 part
  └─myvg-stuff 253:0    0  15G  0 lvm  /mnt/stuff
sdc              8:32   0  10G  0 disk
└─sdc1           8:33   0  10G  0 part
  ├─myvg-stuff 253:0    0  15G  0 lvm  /mnt/stuff
  └─myvg-tiny  253:1    0   2G  0 lvm  /mnt/tiny
sdd              8:48   0  10G  0 disk
└─sdd1           8:49   0  10G  0 part
```

Enlarge a Logical Volume

The lvresize command grows or shrinks a logical volume.[5]
Let's enlarge the LV *stuff* to 25 GB:

```
→ sudo lvresize --resizefs --size 25G /dev/myvg/stuff
→ df -h /mnt/stuff
```

---

5 Old-timers may resize an LV by running lvextend, umount, fsck,
  resize2fs, and mount in sequence. lvresize is easier.

```
Filesystem                Size  Used Avail Use% Mounted on
/dev/mapper/myvg-stuff     25G  24K   24G   1% /mnt/stuff
```

Shrink a Logical Volume

It turns out the LV *stuff* doesn't need to be so large. Shrink it to
8 GB (making sure first that it has less than 8 GB in use):

```
→ sudo lvresize --resizefs --size 8G /dev/myvg/stuff
Do you want to unmount "/mnt/stuff" ? [Y|n] y
⋮
Logical volume myvg/stuff successfully resized.
→ df -h /mnt/stuff
Filesystem                Size Used Avail Use% Mounted on
/dev/mapper/myvg-stuff    7.9G  24K  7.5G   1% /mnt/stuff
```

Delete a Logical Volume

The lvremove command deletes a logical volume. Let's get rid
of the LV *tiny*:

```
→ sudo umount /mnt/tiny              First unmount the LV
→ sudo lvremove /dev/myvg/tiny       Remove the LV
Do you really want to remove and DISCARD
active logical volume myvg/tiny? [y/n]: y
  Logical volume "tiny" successfully removed
```

Reduce a Volume Group

The vgreduce command removes an unused physical volume
from a volume group. The PV remains managed by lvm2, just
not within the VG *myvg*:

```
→ sudo vgreduce myvg /dev/sdd1
  Removed "/dev/sdd1" from volume group "myvg"
```

Delete a Volume Group

The vgremove command removes a volume group and deletes
any logical volumes it contains:

```
→ sudo vgremove myvg
Do you really want to remove volume group "myvg"
```

```
containing 1 logical volumes? [y/n]: y
Do you really want to remove and DISCARD
active logical volume myvg/stuff? [y/n]: y
  Logical volume "stuff" successfully removed
  Volume group "myvg" successfully removed
```

Delete a Physical Volume

The pvremove command removes physical devices from LVM:

```
→ sudo pvremove /dev/sdb1 /dev/sdc1
  Labels on physical volume "/dev/sdb1" wiped.
  Labels on physical volume "/dev/sdc1" wiped.
```

ZFS: A Modern, Do-It-All Filesystem

zpool   Configure a ZFS storage pool.

zfs   Configure a ZFS dataset.

WARNING

ZFS operations can wipe out filesystems without confirmation. Practice the commands on spare drives or a virtual
machine for safety.

ZFS (Zettabyte File System) packs advanced features like RAID,
logical volume management, encryption, and compression into
one convenient package. If you're accustomed to traditional
Linux filesystems like ext4, ZFS may seem like an alien world.
It has its own terminology with "pools" and "vdevs." It doesn't
use */etc/fstab* or the mount command. You don't even need to
partition or format your disks explicitly.

A ZFS *vdev*, short for "virtual device," is a group of physical
disks that work together. They might divide the data among
themselves as if they were one big disk, like a RAID-0 "disk
striping" setup. They might mirror each other for redundancy,

like a RAID-1 setup. They might operate as a disk cache; and there are other possibilities.

A collection of vdevs is called a *pool*. A pool acts like one big storage device. You can carve it up into units that are sort of like partitions, called *datasets*, and you can change their size limits and other attributes flexibly. Dataset names look like Linux paths without a leading slash. For example, a pool named mypool with a dataset named stuff would be named mypool/stuff. (Datasets can contain other datasets too, like mypool/stuff/important.) Add a leading slash, and you get the dataset's default Linux mount point, like */mypool/stuff*.

ZFS isn't the only filesystem with advanced capabilities—another popular one is Btrfs—but it's among the easiest to configure.

NOTE

I discuss only the minimal ZFS functionality to do interesting things. Real ZFS systems need careful configuration, tuning, and plenty of RAM; read the docs at *https://oreil.ly/-t5Fu*.

To demonstrate ZFS with both mirroring and striping, I use two pairs of disks, as in Figure 4-2. Each pair is a vdev with mirroring (RAID-1). ZFS then stripes across the two vdevs (RAID-0), effectively creating a RAID-10 setup. This redundant pool can tolerate one failed drive in each vdev and keep the data safe.

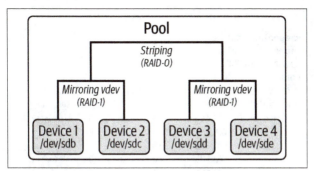

Figure 4-2. Our example ZFS configuration: a RAID-10 pool

Create a ZFS Pool

Use the zpool command to construct the pool of two pairs of mirrored drives. I create a pool called mypool from four 10 GB disk devices, */dev/sdb*, */dev/sdc*, */dev/sdd*, and */dev/sde*:

```
→ sudo zpool create mypool \
  mirror /dev/sdb /dev/sdc \
  mirror /dev/sdd /dev/sde
```

WARNING

The simple device names in my examples, like */dev/sdb*, can change after a reboot. For a more robust setup, use names that are guaranteed not to change, like the symbolic links found in */dev/disk/by-id* or */dev/disk/by-uuid*.

Also, on real systems, be sure to set an appropriate alignment shift value with -o ashift on creation; see the docs.

Use zpool status to view the results.

```
→ zpool status
  pool: mypool
 state: ONLINE
config:
  NAME          STATE     READ WRITE CKSUM
  mypool        ONLINE       0     0     0   The pool
    mirror-0    ONLINE       0     0     0   First vdev
      sdb       ONLINE       0     0     0
      sdc       ONLINE       0     0     0
    mirror-1    ONLINE       0     0     0   Second vdev
      sdd       ONLINE       0     0     0
      sde       ONLINE       0     0     0
```

Create a ZFS Dataset

Traditional filesystems have partitions of fixed size that you mount in the file */etc/fstab*. ZFS has datasets of arbitrary size that it mounts automatically. Create a dataset named data in pool mypool, mounted at the directory */mypool/data*:

```
→ sudo zfs create -o mypool/data
```

Move the mount point if you like, to */mnt/stuff*:

```
→ sudo zfs set mountpoint=/mnt/stuff mypool/data
```

View the results with either of these commands:

```
→ zfs mount
mypool              /mypool         The whole pool
mypool/data         /mnt/stuff      Your dataset
→ zfs get mountpoint mypool/data
NAME           PROPERTY     VALUE         SOURCE
mypool/data    mountpoint   /mnt/stuff    local
```

Now use the dataset like any other mounted partition:

```
→ sudo cp /etc/hosts /mnt/stuff
→ cd /mnt/stuff
→ ls
hosts
```

Create an Encrypted ZFS Dataset

By adding a few options, you can create a dataset that's encrypted and requires a passphrase before mounting. Create an encrypted dataset named mypool/cryptic:

```
→ zfs create \
  -o encryption=on \
  -o keylocation=prompt \
  -o keyformat=passphrase \
  mypool/cryptic
Enter new passphrase: xxxxxxxx
Re-enter new passphrase: xxxxxxxx
```

Use the dataset normally. When you reboot or otherwise need to mount the dataset, run:

```
→ sudo zfs mount -l mypool/cryptic
```

Set Size Limits on ZFS Datasets

By default, a ZFS dataset is the same size as the pool. Limit its size by setting a quota, which you may change anytime:

```
→ sudo zfs set quota=15g mypool/data
→ zfs list
NAME          USED  AVAIL REFER  MOUNTPOINT
mypool        312K  18.4G  25K   /mypool
mypool/data    24K  15.0G  24K   /mnt/stuff    15 GB limit
```

Enable Compression on ZFS Datasets

ZFS can automatically compress data as it's written and uncompress it when read. It supports various compression algorithms; here I use gzip compression and view how effectively files are being compressed (the compression ratio):

```
→ sudo zfs set compression=gzip mypool/data
→ cp hugefile /mnt/stuff          Store a big file
→ zfs get compressratio           See the compression ratio
NAME         PROPERTY       VALUE   SOURCE
mypool       compressratio  122.66x  -
mypool/data  compressratio  126.12x  -
```

After enabling compression, only new data is compressed; existing files are not. To turn off compression:

```
→ sudo zfs set compression=off mypool/data
```

Snapshot a ZFS Dataset

ZFS supports *snapshots*: storing the state of a dataset so you can easily return to that state (roll back) later. Before performing a risky change on your files, for example, take a snapshot, and if something goes wrong, you can revert the change with a single command. Snapshots occupy very little disk space, and you can send them efficiently to other zpools or hosts (with `zfs send` and `zfs recv`). Create a snapshot of mypool/data named safe:

```
→ sudo zfs snapshot mypool/data@safe
```

List your snapshots:

```
→ zfs list -t snapshot
NAME                 USED  AVAIL    REFER  MOUNTPOINT
mypool/data@safe      0B      -      24K  -
```

If you can't list snapshots, set listsnapshots=on and try again:

```
→ sudo zpool set listsnapshots=on mypool
```

Try changing some files in mypool/data. Then roll back to the snapshot safe and see that your changes are gone:

```
→ sudo zfs rollback mypool/data@safe
```

Destroy a ZFS Dataset or Snapshot

Be careful with the `zfs destroy` command—it runs immediately without confirmation.

```
→ sudo zfs destroy mypool/data@safe      A snapshot
→ sudo zfs destroy mypool/data           A dataset
```

Destroy a ZFS Pool

Be careful with the `zpool destroy` command—it runs immediately without confirmation.

```
→ sudo zpool destroy mypool
```

Backups and Remote Storage

rsync	Efficiently copy a set of files, even across a network.
rclone	Sync files with various cloud providers.
dd	Low-level copying of data.
growisofs	Burn a DVD or Blu-ray disc.

You can back up your precious Linux files in various ways:

- Copy them to a remote machine.
- Copy them to a backup medium like an external drive.
- Burn them onto a disc.

I present a few popular Linux commands for backups, but there are others. Some users prefer cpio for its flexibility, and some long-time administrators swear by dump and restore as the only reliable way to back up and restore every type of file. See the manpages for these commands if you are interested in them.

---

rsync   stdin **stdout** -file --opt --help --version

rsync [*options*] *source destination*

The rsync command copies a set of files. It can make an exact copy, including file permissions and other attributes (called *mirroring*), or it can just copy the data. It can run over a network or on a single machine. rsync has many uses and over 50 options; I present just a few common cases relating to backups.

To mirror the directory *mydir* and its contents into another directory *mydir2* on a single machine:

```
→ rsync -a mydir mydir2
```

rsync is finicky about how you specify the first directory. If you write "mydir" as in the example here, that directory is copied into *mydir2*, creating the subdirectory *mydir2/mydir*. If instead, you'd rather have only the contents of *mydir* copied into *mydir2*, append a slash onto "mydir":

```
→ rsync -a mydir/ mydir2
```

rsync can mirror a directory over a network to another host, securing the connection with SSH to prevent eavesdropping. Here I copy directory *mydir* to the account "smith" on remote host *server.example.com*, in a directory *D2*:

```
→ rsync -a mydir smith@server.example.com:D2
```

If you like rsync but also want to have incremental backups and manage them efficiently, try rsnapshot (*https://oreil.ly/VNfb-*).

Useful options

- -o Copy the ownership of the files. (You might need superuser privileges on the remote host.)

- -g Copy the group ownership of the files. (You might need superuser privileges on the remote host.)

- -p Copy the file permissions.

- -t Copy the file timestamps.

- -r Copy directories recursively (i.e., including their contents).

- -l Permit symbolic links to be copied (rather than the files they point to).

- -D Permit devices to be copied. (Superuser only.)

- -a Mirroring: copy all attributes of the original files. This implies all of the options -Dogptrl (think "dog patrol").

- -x   When copying a tree of files, remain within the current filesystem; do not cross over into other mounted filesystems.

- -z   Compress the data for transit. Only useful for remote hosts over slow connections. Avoid compression when copying files locally (it's wasteful).

- -n   Dry-run mode: don't actually copy. Just display what *would* be done.

- -v   Verbose mode: print status information during the copy. Add --progress to display a numeric progress meter while files are copied.

---

rclone
stdin   stdout   - file   -- opt   --help   --version

`rclone subcommand [options] [arguments]`

The rclone command connects your Linux system to popular cloud storage providers to copy files conveniently. It works with Dropbox, Google Drive, Microsoft OneDrive, Amazon S3, and about 50 other destinations. To get started, run `rclone config` and follow the prompts to set up a connection with your cloud provider of choice, which rclone calls a *remote*. Visit rclone.org/docs (*https://oreil.ly/YXVrw*) for detailed instructions on configuration.

After choosing a name for your remote, such as myremote, refer to remote files with the syntax myremote:*path*, where *path* is a Linux-style file path. For example, a file *photo.jpg* in a remote directory *Photos* would be myremote:Photos/photo.jpg.

Backups are usually done with the rclone sync command, which synchronizes a local directory and a remote directory so they contain the same content, adding or deleting as necessary. It works much like the rsync --delete command. You can synchronize in either direction, from your local machine to the remote, or from the remote to your local machine. You can even set up client-side encryption, so files are transparently encrypted before they're copied to the remote and decrypted when they're copied back to your local system (see the docs).

Some common operations for backups include:

`rclone ls remote:`	List files on the remote recursively (append `--max-depth 1` for no recursion).
`rclone lsd remote:`	List only directories on the remote.
`rclone lsl remote:`	Display a long listing like `ls -l` from the remote recursively (append `--max-depth 1` for no recursion).
`rclone copy myfile remote:`	Copy a local file to the remote.
`rclone copy remote:myfile .`	Copy a remote file to your local system.
`rclone move myfile remote:`	Move a local file to the remote.
`rclone move remote:myfile .`	Move a remote file to your local system.
`rclone delete remote:myfile`	Delete a remote file.
`rclone sync mydir remote:mydir`	Synchronize local files onto the remote.
`rclone sync remote:mydir mydir`	Synchronize remote files onto your local system.

Run `rclone help` for a complete list of subcommands. Note that you can access fancier paths on the remote than my earlier examples show:

```
→ rclone copy remote:Photos/Vacation/picture.jpg .
```

Useful options

-n Dry-run mode: don't actually copy. Just display what *would* be done.

-i Run interactively so you're prompted before changes.

dd [*options*]

dd is a low-level copier of bits and bytes. It can copy data from one file to another, say, from *myfile* to */tmp/mycopy*:

```
→ dd if=myfile of=/tmp/mycopy
2+1 records in
2+1 records out
1168 bytes (1.2 kB) copied, 0.000174074 s, 6.7 MB/s
```

It can even convert data while copying, like changing characters to uppercase while copying from *myfile* to */tmp/mycopy*:

```
→ dd if=myfile of=/tmp/mycopy conv=ucase
```

dd does much more than copy files. It can copy raw data directly from one disk device to another. Here's a command to clone a hard disk:

```
→ sudo dd if=/dev/device1 of=/dev/device2 bs=512 \
  conv=noerror,sync              OVERWRITES /dev/device2
```

Or, copy an entire disk device to create an ISO file. Make sure the output file is on a different disk device and has sufficient free space.

```
→ sudo dd if=/dev/device of=disk_backup.iso
```

WARNING

dd, when run as the superuser, can *wipe out your hard drive* in seconds if you're not careful. Always double-check that the output file (the argument of=) is the one you intend. Back up your computer and keep a Linux "live" distro on hand for emergencies (see "What's in This Book?" on page ix) before experimenting with dd as root.

For some great advice on sophisticated uses of dd, visit *https://oreil.ly/R3krx*. My favorite tip is backing up a disk's master boot record (MBR), which is 512 bytes long, to a file called *mbr.txt*:

```
→ sudo dd if=/dev/device of=mbr.txt bs=512 count=1
```

Useful options

if=*file*	Specify an input file or device.
of=*file*	Specify an output file or device. **Double-check that it's the correct one!**
bs=*N*	Copy *N* bytes (the "block size") at a time. (To set different block sizes for the input and output, use ibs and obs, respectively.)
skip=*N*	Skip past *N* blocks of input (of size ibs) before starting the copy.
seek=*N*	Discard *N* blocks of output (of size obs) before starting the copy.
conv=*spec*	Convert the data being copied. *spec* can be ucase (convert to uppercase), lcase (convert to lowercase), ascii (convert to ASCII from EBCDIC), and many others listed on the manpage.

---

growisofs   stdin   stdout   - file   -- opt   --help   --version

```
growisofs [options] tracks
```

The growisofs command burns a writable CD, DVD, or Blu-ray disc. To burn the contents of a Linux directory onto a disc readable on Linux, Windows, and macOS systems:

1. Locate your disc writer devices by running:
   ```
   → grep "^drive name:" /proc/sys/dev/cdrom/info
   drive name:    sr1     sr0
   ```

   The available devices here are */dev/sr1* and */dev/sr0*.

2. Put the files you want to burn into a directory, say, *dir*. Arrange them exactly as you'd like on the disc. The directory *dir* itself is not copied to the disc, just its contents.

---

3. Use the mkisofs command to create an ISO (disc) image file, and burn it onto a disc using growisofs, assuming your device is */dev/sr1*:

```
→ mkisofs -R -l -o $HOME/mydisk.iso dir
→ growisofs -dvd-compat -Z /dev/sr1=$HOME/mydisk.iso
→ rm $HOME/mydisk.iso
```

To burn audio CDs, use a friendly graphical program like k3b.

Networking Commands

Host Information

uname   Print basic system information.

hostname   Print the system's hostname.

ip   Set and display network interface information.

Every Linux machine or *host* has a name, a network IP address, and other properties. Here's how to display this information.

---

uname   stdin **stdout** - file **-- opt** **--help**   **--version**

uname [*options*]

The uname command prints fundamental information about the OS, particularly the kernel:

```
→ uname -a
Linux myhost 5.15.0-76-generic #83-Ubuntu
  SMP Thu Jun 15 19:16:32 UTC 2023 x86_64
  x86_64 x86_64 GNU/Linux
```

This includes the kernel name (Linux), hostname (myhost), kernel release (5.15.0-76-generic), kernel version (#83-Ubuntu

---

SMP Thu Jun 15 19:16:32 UTC 2023), hardware name (x86_64), processor type (also x86_64), hardware platform (also x86_64) and OS name (GNU/Linux).

Useful options

- `-a`   All information
- `-s`   Only the kernel name (the default)
- `-n`   Only the hostname, as with the `hostname` command
- `-r`   Only the kernel release
- `-v`   Only the kernel version
- `-m`   Only the hardware name
- `-p`   Only the processor type
- `-i`   Only the hardware platform
- `-o`   Only the OS name

---

hostname   stdin **stdout** · file **-- opt** **--help** **--version**

`hostname [options] [name]`

The `hostname` command prints the name of your computer. Depending on how you have things set up, this might be the fully qualified hostname:

```
→ hostname
myhost.example.com
```

or your short hostname:

```
→ hostname
myhost
```

You can also set your hostname, as root:

```
→ sudo hostname orange
```

Useful options

-s	Print your host's short name.
-f	Print your host's fully qualified name.
-d	Print your host's DNS domain name.
-a	Print all of your host's aliases.
-I	Print all of your host's network addresses.
-F *hostfile*	Set your hostname by reading it from file *hostfile*.

ip

stdin **stdout** -file --opt **--help** --version

ip [*options*] *object command*…

The ip command displays and sets various aspects of your computer's network interface. This topic is beyond the scope of the book, but I'll teach you a few tricks.

If you know the name of your default interface, such as *eth0*, *ens160*, or *enp68s0*, view its details with this command:

```
→ ip addr show eth0
2: eth0: <BROADCAST,MULTICAST,UP,LOWER_UP> ...
   link/ether 00:50:ba:48:4f:ba brd ff:ff:ff: ...
   inet 192.168.0.21/24 brd 192.168.0.255 scope ...
   inet6 fe80::21e:8cff:fe53:41e4/64 ...
```

They include the IPv4 address (192.168.0.21), IPv6 address (fe80::21e:8cff:fe53:41e4/64), MAC address (00:50:ba:48:4f:ba),

and other details. If you don't know the interface name, view all
loaded network interfaces:

→ **ip addr show | less**

Another command, ifconfig, presents information similar to
ip addr show. It's considered mostly obsolete but you'll still
find it on many systems.

→ **ifconfig eth0**   *Details of one network interface*
→ **ifconfig -a**   *Details of all network interfaces*

Display other network information with the following ip commands. Add help on the end of any command (e.g., ip link
help) for usage details.

ip addr	Display IP addresses of your network devices.
ip maddr	Display multicast addresses of your network devices.
ip link	Display attributes of your network devices.
ip route	Display your routing table.
ip monitor	Begin monitoring your network devices; press ^C to stop.
ip help	See usage information for all these commands.

Superusers can also use ip to configure network devices, manage routing tables and rules, create tunnels, and more. Learn
more about ip and related tools (*https://oreil.ly/jT5FF*) (known
as iproute2) and on the ip manpage.

Host Location

host	Look up hostnames, IP addresses, and DNS info.
whois	Look up the registrants of internet domains.
ping	Check if a remote host is reachable.
traceroute	View the network path to a remote host.

When dealing with remote computers, you might want to know more about them. Who owns them? What are the IP addresses? Where on the network are they located?

---

host

```
host [options] name [server]
```

The host command looks up the hostname or IP address of a remote machine by querying DNS:

```
→ host www.ubuntu.org
www.ubuntu.com has address 69.16.230.226
→ host 69.16.230.226
226.230.16.69.in-addr.arpa domain name pointer
 lb05.parklogic.com.
```

It can also find out much more:

```
→ host -a www.ubuntu.org
Trying "www.ubuntu.org"
;; ->>HEADER<<- opcode: QUERY, status: NOERROR ...
;; flags: qr rd ra; QUERY: 1, ANSWER: 2, ...

;; QUESTION SECTION:
;www.ubuntu.org.                    IN      ANY

;; ANSWER SECTION:
www.ubuntu.org.      60     IN      CNAME   ubuntu.org.
```

though a full discussion of this output is beyond the scope of this book. The final, optional "server" parameter specifies a particular nameserver for the query:

```
→ host www.ubuntu.org ns1.parklogic.com
Using domain server:
Name: ns1.parklogic.com
Address: 69.16.230.48#53
Aliases:
www.ubuntu.org has address 69.16.230.226
www.ubuntu.org mail is handled by ...
```

Useful options

To see all options, run host by itself.

- -a   Display all available information about a host.

- -t   Choose the type of nameserver query: A, AXFR, CNAME, HINFO, KEY, MX, NS, PTR, SIG, SOA, and so on.

Here's an example of the -t option to locate MX records:

```
→ host -t MX centos.org
centos.org mail is handled by 10 mail.centos.org.
```

If the host command doesn't meet your needs, try dig, another DNS lookup utility, or the nslookup command, which is mostly obsolete but still around.

---

whois

whois [*options*] *domain_name*

The whois command prints the registration of an internet domain. The output is long, so pipe it through less:

```
→ whois linuxmint.com | less
  Domain name: LINUXMINT.COM
  Registrar: Ascio Technologies, Inc. Danmark
  Updated Date: 2023-05-16T22:22:38Z
  Creation Date: 2006-06-07T10:45:34Z
  Name Server: NS01.SERVAGE.NET
  ⋮
```

Useful options

- -h *server*   Perform the lookup at the given registrar's whois server. For example:
  ```
  → whois -h whois.comlaude.com redhat.com
  ```

- -p *port*   Query the given TCP port instead of the default (43).

---

ping

stdin **stdout** -file **--opt** --help --version

ping [*options*] *host*

The ping command tells you if a remote host is reachable. It sends small messages called ICMP packets to a remote host, waits for responses, and prints how long they took:

```
→ ping slackware.com
PING slackware.com (64.57.102.36) 56(84) bytes of data.
64 bytes from connie.slackware.com (64.57.102.36):
 icmp_seq=1 ttl=52 time=107 ms
64 bytes from connie.slackware.com (64.57.102.36):
 icmp_seq=2 ttl=52 time=107 ms
^C
--- slackware.com ping statistics ---
2 packets transmitted, 2 received, 0% packet loss, ...
rtt min/avg/max/mdev = 107.207/107.350/107.494/0.143 ms
```

Here, the host slackware.com replied in 107 milliseconds. (Notice that its real name is connie.slackware.com.) Pings may be blocked by firewalls, so a running host might not respond.

Useful options

-c *N* Ping at most *N* times. (Note that "ping" is a verb.)

-i *N* Wait *N* seconds (default 1) between pings. (Here "ping" is a noun.)

-n Print IP addresses in the output, rather than hostnames.

-6 Use IPv6 instead of the default IPv4.

traceroute

stdin **stdout** -file **--opt** --help --version

traceroute [*options*] *host* [*packet_length*]

The traceroute command prints the network path from your local host to a remote host, and the time it takes for packets to traverse the path:

```
→ traceroute archlinux.org
 1 server.mydomain.com (192.168.0.20) 1.397 ms ...
 2  10.221.16.1 (10.221.16.1) 15.397 ms ...
 3  router.example.com (92.242.140.21) 4.952 ms ...
   ⋮
12  archlinux.org (95.217.163.246)  117.100 ms ...
```

traceroute sends three "probes" to each host in the path and
reports the return times. If five seconds pass with no response,
traceroute prints an asterisk. If traceroute is blocked by firewalls or cannot proceed for other reasons, it prints a symbol:

Symbol	Meaning
!F	Fragmentation needed
!H	Host unreachable
!N	Network unreachable
!P	Protocol unreachable
!S	Source route failed
!X	Communication administratively prohibited
!N	ICMP unreachable code N

The default packet size is 40 bytes. Change this value with
the final, optional *packet_length* parameter (e.g., traceroute
myhost 120). For a more interactive experience, try the mtr
command ("my traceroute").

Useful options

-n   Numeric mode: print IP addresses instead of hostnames.

-w N Change the timeout from five seconds to N seconds.

-6   Use IPv6 instead of the default IPv4.

Network Connections

ssh   Log into a remote host, or run commands on it.

`scp`	Copy files between two hosts.
`sftp`	Interactively copy files between two hosts.
`netcat`	Create arbitrary network connections.

Linux makes it easy to connect from one host to another securely for remote logins, file transfers, and other purposes.

---

ssh   stdin stdout -file --opt --help --version

`ssh [options] host [command]`

The ssh (Secure Shell) command securely logs you into a remote machine. If your local and remote usernames are the same, just provide the remote hostname:

```
→ ssh remote.example.com
smith@remote.example.com's password: xxxxxxxx
```

Otherwise, provide your remote username as well:

```
→ ssh sandy@remote.example.com          One syntax
→ ssh -l sandy remote.example.com       Another syntax
```

If you provide a command, ssh invokes it on the remote machine without starting an interactive login session:

```
→ ssh sandy@remote.example.com df       Check free disk space
```

ssh encrypts all data that travels across its connection, including your username and password. The SSH protocol also supports other ways to authenticate, such as public keys: see the sidebar "Public Key Authentication with SSH" on page 240.

Useful options

- `-l user` Specify your remote username; otherwise, ssh assumes it equals your local username. Or use the syntax *username@host*:

    ```
    → ssh sandy@remote.example.com
    ```

- p *port*   Connect to a *port* number other than the default (22).

- t   Allocate a tty on the remote system; useful when trying to run a remote command with an interactive UI, such as a text editor.

- v   Produce verbose output, useful for debugging. Repeat -v for more detailed messages.

Public Key Authentication with SSH

Public key authentication is a more secure way to log into remote hosts with SSH. It uses a pair of cryptographic keys. Your private key remains on your local host in the directory *~/.ssh*, protected by a passphrase. Your public key is copied to remote hosts. First, generate a key pair:

```
→ ssh-keygen
Enter file to save the key (~/.ssh/id_rsa): <Enter>
Enter passphrase (empty for no passphrase): xxxxxxx
Enter same passphrase again:  xxxxxxx
Your identification has been saved in ~/.ssh/id_rsa
```

Then, copy your public key to the remote host and log in:

```
→ ssh-copy-id sandy@remote.example.com
sandy@remote.example.com's password: xxxxxxxx
Number of key(s) added: 1
→ ssh sandy@remote.example.com
Enter passphrase for '/home/sandy/.ssh/id_rsa': xxxxxxx
```

If the final ssh command fails to log you in, check that:

- The local and remote *~/.ssh* directories have mode 0700.
- The local private key file *~/.ssh/id_rsa* has mode 0600.
- The remote file *~/.ssh/authorized_keys* has mode 600.
- The public key in local file *~/.ssh/id_rsa.pub* appears in remote file *~/.ssh/authorized_keys*. If not, append the local file's contents to the remote *authorized_keys* and try again.

Also run ssh -v to print debug messages and look for clues. Run ssh -vvv for more verbose detail.

```
scp local_spec remote_spec
```

The scp (secure copy) command copies files and directories from one computer to another in batch. (For an interactive UI, see sftp.) It encrypts all communication between the two machines using SSH. As a simple example, scp can copy a local file to a remote machine:

→ `scp myfile remote.example.com:newfile`

recursively copy a directory to a remote machine:

→ `scp -r mydir remote.example.com:`

copy a remote file to your local machine:

→ `scp remote.example.com:myfile .`

or recursively copy a remote directory to your local machine:

→ `scp -r remote.example.com:mydir .`

You can even copy files from one remote machine to another if you have SSH access to both machines:

→ `scp remote1.example.com:myfile remote2.example.com:`

To specify an alternate username on the remote system, use the *username@host* syntax:

→ `scp myfile sandy@remote.example.com:`

Useful options

-P *port*	Connect on the given TCP port number (default is 22).
-p	Preserve all file attributes (permissions, timestamps) when copying.
-r	Recursively copy directories and their contents.
-v	Produce verbose output, useful for debugging.

sftp

sftp (*host* | *username@host*)

The sftp command is an interactive program that copies files securely between two computers using SSH. (Avoid the similarly named command ftp—most implementations send usernames, passwords, and files insecurely over the network.)

```
→ sftp remote.example.com
smith@remote.example.com's password: xxxxxxxx
sftp> cd MyFiles                    Change remote directory
sftp> ls                            List remote directory
README
file1
file2
file3
sftp> get file2                     Transfer a remote file
Fetching /home/sandy/MyFiles/file2 to file2
sftp> quit
```

If your username on the remote system is different from your local one, use the *username@host* argument:

```
→ sftp sandy@remote.example.com
```

Command	Meaning
help	View a list of available commands.
ls	List the files in the current remote directory.
lls	List the files in the current local directory.
pwd	Print the remote working directory.
lpwd	Print the local working directory.
cd *dir*	Change your remote directory to be *dir*.
lcd *dir*	Change your local directory to be *dir*.
get *file1* [*file2*]	Copy remote *file1* to local machine, optionally renamed as *file2*.

Command	Meaning
put *file1* [*file2*]	Copy local *file1* to remote machine, optionally renamed as *file2*.
mget *file**	Copy multiple remote files to the local machine using patterns * and ?.
mput *file**	Copy multiple local files to the remote machine using patterns * and ?.
quit	Exit sftp.

netcat

stdin stdout -file --opt --help --version

netcat [*options*] [*destination*] [*port*]

nc [*options*] [*destination*] [*port*]

netcat, or equivalently, nc, is a general-purpose tool to make network connections. It's handy for debugging, learning about networking, and many other uses. For example, netcat can speak directly to any TCP or UDP service, such as an SSH server (if one is running) on your local TCP port 22:

```
→ netcat localhost 22
SSH-2.0-OpenSSH_8.9p1 Ubuntu-3ubuntu0.1
^C
```

This feature, which can determine if a particular service is up or down, also works with service names as listed in the file */etc/services*. For example, you could connect to Google's web service (port 80) with:

```
→ netcat www.google.com http
abc <Enter>                    Type some junk and press Enter
HTTP/1.0 400 Bad Request
Content-Type: text/html; charset=UTF-8
Content-Length: 1555
Date: Tue, 18 Jul 2023 03:14:36 GMT
⋮
```

For old-school Linux users who run `telnet` to connect to TCP ports, `netcat` is more flexible. For example, create a client and a service that talk to each other. Begin with a service listening on port 55555:

```
→ netcat -l 55555
```

In another window, run a client that talks to that same port, and type a message:

```
→ netcat localhost 55555
Hello world, how are you? <Enter>
```

Your message is sent to your service, which prints "Hello world, how are you?" and any subsequent lines you enter. Press ^C in the client to close the connection.

Useful options

-u   Establish a UDP connection instead of TCP.

-l   Listen for connections on the given port.

-p *N*   Use port *N* as the source port.

-w *N*   Time out after *N* seconds.

-h   Get help.

Email in Daily Use

mutt   Text-based mail client.

mail   Minimal text-based mail client.

mailq   View the outgoing mail queue on your system.

Most users receive their email in the cloud and read it in a web browser or a graphical email application. Few people read their email at the command line. Nevertheless, text-based email programs have interesting uses, particularly in scripts. I present one full-featured email client (`mutt`) that runs on the command line, followed by a few other mail-related commands. I assume your system is already configured to accept email; otherwise, some commands will not work.

mutt

mutt [options]

Mutt is a text-based mailer that runs in a shell, so it can be used both locally (e.g., in a terminal window) or remotely over an SSH connection. To invoke it, run:

→ mutt

When the main screen appears, mutt briefly lists messages in your mailbox, one per line. Try the following operations:

Keystroke	Meaning
Up arrow	Move to the previous message.
Down arrow	Move to the next message.
PageUp	Scroll up one pageful of messages.
PageDown	Scroll down one pageful of messages.
Home	Move to the first message.
End	Move to the last message.
m	Compose a new mail message. This invokes your default text editor. After editing the message and exiting the editor, type y to send the message or q to postpone it.
r	Reply to current message. Works like m.
f	Forward the current message. Works like m.
i	View the contents of your mailbox.
C	Copy the current message to another mailbox.
d	Delete the current message.

When you've finished editing a message, try these operations:

Keystroke	Meaning
a	Attach a file (an attachment) to the message.
c	Set the CC list.
b	Set the BCC list.
e	Edit the message again.
r	Edit the Reply-To field.
s	Edit the subject line.
y	Send the message.
C	Copy the message to a file.
q	Postpone the message without sending it.

The following operations are always available:

Keystroke	Meaning
?	See a list of all commands (press the space bar to scroll down, q to quit).
^G	Cancel the command in progress.
q	Quit.

mail

stdin   stdout -file --opt --help --version

```
mail [options] recipient
```

The mail command is a simple email client. It's best for quick messages from the command line or in scripts. Send a message:

```
→ mail smith@example.com
Subject: my subject
I'm typing a message.
To end it, I type a period by itself on a line.
.
Cc: jones@example.com
→
```

Pipe any command's output to `mail` to send it in an email message. This feature is particularly useful in shell scripts.

```
→ echo "Wake up!" | mail -s "Alert" smith@example.com
```

To mail the contents of a text file, simply redirect the file to `mail`. This won't work for binary files like images, which must be converted to attachments first.

```
→ mail -s "my subject" smith@example.com < file.txt
```

Useful options

-s *subject*	Set the subject line of an outgoing message.
-c *addresses*	CC to the given addresses, a comma-separated list.
-b *addresses*	BCC to the given addresses, a comma-separated list.
-v	Verbose mode: print messages about mail delivery.

---

mailq

stdin **stdout** -file --opt --help --version

`mailq`

The `mailq` command lists outgoing email messages awaiting delivery, if any.

```
→ mailq
... Size-- ----Arrival Time--  -Sender/Recipient---
      333 Tue Jan 10 21:17:14 smith@example.com
                              jones@elsewhere.org
```

Mail delivery is often so quick that `mailq` has no output. Sent messages are also recorded in a log file such as */var/log/mail.log*. The name may differ from distro to distro. View the last few lines with `tail`:

```
→ tail /var/log/mail.log
```

Beyond Mail Readers

Email is more "transparent" on Linux than on other platforms that merely display your mailbox and send and receive messages. The ability to list outgoing email messages with mailq is just one example. Here are some other options to whet your appetite and encourage you to explore.

- Process your mailboxes with any command-line tools, such as grep, because mail files are plain text.

- Manually retrieve messages from a remote mail server at the command line with the fetchmail command. Using a simple configuration file, this command can reach out to IMAP and POP servers and download mail in batch. See man fetchmail.

- Run a mail server, such as postfix, for complex mail delivery situations; see "Email Servers" on page 248.

- Control local mail delivery in sophisticated ways with the procmail command, which filters arriving email messages through any arbitrary program. See man procmail.

- Perform spam filtering with the SpamAssassin suite of programs. Run it personally on your incoming email or at the server level for large numbers of users.

In short, email is not limited to the features of your mail-reading program. Investigate and experiment!

Email Servers

Configuring a mail server is a complex job that can't be taught in a few pages, so I just present some common operations. For Postfix, one of the most popular mail servers, I assume it's already running on your local host. In case you don't have a mail server yet, I also present Nullmailer, a simpler service that relays your mail to another server for delivery.

Postfix: A Full-Featured Mail Server

Postfix is a powerful and popular mail server, and it's controlled by the postfix command. Important configuration files for the server are located in the directory */etc/postfix*:

main.cf

> Variables that control Postfix's behavior, such as your server's name and domain, locations of important files, size limits on mailboxes and incoming mail, and more. After changing this file, run sudo postfix reload for the changes to take effect.

master.cf

> Defines how Postfix runs various services. Most users don't commonly edit this file, but if you do, run sudo postfix reload for the changes to take effect.

postfix-files

> Defines the correct permissions for all Postfix files. These permissions are critical for email security. Most users won't modify this file. To restore a Postfix installation to these permissions, run sudo postfix set-permissions.

sasl_passwd

> Authentication information for connecting to a remote SMTP provider. After changing this file, run sudo postmap /etc/postfix/sasl_passwd for the changes to take effect. The file format is:

> `[smtpserver]:port  username:password`

> where *smtpserver* is the remote SMTP server, *port* is its TCP port number (optional), and *username* and *password* are the authentication credentials. For example:

> `[smtp.example.com]:587  smith:SEEKRIT_PASSWURD`

Postfix usually runs automatically, but you can start and stop it
by hand:

→ **sudo postfix start**   *Run the server*
→ **sudo postfix status**   *Check that the server is running*
→ **sudo postfix stop**   *Halt the server gracefully*
→ **sudo postfix abort**   *Kill the server ungracefully*

After a mail delivery problem, to deliver all queued mail immediately, run:

→ **sudo postfix flush**

For more information on Postfix, visit postfix.org (*https://
oreil.ly/NzFRZ*).

Nullmailer: Simple Outgoing Email

Postfix is complicated. A simpler solution is to forward your
local host's email to another mail server for delivery. (You'll
need an account on the remote mail server.) This is called
setting up a relay-only mail server.

Suppose you have an account "smith" on a Linux host
example.com, and you want to configure that host to send
email. You also have an account "sandy" on a remote server,
mail.example.com, that already runs Postfix for delivering mail.
Install Nullmailer on your local host, either using your distro's
package manager (preferred) or from *https://oreil.ly/82aMq*.
Then, as the superuser, create three local files in the directory */etc/nullmailer*:

adminaddr

> Contains the email address to receive administrative emails, such as Nullmailer notices.

defaultdomain

> Contains the domain to set for all outgoing emails.

remotes

> Contains the login information for the remote mail server, including the password in plain text, so make sure this file is readable only by root:

```
→ chmod 0600 /etc/nullmailer/remotes
```

Here's what the three files look like in a typical installation:

```
→ cd /etc/nullmailer
→ cat adminaddr
smith@example.com
→ cat defaultdomain
example.com
→ cat remotes
cat: remotes: Permission denied
→ sudo cat remotes          The content must be on a single line
mail.example.com smtp --port=587 --tls --user=sandy
  --pass=...
```

Your *remotes* file will require different values specific to your remote mail server. Run `man nullmailer-send` to learn about them. Once the three files are in place, enable and start the Nullmailer service:

```
→ sudo systemctl enable nullmailer
→ sudo systemctl start nullmailer
```

Send a test message:

```
→ echo hi | mail funkydance@another.example.com
```

Check that the message was relayed to mail.example.com:

```
→ tail /var/log/mail          Or other mail log file
...nullmailer-send: Starting delivery:
                   host: mail.example.com
...nullmailer-send: From: <smith@example.com> to:
```

```
    <funkydance@another.example.com>
...nullmailer-send: Delivery complete
```

Web Browsing

lynx   Text-only web browser.

curl   Access online content from the command line.

wget   Download web pages and files.

Besides the usual web browsers such as Chrome and Firefox, Linux offers several ways to explore the World Wide Web via the command line.

---

lynx   stdin   stdout   -file   -- opt   --help   --version

lynx [*options*] [*URL*]

Lynx is a stripped-down text-only web browser. It doesn't display pictures or play audio or video. All browsing is done by keyboard, not with a pointing device. But Lynx is incredibly useful when you just want a quick look at a page, when the network is slow, or for downloading the HTML of a website. It's particularly good for checking out a suspicious URL because Lynx doesn't run JavaScript and won't even accept a cookie without asking you first.

→ **lynx https://danieljbarrett.com**

Many pages won't look right, especially if they use tables or frames, but usually you can find your way around a site.

Keystroke	Meaning
?	Get help.
k	List all keystrokes and their meanings.
^G	Cancel a command in progress.
q	Quit Lynx.

Keystroke	Meaning
Down arrow	Go to the next link or form field.
Up arrow	Go to the previous link or form field.
Enter	"Click" the current link, or finish the current form field.
Right arrow	Go forward to next page, or "click" the current link.
Left arrow	Go back to previous page.
g	Go to a URL (you'll be prompted to enter it).
p	Save, print, or mail the current page.
Space bar	Scroll down.
b	Scroll up.
^A	Go to top of page.
^E	Go to end of page.
m	Return to the main/home page.
/	Search for text on the page.
a	Bookmark the current page.
v	View your bookmark list.
r	Delete a bookmark.
=	Display properties of the current page and link.
\	View HTML source (press again to return to normal view).

Lynx has over one hundred options, so the manpage is worth reading. Other text-based browsers include w3m, links, and elinks.

Useful options

-dump	Print the rendered page to standard output and exit. (Compare to the -source option.)
-source	Print the HTML source to standard output and exit. (Compare to the wget command.)

-useragent=*name*	If a site is blocking `lynx`, set the useragent to present as a different browser. Try -useragent=mozilla.
-emacskeys	Make Lynx obey emacs-like keystrokes.
-vikeys	Make Lynx obey Vim-like keystrokes.
-homepage=*URL*	Set your home page URL to be *URL*.
-color	Turn colored text mode on.
-nocolor	Turn colored text mode off.

curl

stdin   stdout   - file   -- opt   --help   --version

curl [*options* | *URLs*]

The curl command accesses online content. It can download web pages, test a web service, or do any other task that hits a URL. By default, curl writes to standard output, so redirect the output as needed or use the -o option:

```
→ curl https://www.yahoo.com > mypage.html        Redirect
→ curl -o mypage.html https://www.yahoo.com        -o option
→ curl https://www.yahoo.com | wc -l               Pipelines
```

curl is great for quickly testing a REST API. Search Wikipedia for the word "Linux" and receive a JSON response:

```
→ curl "https://en.wikipedia.org/w/rest.php/v1/search/\
page?q=Linux"
{"pages":[{"id":6097297,"key":"Linux","title":"Linux" ...
```

Curl has dozens of options and can speak numerous protocols besides HTTP, such as IMAP, FTP, and SMB. It can add web headers, post data to web pages, authenticate with usernames and passwords, handle SSL certificates, simulate cookies, and much more (see the manpage).

Useful options

-o *file*   Write output to the given file.

`-A` *name*	Set the user agent to *name*. Try `-A mozilla`.
`-v`	Verbose mode: print lots of diagnostic output.
`-s`	Silent mode: no diagnostic output.

wget

stdin   stdout   - file   -- opt   --help   --version

`wget [options] URL`

The `wget` command downloads data from a URL to a file. It's great for capturing individual web pages, downloading files, or duplicating entire website hierarchies to arbitrary depth. For example, let's capture the Yahoo! home page:

```
→ wget https://www.yahoo.com
2023-10-22 13:56:53 (3.45 MB/s) - 'index.html' saved
```

which is saved to a file *index.html* in the current directory. `wget` can resume a download if it gets interrupted in the middle, say, due to a network failure: just run `wget -c` with the same URL and it picks up where it left off.

Perhaps the most useful feature of `wget` is its ability to download files without needing a web browser:

```
→ wget https://linuxpocketguide.com/sample.pdf
```

This is great for large files like videos and ISO images. You can even write shell scripts to download sets of files if you know their names. Here's a script that downloads three MP4 videos named *1.mp4*, *2.mp4*, and *3.mp4* from the root of a website.

```
→ for i in 1 2 3
do
  wget https://example.com/$i.mp4
done
```

`wget` has over 70 options, so I cover just a few important ones.

Useful options

-U *name*	If a site is blocking `wget`, set the useragent to present as a different browser. Try `-U mozilla`.
-O *filename*	Write all the captured HTML to the given file.
-i *filename*	Read URLs from the given file and retrieve them in turn.
-c	Continue an interrupted download. For example, if `wget` downloaded 100K of a 150K file, `wget -c` retrieves just the remaining 50K. `wget` can be fooled, however, if the remote file has changed since the first (partial) download, so use `-c` only if the remote file hasn't changed.
-t *N*	Try *N* times before giving up. *N*=0 means try forever.
--progress=dot	Print dots instead of bars to show download progress.
--spider	Don't download, just check existence of remote pages.
-nd	Retrieve all files into the current directory, instead of duplicating the remote directory hierarchy.
-r	Retrieve a whole tree of pages recursively.
-l *N*	Retrieve files at most *N* levels deep (5 by default).
-k	Inside retrieved files, modify URLs so the files can be viewed locally in a web browser.
-p	Download all necessary files to make a page display completely, such as stylesheets and images.
-L	Follow relative links (within a page) but not absolute links.
-A *pattern*	Accept mode: download only files whose names match a given pattern, using standard shell pattern-matching.
-R *pattern*	Reject mode: download only files whose names *do not* match a given pattern.
-I *pattern*	Directory inclusion: download files only from directories that match a given pattern.
-X *pattern*	Directory exclusion: download files only from directories that *do not* match a given pattern.

Getting Stuff Done

Screen Output

echo	Print simple text on standard output.
printf	Print formatted text on standard output.
yes	Print repeated text on standard output.
seq	Print a sequence of numbers on standard output.
clear	Clear the screen or window.

Linux provides several commands to print messages on standard output. Each has different strengths and intended purposes. These commands are invaluable for learning about Linux, debugging, writing shell scripts (see "Programming with Shell Scripts" on page 293), or just talking to yourself.

---

echo
stdin **stdout** - file -- opt --help --version

```
echo [options] strings
```

The echo command simply prints its arguments:

```
→ echo We are having fun
We are having fun
```

Confusingly, there are several different echo commands with slightly different behavior. There's */bin/echo*, but Linux shells typically override this with a built-in command called echo. To find out which you're using, run the following command:

```
→ type echo
echo is a shell builtin
```

Useful options

- -n Don't print a final newline character.

- -e Recognize and interpret escape characters. For example, try echo 'hello\a' and echo -e 'hello\a'. The first prints literally and the second produces a beep.

- -E Don't interpret escape characters: the opposite of -e.

Available escape characters are:

\a Alert (play a beep)

\b Backspace

\c Don't print the final newline (same effect as -n)

\f Form feed

\n Line feed (newline)

\r Carriage return

\t Horizontal tab

\v Vertical tab

\\ A backslash

\' Single quote

\" Double quote

nnn The character whose ASCII value is *nnn* in octal (base 8)

printf

printf *format_string* [*arguments*]

The printf command is an enhanced echo: it prints formatted strings on standard output. It operates much like the C programming language function printf(), which applies a format string to a sequence of arguments to create some specified output. For example:

```
→ printf "User %s is %d years old.\n" sandy 29
User sandy is 29 years old.
```

The first argument is the format string, which in our example contains two format specifications, %s and %d. The subsequent arguments, sandy and 29, are substituted by printf into the format string and then printed. Format specifications can get fancy with floating-point numbers:

```
→ printf "That'll be $%0.2f, my friend.\n" 3
That'll be $3.00, my friend.
```

Linux has two printf commands: one built into bash, and one in */usr/bin/printf*. The two behave almost identically with small differences; for example, only the built-in printf can store output in a shell variable (with the -v option).

Make sure the number of format specifications (%) equals the number of arguments to printf. With too few arguments, printf outputs default values (0 for numeric formats, an empty string for string formats). With too many arguments, printf iterates over the extras until they run out. Treat such mismatches as errors, even though printf is forgiving: they are bugs waiting to happen.

```
→ printf "%d %d\n" 10                    Too few arguments
10 0
→ printf "%d %d\n" 10 20 30 40           Too many arguments
10 20
30 40
```

Format specifications are described in detail on the manpage for the C function printf (see man 3 printf). Here are some useful ones:

%d	Decimal integer
%ld	Long decimal integer
%o	Octal integer
%x	Hexadecimal integer
%f	Floating point
%lf	Double-precision floating point
%c	A single character
%s	String
%q	String with any special shell characters escaped
%%	A percent sign by itself

Set the minimum width of the output by inserting a numeric expression just after the leading percent sign. For example, "%5d" means to print a decimal number in a five-character-wide field, and "%6.2f" means a floating-point number in a six-character-wide field with two digits after the decimal point. Some useful numeric expressions are:

n	Minimum width *n*
0*n*	Minimum width *n*, padded with leading zeros
n.m	Minimum width *n*, with *m* digits after the decimal point

printf also interprets escape characters like "\n" (print a new-line character) and "\a" (ring the bell). See the echo command for the full list.

yes

yes [*string*]

The yes command prints "y" or a given string forever, one string per line:

→ **yes**
y
y
y
⋮

Though it might seem useless at first glance, yes can be perfect for commands that prompt the user to continue. Pipe the output of yes into the input of the command to answer every prompt affirmatively:

→ **yes | *any_interactive_command***

When *any_interactive_command* terminates, so does yes.

---

seq

seq [*options*] *specification*

The seq command prints a sequence of integers or real numbers that's suitable to pipe to other programs. It supports three kinds of arguments:

A single number: an upper limit
    seq begins at 1 and counts up to the number:

    → **seq 3**
    1
    2
    3

Two numbers: lower and upper limit
    seq begins at the first number and counts as far as it can without passing the second number:

```
→ seq 2 5
2
3
4
5
```

Three numbers: lower limit, increment, and upper limit

seq begins at the first number and increments by the second number as far as possible without passing the third
number:

```
→ seq 1 .3 2
1
1.3
1.6
1.9
```

You can also go backward with a negative increment:

```
→ seq 5 -1 2
5
4
3
2
```

Useful options

-w   Print leading zeros, as necessary, to give all lines the same width:
```
→ seq -w 8 10
08
09
10
```

-f *format*   Format the output lines with a printf-like format string, which
                must include either %g (the default), %e, or %f:
```
→ seq -f '**%g**' 3
**1**
**2**
**3**
```

-s *string*	Use the given string as a separator between the numbers. By default, a newline is printed (i.e., one number per line):

```
→ seq -s ':' 10
1:2:3:4:5:6:7:8:9:10
```

Bash and other shells have a similar feature to produce a sequence of numbers; see "Brace Expansion" on page 21.

```
→ echo {1..10}
1 2 3 4 5 6 7 8 9 10
```

---

clear
stdin **stdout** -file   --opt   --help   --version

```
clear
```

This command simply clears your display or shell window. Alternatively, press ^L.

Copy and Paste

xclip   Copy and paste between the shell and the clipboard.

xsel   Manipulate the clipboard from the shell.

Linux has a clipboard to copy and paste between graphical applications. Actually, Linux has three different clipboards, called *selections*. You can access the selections from the command line, send the output of any shell command to the selection, or read the selection like standard input.

These commands work only if your shell runs in an X11 environment such as GNOME or KDE. Wayland has other clipboard mechanisms such as wl-copy and wl-paste. In a non-graphical environment, the tmux and screen commands provide clipboards while running. If you're using none of these environments, no clipboard exists.

xclip

```
xclip [options]
```

xclip reads and writes the three Linux selections (clipboards) to copy and paste text between the shell and graphical applications. To see it in action, copy some text with your mouse to a selection—say, double-click a word in your terminal window—and then run:

```
→ xclip -o
```

The text you copied is printed on standard output. As another example, copy the contents of a file to a selection, and then print the selection:

```
→ cat poem                          See the file
Once upon a time, there was
a little operating system named
Linux, which everybody loved.
→ cat poem | xclip -i               Pipe file to selection
→ xclip -o                          Print selection
Once upon a time, there was
a little operating system named
Linux, which everybody loved.
```

All command-line options for xclip use single dashes, even -help and -version.

Useful options

-selection *name*	Choose a selection: primary (default), secondary, or clipboard. In my terminal windows, the middle mouse button pastes from primary, and "Paste" in the right-button menu uses clipboard.
-i	Read the selection contents from standard input (default behavior).
-o	Write the selection contents to standard output.

xsel

`xsel [options]`

xsel is a more powerful version of xclip. Along with reading and writing the three selections (clipboards), it can also append to them, swap them, and clear them:

```
→ echo Hello | xsel -i
→ xsel -o
Hello
→ echo World | xsel -a        Append
→ xsel -o
Hello
World
```

Useful options

-p   Use the primary selection (default).

-s   Use the secondary selection.

-b   Use the clipboard selection.

-i   Read the selection contents from standard input (default behavior).

-a   Append to the selection.

-o   Write the selection contents to standard output.

-c   Clear the selection contents.

-x   Swap (exchange) the contents of the primary and secondary selection.

Math and Calculations

expr   Do simple math on the command line.

bc   Text-based calculator.

dc   Text-based RPN calculator.

Need a calculator? Linux provides some commands to compute mathematical truths for you.

expr

expr *expression*

The expr command does simple math (and other expression evaluation) on the command line:

```
→ expr 7 + 3
10
→ expr '(' 7 + 3 ')' '*' 14      Quote any shell characters
140
→ expr length ABCDEFG
7
→ expr 15 '>' 16
0                                Zero means false
```

Bash provides a shorthand for expr using a dollar sign and a double parenthesis: $((…)). It's convenient for calculations within a command line:

```
→ echo The answer is: $((7 + 3))
The answer is: 10
```

Each argument must be separated by whitespace. Notice that you have to quote or escape any characters that have special meaning to the shell. Parentheses (escaped) may be used for grouping. Operators for expr include:

Operator	Numeric operation	String operation
+, -, *, /	Addition, subtraction, multiplication, and integer division, respectively	
%	Remainder (mod)	
<	Less than	Earlier in dictionary
<=	Less than or equal	Earlier in dictionary, or equal
>	Greater than	Later in dictionary

Operator	Numeric operation	String operation
>=	Greater than or equal	Later in dictionary, or equal
=	Equality	Equality
!=	Inequality	Inequality
|	Boolean "or"	Boolean "or"
&	Boolean "and"	Boolean "and"
s:regexp		Does the regular expression *regexp* match string *s*?
substr s p n		Print *n* characters of string *s*, beginning at position p (the first character is p=1)
index s chars		Return the index of the first position in string *s* containing a character from string *chars*. Return 0 if not found. Same behavior as the C function index().

For Boolean expressions, the number 0 and the empty string are considered false; any other value is true. When returning Boolean results, 0 is false and 1 is true.

---

bc

bc [*options*] [*files*]

bc is a text-based calculator that reads arithmetic expressions, one per line, and prints the results. Unlike most other calculators, bc can handle numbers of unlimited size and any number of decimal places:

```
→ bc
1+2+3+4+5                    Add five numbers
```

```
15
scale=2                          Set precision to 2 decimal places
(1 + 2 * 3 / 4) - 5
-2.50
2^100                            Raise 2 to the power 100
1267650600228229401496703205376
^D                               Exit
```

Programmers may enjoy the ability to switch bases to perform calculations and conversions in binary, octal, hexadecimal, or even custom bases:

```
→ bc
obase=2                          Display results in base 2
999
1111100111
obase=16                         Or base 16
999
3E7
```

But bc doesn't stop there. It's also a programmable calculator that can define functions. Here's a function that implements the quadratic formula from algebra and prints the real roots of a given equation, stored in a file called *quadratic.txt*:[1]

```
→ cat quadratic.txt
scale=2
define quadform ( a, b, c ) {
 root1 = (-b + sqrt(b^2 - 4*a*c)) / (2*a)
 root2 = (-b - sqrt(b^2 - 4*a*c)) / (2*a)
 print root1, "   ", root2, "\n"
}

quadform(1, 7, 12)               Solve x² + 7x + 12 = 0
```

Solve $x^2 + 7x + 12 = 0$

Redirect the file to bc to run the function and see the results:

```
→ bc < quadratic.txt
    -3.00   -4.00
```

---

1 This demonstration code fails if the roots are imaginary.

In its most powerful form, bc is a programming language for arithmetic. You can assign values to variables, manipulate arrays, execute conditional expressions and loops, and even write scripts that prompt you for values and run any sequence of math operations. For full details, see the manpage.

Useful arithmetic operations

+, -, *, /	Addition, subtraction, multiplication, and division, respectively. Results of division are truncated to the current scale (see below).
%	Remainder (mod).
^	Exponentiation, as in 10^5 for "ten to the fifth power."
sqrt(*N*)	Square root of *N*.
ibase=*N*	Treat all input numbers as base *N*.
obase=*N*	Output all numbers in base *N*.
scale=*N*	Set the number of significant digits after the decimal point to *N*.
(...)	Parentheses for grouping (changing precedence).
name=value	Assign a value to the variable *name*.

---

dc

stdin   stdout   - file   -- opt   --help   --version

dc [*options*] [*files*]

The dc (desk calculator) command is a reverse Polish notation (RPN), stack-based calculator that reads expressions from standard input and writes results to standard output. If you know how to use a Hewlett-Packard RPN calculator, dc is pretty easy once you understand its syntax. If you're accustomed to traditional calculators, however, dc may seem inscrutable. I cover only some basic commands.

For stack and calculator operations:

---

q	Quit dc.
f	Print the entire stack.
c	Delete (clear) the entire stack.
p	Print the topmost value on the stack.
P	Pop (remove) the topmost value from the stack.
n k	Set precision of future operations to be *n* decimal places (default is 0k, meaning integer operations).

To pop the top two values from the stack, perform a requested operation, and push the result:

+, -, *, /	Addition, subtraction, multiplication, and division, respectively.
%	Remainder (mod).
^	Exponentiation (second-to-top value is the base, top value is the exponent).

To pop the top value from the stack, perform a requested operation, and push the result:

v	Square root.

Examples:

```
→ dc
4 5 + p           Print the sum of 4 and 5
9
2 3 ^ p           Raise 2 to the 3rd power and print the result
8
10 * p            Multiply the stack top by 10 and print the result
80
f                 Print the stack
80
9
+p                Pop the top two values and print their sum
89
^D                Exit
```

Dates and Times

cal   Print a calendar.

date   Print or set the date and time.

Need a date? How about a good time? Try these commands to display and set dates and times on your system.

---

cal

cal [*options*] [*month* [*year*]]

The cal command prints a calendar—by default, the current month:

```
→ cal
      January 2024
 Su Mo Tu We Th Fr Sa
     1  2  3  4  5  6
  7  8  9 10 11 12 13
 14 15 16 17 18 19 20
 21 22 23 24 25 26 27
 28 29 30 31
```

To print a different calendar, supply a month and four-digit year: cal 8 2024 or cal aug 2024. If you omit the month (cal 2024), the entire year is printed. Note that several different cal programs exist and yours may behave differently.

Useful options

- -y   Print the current year's calendar.

- -3   Three-month view: print the previous and next month as well.

- -j   Print each date by its position in the year. February 1 would be displayed as 32, February 2 as 33, and so on.

---

date

date [*options*] [*format*]

The date command prints dates and times. The results depend on your system's locale settings (for your country and language). In this section, I assume an English, US-based locale.

By default, date prints the system date and time in the local timezone:

```
→ date
Sun Jun  4 02:09:05 PM EDT 2023
```

Format the output differently by supplying a format string beginning with a plus sign:

```
→ date +%x
06/04/2023
→ date '+The time is %l:%M %p on a lovely %A in %B'
The time is  2:09 PM on a lovely Sunday in June
```

Here is a sampling of the date command's many formats:

Format	Meaning	Example (US English)
Whole dates and times:		
%c	Full date and time, 12-hour clock	Sun 04 Jun 2023 02:09:05 PM EDT
%D	Numeric date, 2-digit year	06/04/23
%x	Numeric date, 4-digit year	06/04/2023
%T	Time, 24-hour clock	14:09:05
%X	Time, 12-hour clock	02:09:05 PM
Words:		
%a	Day of week (abbreviated)	Sun
%A	Day of week (complete)	Sunday
%b	Month name (abbreviated)	Jun

Format	Meaning	Example (US English)
%B	Month name (complete)	June
%Z	Time zone	EDT
%p	AM or PM	PM
Numbers:		
%w	Day of week (0–6, 0=Sunday)	0
%u	Day of week (1–7, 1=Monday)	7
%d	Day of month, leading zero	04
%e	Day of month, leading blank	4
%j	Day of year, leading zeros	144
%m	Month number, leading zero	06
%y	Year, 2 digits	23
%Y	Year, 4 digits	2023
%M	Minute, leading zero	09
%S	Seconds, leading zero	05
%l	Hour, 12-hour clock, leading blank	2
%I	Hour, 12-hour clock, leading zero	02
%k	Hour, 24-hour clock, leading blank	14
%H	Hour, 24-hour clock, leading zero	14
%N	Nanoseconds	384789400
%s	Seconds since the beginning of Linux time: midnight January 1, 1970	1685902145
Other:		
%n	Newline character	
%t	Tab character	
%%	Percent sign	%

date also displays other dates and times via options.

Useful options

-d *string*	Display the given date or time *string*, formatted as you wish.
-r *filename*	Display the last-modified timestamp of the given file, formatted as you wish.
-s *string*	Set the system date and/or time to be *string*; only the superuser can do this.

Version Control

git	Perform version control using Git.
svn	Perform version control using Subversion.

Version control systems like Git and Subversion let you keep track of changes to files, safely revert risky edits, and collaborate with teams to modify the same files without clobbering each others' work. I'll assume you already understand version control concepts like repositories, branches, and commits.

---

git   stdin **stdout** · file **-- opt** **--help** **--version**

git [*options*] subcommand [*arguments*]

Git is a popular and powerful version control system. It gives every participant their own full-featured repository and lets them share changes with other repositories. The git command has a rich set of features too large to teach here, but let's check out some common operations.

To get started, either create a local repository:

```
→ mkdir project
→ cd project
→ git init .
```

---

or download a copy of a remote repository by its URL:

```
→ git clone url
```

After you edit some files, a common sequence of `git` commands is as follows:

→ `git status`	*List the changed files*
→ `git diff`	*Check changes line by line*
→ `git add -A`	*Stage the changed files*
→ `git diff --staged`	*Check the staged changes*
→ `git commit -m"comment"`	*Commit the staged changes locally*
→ `git show .`	*View the committed changes*

Staging and Undoing Changes

Staging means copying files to a hidden "staging area" to commit in the next `git commit`. The opposite is `git reset`, which removes ("unstages") files from the staging area.

→ `git reset files...`	*Unstage some files*
→ `git reset`	*Unstage ALL files*

You can also undo changes that aren't staged yet, restoring some or all files to their most recent commit.

→ `git restore files...`	*Undo unstaged changes in files*
→ `git reset --hard`	*Unstage, then undo ALL changes*

Older versions of Git use `git checkout` instead of `git restore`.

WARNING

`git reset --hard` destroys *all* uncommitted changes, whether they're staged or not. Be sure you mean it!

If you're working with a remote repository, push your changes there at your convenience. The following `git` command pushes your changes to the remote branch that matches your local one.

→ `git push origin HEAD`

Pull your teammates' changes into your local repository. This is a good practice to ensure your changes work with your teammates' before you push.

→ `git pull`

Another common workflow is to create a branch, commit various changes to it, merge the changes into the main branch when you're ready, and delete the branch when you're done.[2]

→ `git switch -c branch_name`	*Create local branch*
→ `...`	*Edit files and commit changes*
→ `git switch main`	*Switch to your main branch*
→ `git merge branch_name`	*Merge your changes*
→ `git branch -d branch_name`	*Delete local branch*

You can also push changes to a remote branch other than the main one:

→ `git push origin branch`   *Push changes*

and delete a remote branch when your collaborators are finished with it:

→ `git push origin --delete branch`   *Delete remote branch*

View your branch's change history:

→ `git log`

Each commit has a revision ID: a string of 40 hexadecimal digits, sometimes abbreviated to the first 7 digits. Many `git`

---

2 Older Git versions use `git checkout [-b]` instead of `git switch [-c]`.

commands accept revision IDs as arguments, like `git log b77eb6b`.

Other common operations:

→ `git branch`	*List all branches*
→ `git mv source dest`	*Move a file/directory*
→ `git cp source dest`	*Copy a file/directory*
→ `git rm file`	*Delete a file*
→ `git rm -r dir`	*Delete a directory*

---

svn
stdin   **stdout** - file -- opt **--help** **--version**

`svn subcommand [options] [arguments]`

Subversion is a version control system for a tree of files. Unlike Git, Subversion requires an existing repository before you can work on files, so I assume you already have access to a repository. The svn command has a rich set of features too large to teach here, but let's check out some common operations.

To get started, locate the URL of an existing repository and check it out, creating a local workspace called the *working copy*:

→ `svn checkout URL`

After you edit files in the working copy, a common sequence of svn commands is as follows:

→ `svn status`	*List the changed files*
→ `svn diff`	*Review your changes*
→ `svn commit -m"comment"`	*Commit your changes*

If you create new files, you must tell Subversion that they're part of your working copy before committing them:

→ `svn add new_files...`	*Add to working copy*
→ `svn commit -m"comment"`	*Commit your changes*

Pull your teammates' changes into your working copy. This is a good practice to ensure your changes work with your teammates' before you commit.

```
→ cd root_of_your_working_copy
→ svn update
```

Another common workflow is to create a branch in the repository, commit various changes to it, and merge the changes into the main branch when you're ready. Subversion's branching syntax is trickier than Git's. A branch name is typically a URL within the repository, like the following examples:

```
https://example.com/path        Remote server, SSL
svn://example.com/path          Remote server, SVN protocol
svn://localhost/path            Local server, SVN protocol
```

The following commands create a branch by copying the main branch, often called the *trunk*. They then commit changes to the new branch and merge it back into the trunk.

```
→ ls
my_project
→ svn cp my_project my_branch            Create branch
→ nano my_branch/file.py                 Edit a file
→ svn commit -m"edited in a branch"      Commit to branch
Adding          my_branch
Sending         my_branch/file.py
Transmitting file data .done
Committing transaction...
Committed revision 966.
→ cd my_project
→ svn merge -c966 svn://example.com/my_branch .    Merge
--- Merging r966 into .:
U    file.py
→ svn commit -m"merging into trunk"      Commit to trunk
Sending         file.py
Transmitting file data .done
Committing transaction...
Committed revision 967.
```

View your change history:

→ `svn log`

Each commit has a revision ID: a positive integer that increases by 1 with each commit. IDs appear in the log. Many svn commands accept revision IDs as options, like svn log -r25. Specify a range of revisions with two IDs separated by a colon: svn log -r25:28.

Other operations:

→ `svn mv source dest`	*Move a file/directory*
→ `svn rm path`	*Delete a file/directory*
→ `svn cat [-r revision] file`	*Print file on stdout*
→ `svn info path`	*Print info about files*

Containers

docker Package and run applications in containers.

Have you ever installed an application and discovered that your Linux system isn't configured to run it? Containers are a way to package up an application's code plus all its dependencies so it's ready to run on other systems. Even better, each running container is an isolated, miniature environment, sort of like a virtual machine but much lighter weight, which is great for scaling up applications, especially in the cloud.

Docker is a popular infrastructure for containers. I present its common uses and assume you have a Docker environment.

---

docker

stdin **stdout** -file --opt **--help** **--version**

docker *subcommand* [*options*] [*arguments*]

The docker command creates, runs, and manages containers. Begin with a text file named *Dockerfile* that specifies a running container's contents and behavior. Here's a simple *Dockerfile* for

---

an image that simply sleeps for five minutes, but it could just as easily run a web server or do calculations.

```
# A image that sleeps for 5 minutes.
# Based on a minimal image called alpine.
FROM alpine
CMD ["sleep", "300"]
```

Then "build" the Dockerfile to create an *image* that's ready to run. Finally, run one or more instances of the image, each inside a container that is an isolated (sandboxed) process. A typical workflow is:

```
→ docker build -t example .      Build an image named "example"
→ docker run example &           Run image in a container
→ docker run example &           Run image in another container
→ docker ps                      List running containers
CONTAINER ID   IMAGE     COMMAND        ...
ff6d0f5ad309   example   "sleep 300"    ...
f80519480635   example   "sleep 300"    ...
```

Or, instead of creating a Dockerfile, download and run an image created by others. The Docker Registry is an infrastructure for sharing images. A typical workflow is:

```
→ docker search hello           Search the Registry
NAME            DESCRIPTION
hello-world     Hello World! (an example of minimal...
⋮
→ docker pull hello-world       Download an image
→ docker run hello-world        Run image in a container
```

NOTE

Depending on how docker is installed on your system, you may need to run docker commands as root (sudo docker) or join the Linux group "docker" to run commands as yourself (sudo usermod -aG docker $USER).

Common Docker Operations

For operations that need a container name or ID, run docker ps to find them. Most docker subcommands have options, and there are other subcommands I don't cover. The Docker site (*https://oreil.ly/6eNA6*) has full details.

Images and Containers

docker search *string*   Locate an image in a central registry with a name or description matching *string*.

docker pull *image*   Download an image from a central registry.

docker build *image*   Given a Dockerfile, build an image.

docker create *image*   Given an image, create a container and don't run it.

Executing Containers

docker run *image*   Create a container and run an instance of an image.

docker stop *names*   Stop the execution of containers with the given names or IDs. For a time, the containers can be restarted with docker start, but if they're stopped for long enough, they are killed.

docker start *names*   Start any stopped containers with the given names or IDs.

docker restart *names*   Same as docker stop followed by docker start.

docker pause *names*   Suspend all processes in containers with the given names or IDs. The container itself continues to run.

docker unpause *names*   Unpause containers with the given names or IDs.

docker kill *names*   Kill containers with the given names or IDs.

Manipulating Containers and Images

docker cp *path1 path2*	Copy files to and from a container. One path is in your local filesystem and the other is within the container. Paths within a container begin with the container name or ID, a colon, and then a file path, like *45171c25a5a0:/etc*.
docker exec *name cmd*	Execute a command inside a container, such as docker exec dcf10812030b ls -l.
docker diff *name*	List file additions, removals, and changes in a container since it was run.
docker rename *old new*	Rename a container.
docker rm [-f] *name*	Remove (delete) a container. Use -f to force a deletion.
docker rmi [-f] *image*	Remove (delete) an image. Use -f to force a deletion.

Monitoring Containers

docker ps [-a]	List all running containers. Add -a to list all containers.
docker top *name*	List processes running in the given container.
docker logs [*options*] *name*	View the system log of a given container. The option --follow prints the logs and continues monitoring them. The option --tail *N* prints the last *N* log lines. The option --since *T* begins the logs at timestamp *T*, such as --since 2024-01-31.

I've covered just the basics of the docker command. See the manual (*https://oreil.ly/6eNA6*) to learn more.

Displaying and Processing Images

display   Display a graphics file.

convert   Convert files from one graphical format into another.

mogrify   Modify a graphics file.

montage   Combine graphics files.

For viewing or editing graphics, Linux has handy tools with tons of options. Let's focus on command-line tools from a package called ImageMagick (*https://oreil.ly/HyBKC*). Its commands all have similar usage, and a full explanation is at *https://oreil.ly/nJZnm*.

---

display   stdin   stdout   -file   -- opt   --help   --version

display [*options*] *files*

The display command displays images of numerous formats: JPEG, PNG, GIF, BMP, and more. It also includes a small suite of image editing tools that appear if you left-click the displayed image. Type q to exit the program.

→ **display photo.jpg**

The command is very powerful, with more than 100 options listed on its manpage.

Useful options

-resize *size*   Resize the image. The size values are extremely flexible, including setting the width (800), the height (x600), both (800x600), a percentage to grow or shrink (50%), an area in pixels (480000@), and more.

-flip   Reverse the image vertically.

-flop   Reverse the image horizontally.

-rotate *N*   Rotate the image by *N* degrees, positive or negative.

-backdrop	Display the image on a backdrop of solid color that covers the rest of your screen.
-fill	Set the solid color used by the -backdrop option.
-delay *N*	Show the image for *N* seconds and then exit. If you list multiple images, you get a slideshow with a delay of *N* seconds between images.
-identify	Print information about the image's format, size, and other statistics to standard output.

convert   **stdin**   **stdout**   **- file**   **-- opt**   **--help**   **--version**

convert [*input_options*] *infile* [*output_options*] *outfile*

The convert command copies an image and converts it to a different graphics format. For example, if you have a JPEG file, produce a PNG or PDF file of the same image:

→ **convert photo.jpg newphoto.png**
→ **convert photo.jpg newphoto.pdf**

Modify the copy at the same time, such as resizing or reversing it:

→ **convert photo.jpg -resize 50% -flip newphoto.png**

convert accepts largely the same options as display.

mogrify   **stdin**   **stdout**   **- file**   **-- opt**   **--help**   **--version**

mogrify [*options*] *file*

The mogrify command transforms an image like convert does, but it changes the original image file you provide, not a copy. (So convert is a safer command when experimenting on a favorite photo.) It accepts largely the same options as display:

→ **mogrify -resize 25% photo.jpg**

montage

```
montage infiles [options] outfile
```

montage produces a single image file from a collection of input files. For example, create a sheet of thumbnails as a single image, labeling each thumbnail with its original filename:

```
→ montage photo.jpg photo2.png photo3.gif \
  -geometry 120x176+10+10 -label '%f' outfile.jpg
```

montage provides great control over how those images appear. The preceding command, for example, produces thumbnails of size 120 × 176 pixels, offset by 10 pixels horizontally and vertically (creating space between the thumbnails), and labeled with their input filename.

Useful options

-geometry $WxH[+|-]X[+|-]Y$	Set the width (W), height (H), and (X,Y) offset of the images. Example value: 120x176+10-10.
-frame N	Draw a frame of N pixels around each image.
-label $string$	Label each image with any $string$, which can contain special escape characters beginning with a percent sign: %f for the original filename, %h and %w for height and width, %m for file format, and about 40 others.

Audio and Video

mediainfo	Print details about a multimedia file.
cdparanoia	Rip audio from CDs to WAV files.
lame	Convert from WAV to MP3.
id3info	View ID3 tags in an MP3 file.

id3tag	Edit ID3 tags in an MP3 file.
ogginfo	View information about an OGG file.
metaflac	View and edit information about a FLAC file.
sox	Convert between audio file formats.
mplayer	Play a video or audio file.
ffmpeg	Convert between video and/or audio file formats.

There are numerous Linux programs with graphical interfaces for playing and editing audio and video, but let's focus once again on command-line tools.

mediainfo

stdin   **stdout**   - file   -- opt   --help   --version

mediainfo [*options*] *files*

The mediainfo command displays details about video and audio files.

```
→ mediainfo clip.mp4
General
Complete name        : clip.mp4
Format               : MPEG-4
Format profile       : Base Media / Version 2
Codec ID             : mp42 (mp42/mp41/isom/avc1)
File size            : 1.11 MiB
Duration             : 23 s 275 ms
Overall bit rate     : 399 kb/s
⋮
```

mediainfo has options, but usually the default output is sufficient. If you need more, add the option -f ("full") to print every picky detail about a media file.

cdparanoia

cdparanoia [*options*] *span* [*outfile*]

The cdparanoia command reads (rips) audio data from a CD and stores it in WAV files (or other formats: see the manpage). Common uses are:

cdparanoia *N*
> Rip track *N* to a file.

cdparanoia -B
> Rip all tracks on the CD into separate files.

cdparanoia -B 2-4
> Rip tracks 2, 3, and 4 into separate files.

cdparanoia 2-4
> Rip tracks 2, 3, and 4 into a single file.

If you experience difficulty accessing your drive, try running cdparanoia -Qvs (meaning "search for CD-ROM drives verbosely") and look for clues.

lame

lame [*options*] *file*.wav

The lame command converts a WAV audio file (say, *song.wav*) into an MP3 file:

→ **lame song.wav song2.mp3**

It has over one hundred options to control bit rate, convert other formats, add ID3 tags, and much more.

id3info

id3info [*options*] [*files*]

The id3info command displays information about an MP3 audio file, such as the song title, recording artist, album name, and year. The file must contain ID3 tags. There are no options except --help and --version:

```
→ id3info knots.mp3
*** Tag information for knots.mp3
=== TIT2 (Title/songname/content description): Knots
=== TPE1 (Lead performer(s)/Soloist(s)): Gentle Giant
=== TALB (Album/Movie/Show title): Octopus
=== TYER (Year): 1972
*** mp3 info
MPEG1/layer III
Bitrate: 320KBps
Frequency: 44KHz
```

id3tag

id3tag [*options*] *files*

The id3tag command adds or modifies ID3 tags in an MP3 file. For example, to tag an MP3 file with a new title and artist, run:

```
→ id3tag -A "My Album" -a "Loud Linux Squad" song.mp3
```

Useful options

-A *name*   Set the artist's name.

-a *title*   Set the album title.

-s *title*   Set the song title.

-y *year*   Set the year.

-t *number*   Set the track number.

-g *number*   Set the genre number.

ogginfo

ogginfo [*options*] [*files*]

ogginfo is a simple command that displays information about an Ogg Vorbis audio file:

```
→ ogginfo knots.ogg
Processing file "knots.ogg"...
⋮
User comments section follows...
        Title=Knots
        Artist=Gentle Giant
        Album=Octopus
⋮
Vorbis stream 1:
        Total data length: 69665 bytes
        Playback length: 0m:05.067s
        Average bitrate: 109.973744
```

Add the -h option for more detailed usage information.

---

metaflac

metaflac [*options*] [*files*]

The metaflac command displays or changes information about a FLAC audio file. To display information, run:

```
→ metaflac --list knots.flac
⋮
  sample_rate: 44100 Hz
  channels: 2
  bits-per-sample: 16
  total samples: 223488
⋮
  comments: 4
    comment[0]: Title=Knots
    comment[1]: Artist=Gentle Giant
    comment[2]: Album=Octopus
    comment[3]: Year=1972
```

The simplest way to change information, such as the title and artist, is to export the information to a text file, edit the file, and then reimport it:

```
→ metaflac --export-tags-to info.txt knots.flac
→ cat info.txt
Title=Knots
Artist=Gentle Giant
Album=Octopus
Year=1972
→ nano info.txt          Make changes and save the file
→ metaflac --import-tags-from info.txt knots.flac
```

Useful options

--show-tag *name*	Display the value for the named tag, such as title, artist, album, year, etc. There are many other "show" options for other information: see the manpage.
--remove-tag *name*	Remove all occurrences of the named tag (title, artist, etc.) from the FLAC file.

SOX   stdin stdout -file -- opt --help --version

sox [*options*] *infile outfile*

sox is the simplest command to convert from one audio file format to another. It supports MP3, OGG, FLAC, WAV, and dozens of other formats. (Run man soxformat for a list.) Simply specify the new format using the correct file extension, as in these examples:

```
→ sox knots.mp3 knots2.wav      MP3 to WAV
→ sox knots.ogg knots2.mp3      OGG to MP3
→ sox knots.flac knots2.ogg     FLAC to OGG
```

sox has *many* other uses, including combining audio files and adding special effects. See the manpage for details.

Useful options

-S	Show a progress meter; useful for long conversions.
--no-clobber	Don't overwrite the output file if it already exists.
-t *type*	Specify the type of the input file, if sox cannot figure it out. See man soxformat for the list of types.

---

mplayer   stdin stdout - file -- opt --help --version

mplayer [*options*] *video_files*...

The mplayer command plays video and audio files in many formats (MPEG, AVI, MOV, and more):

→ **mplayer clip.mp4**

Press the space bar to pause and resume the video, the cursor keys to jump forward and backward, and Q to quit. mplayer also plays audio files and has dozens of options on its manpage. Learn more at *https://oreil.ly/96S5B*.

Other popular video players for Linux include (vlc) (*https://oreil.ly/hBGP0*), (kaffeine) (*https://oreil.ly/mROWt*), and (xine) (*https://oreil.ly/IyQw6*).

---

ffmpeg   stdin stdout - file -- opt **--help** --version

ffmpeg [*input_options*] -i *input* [*output_options*] *output*

The ffmpeg command converts video file formats, splits and appends videos, extracts audio tracks, creates thumbnail images for videos, and much more. To understand ffmpeg thoroughly, it helps to know digital video concepts like frame rates, demuxing, and codecs; but in this pocket guide I cover just a few common uses. For more complicated tasks, your best bet is to search the web for someone else's ffmpeg solution.

---

ffmpeg is sensitive to the order of its options, unlike most other Linux commands. Wherever you place the option -i *filename* on the command line, input file options come before it and output file options come after. If an input option sits among output options or vice versa, ffmpeg may fail mysteriously.

Convert a video file *myvideo.mp4* from MP4 to MOV format:

```
→ ffmpeg -i myvideo.mp4 myvideo.mov
```

Extract 10 seconds of video (-t 10) beginning at the two minute mark (-s 00:02:00) and store it in a file *extract.mp4*:

```
→ ffmpeg -i myvideo.mp4 -ss 00:02:00 -t 10 \
  -codec copy extract.mp4
```

Extract audio from *myvideo.mp4* into an MP3 file *audio.mp3*:

```
→ ffmpeg -i myvideo.mp4 -q:a 0 -map a audio.mp3
```

Append multiple videos to create *movie.mp4*. Start with a text file that lists the paths to the source videos, then run ffmpeg:

```
→ cat videos.txt
file 'video1.mp4'
file 'video2.mp4'
file 'video3.mp4'
→ ffmpeg -f concat -safe 0 -i videos.txt -c copy \
  movie.mp4
```

Create a thumbnail image from a video file *myvideo.mp4* by extracting a single frame (-vframes 1) at the five-second mark (ss 5) into a JPEG file *thumb.jpg*, sized 160 × 120 pixels:

```
→ ffmpeg -ss 5 -i myvideo.mp4 -vcodec mjpeg \
  -vframes 1 -an -f rawvideo -s 160x120 thumb.jpg
```

ffmpeg has an extensive help system built in (see the manpage):

```
→ ffmpeg -encoders          List supported encoders
→ ffmpeg --help encoder=mpeg4   Get details about one
```

Programming with Shell Scripts

Bash has a built-in programming language. You can write *shell scripts* (bash programs) to accomplish tasks that a single command cannot. The command reset-lpg, supplied in the book's examples directory, is a shell script that you can read:

```
→ less ~/linuxpocketguide/reset-lpg
```

Like any good programming language, bash has variables, conditionals (if-then-else), loops, input and output, and more. Entire books and online courses have been written on shell scripting; I cover the bare minimum to get you started. For greater detail, run info bash, pick up a bash scripting book, or search the web for bash scripting tutorials.

Creating and Running Shell Scripts

To create a shell script, simply put bash commands into a file as you would type them. To run the script, you have three choices:

Prepend #!/bin/bash and make the file executable
  This is the most common way to run scripts. Add the line:

```
#!/bin/bash
```

  to the very top of the script file. It must be the first line of the file, left-justified. Then make the file executable:

```
→ chmod +x myscript
```

  Then run the script. For a script in the current directory, you will probably have to prepend "./" so the shell can locate the script. (The current directory is generally not in your search path for security reasons. You wouldn't want a malicious script named "ls" in the current directory to silently override the real ls command.)

```
→ ./myscript
```

Alternatively, move the script into a directory in your search path and run it like any other command:

```
→ myscript
```

Pass to bash

Run bash with the script filename as an argument.

```
→ bash myscript
```

Run in current shell with source or a dot

The preceding methods run your script as an independent entity that has no effect on your current shell.[3] If you want a script to make changes to your current shell (setting variables, changing directory, etc.), run it with the source command or a single dot:

```
→ source myscript
→ . myscript
```

Whitespace and Linebreaks

Bash shell scripts are sensitive to whitespace and linebreaks. Because the "keywords" of this programming language are actually commands evaluated by the shell, you must separate arguments with whitespace. Likewise, a linebreak tells the shell that a command is complete, so a linebreak in the middle of a command can cut the command short. Follow the conventions I present here and you should be fine. (Also see my formatting advice in the sidebar "Style in Shell Scripts" on page 299.)

To split a long command into multiple lines, end each line (except the last) with a single \ character, which means "continued on next line." Here's a script with a long grep command:

```
#!/bin/bash
grep abcdefghijklmnopqrstuvwxyz file1 file2 file3 \
file4 file5
```

---

3 That's because the script runs in a separate shell (a *child shell*) that cannot alter the original shell.

Variables

I described shell variables in "Shell Variables" on page 21:

```
→ MYVAR=6
→ echo $MYVAR
6
```

All values held in variables are strings, but if they are numeric, the shell treats them as numbers when appropriate:

```
→ NUMBER="10"
→ expr $NUMBER + 5
15
```

When you refer to a variable's value in a shell script, it's a good idea to surround it with double quotes to prevent certain run-time errors. An undefined variable, or a variable with spaces in its value, evaluates to something unexpected if not surrounded by quotes, causing your script to malfunction:

```
→ FILENAME="My Document"                            Space in the name
→ ls $FILENAME                                       Try to list it
ls: My: No such file or directory       ls saw 2 arguments
ls: Document: No such file or directory
→ ls -l "$FILENAME"                                  List it properly
My Document                                          ls saw only 1 argument
```

If a variable name is evaluated adjacent to another string, surround it with curly braces to prevent unexpected behavior:

```
→ HAT="fedora"
→ echo "The plural of $HAT is $HATs"
The plural of fedora is                 No variable "HATs"
→ echo "The plural of $HAT is ${HAT}s"
The plural of fedora is fedoras         What we wanted
```

Input and Output

Scripts can print to standard output with the echo and printf commands, which I described in "Screen Output" on page 257:

```
→ echo "Hello world"
Hello world
→ printf "I am %d years old\n" `expr 20 + 20`
I am 40 years old
```

Scripts can read from standard input with the read command, which grabs one line of input and stores it in a variable:

```
→ read name
Sandy Smith <ENTER>
→ echo "I read the name $name"
I read the name Sandy Smith
```

See also "Command-Line Arguments" on page 305.

Booleans and Exit Codes

Before I describe conditionals and loops, you need the concept of a Boolean (true/false) test. To the shell, the value 0 means true or success, and anything else means false or failure. (Think of zero as "no error" and other values as error codes.)

Additionally, every Linux command returns an integer value to the shell when the command exits. This value is called an *exit code*, *exit value*, or *exit status*.

You can see this value in the special variable $?:

```
→ cat exittest
My name is Sandy Smith and
I really like Ubuntu Linux
→ grep Smith exittest
My name is Sandy Smith and     A match was found...
→ echo $?
0                              ...so exit code is "success"
→ grep aardvark exittest
→ echo $?                      No match was found...
1                              ...so exit code is "failure"
```

A command's exit codes are documented on its manpage.

The test Command

The `test` command (built into the shell) evaluates simple Boolean expressions involving numbers and strings, and sets its exit status to 0 (true) or 1 (false):

```
→ test 10 -lt 5          Is 10 less than 5?
→ echo $?
1                         No, it isn't
→ test -n "hello"         Does "hello" have nonzero length?
→ echo $?
0                         Yes, it does
```

Here are common `test` arguments to check properties of integers, strings, and files:

File tests

-d *name*	File *name* is a directory.
-f *name*	File *name* is a regular file.
-L *name*	File *name* is a symbolic link.
-r *name*	File *name* exists and is readable.
-w *name*	File *name* exists and is writable.
-x *name*	File *name* exists and is executable.
-s *name*	File *name* exists and its size is nonzero.
f1 -nt *f2*	File *f1* is newer than file *f2*.
f1 -ot *f2*	File *f1* is older than file *f2*.

String tests

s1 = *s2*	String *s1* equals string *s2*.
s1 != *s2*	String *s1* does not equal string *s2*.
-z *s1*	String *s1* has zero length.
-n *s1*	String *s1* has nonzero length.

Numeric tests

a `-eq` b	Integers a and b are equal.
a `-ne` b	Integers a and b are not equal.
a `-gt` b	Integer a is greater than integer b.
a `-ge` b	Integer a is greater than or equal to integer b.
a `-lt` b	Integer a is less than integer b.
a `-le` b	Integer a is less than or equal to integer b.

Combining and negating tests

`t1 -a t2`	And: Both tests *t1* and *t2* are true.
`t1 -o t2`	Or: Either test *t1* or *t2* is true.
`! your_test`	Negate the test (i.e., *your_test* is false).
`\( your_test \)`	Use parentheses for grouping, as in algebra.

You can write tests in bash in three ways. The first uses the test command as I've already shown. The second is to surround a condition with double square brackets:

```
→ [[ 10 -lt 5 ]]          Is 10 less than 5?
→ echo $?
1                          No, it isn't
→ [[ -n "hello" ]]         Does "hello" have nonzero length?
→ echo $?
0                          Yes, it does
```

The third way, which is also supported by some other shells, is to use a single square bracket:

```
→ [ 10 -lt 5 ]            Is 10 less than 5?
→ echo $?
1                          No, it isn't
→ [ -n "hello" ]           Does "hello" have nonzero length?
→ echo $?
0                          Yes, it does
```

The single square bracket is an older syntax with some odd quirks. You *must* add whitespace after the left bracket and before the right bracket. That's because the left bracket is actually a *command* named "[" —it is an alias for `test`. You must therefore follow the left bracket with *individual arguments separated by whitespace*. You also must ensure that the final argument is a right square bracket, signifying the end of the test. If you mistakenly forget some whitespace:

```
→ [ 5 -lt 4]              No space between 4 and ]
bash: [: missing ']'
```

then `test` sees the final argument is the string "4]" and complains that the final bracket is missing.

Conditionals

The `if` statement chooses between alternatives, each of which may have a complex test. The simplest form is the `if-then` statement:

```
if command              If exit status of command is 0
then
  body
fi
```

Style in Shell Scripts

Shell scripting keywords (`if`, `then`, `fi`, etc.) must be the first word on their line. That means the keyword must follow either a newline character or a semicolon (plus optional whitespace). Here are two other common layouts for an `if` statement. Other conditionals and loops can be styled similarly.

```
if command; then              Semicolon before then
  body
fi
```

```
if command; then body; fi     Semicolons before then and fi
```

Here's an example script with an `if` statement. Try running it with and without sudo and view the results.

```
→ cat script-if
#!/bin/bash
if [ `whoami` = "root" ]
then
  echo "You are the superuser"
fi
→ ./script-if                        No output
→ sudo ./script-if
[sudo] password: xxxxxxxx
You are the superuser
```

Next is the if-then-else statement:

```
if command
then
  body1
else
  body2
fi
```

For example:

```
→ cat script-else
#!/bin/bash
if [ `whoami` = "root" ]
then
  echo "You are the superuser"
else
  echo "You are a mere mortal"
fi
→ ./script-else
You are a mere mortal
→ sudo ./script-else
[sudo] password: xxxxxxxx
You are the superuser
```

Finally, there's the form if-then-elif-else, which can have as many tests as you like:

```
if command1
then
  body1
elif command2
then
```

```
  body2
elif ...
  ⋮
else
  bodyN
fi
```

For example:

```
→ cat script-elif
#!/bin/bash
bribe=20000
if [ `whoami` = "root" ]
then
  echo "You are the superuser"
elif [ "$USER" = "root" ]
then
  echo "You might be the superuser"
elif [ "$bribe" -gt 10000 ]
then
  echo "You can pay to be the superuser"
else
  echo "You are still a mere mortal"
fi
→ ./script-elif
You can pay to be the superuser
```

The case statement evaluates a single value and branches to an appropriate piece of code:

```
→ cat script-case
#!/bin/bash
echo -n "What would you like to do (eat, sleep)? "
read answer
case "$answer" in
  eat)
    echo "OK, have a hamburger."
    ;;
  sleep)
    echo "Good night then."
    ;;
  *)
    echo "I'm not sure what you want to do."
```

```
    echo "I guess I'll see you tomorrow."
    ;;
esac
→ ./script-case
What would you like to do (eat, sleep)? sleep
Good night then.
```

The general form is:

```
case value in
  expr1)
    body1
    ;;
  expr2)
    body2
    ;;
  ⋮
  exprN)
    bodyN
    ;;
  *)
    body_of_else
    ;;
esac
```

The *value* is any value, usually a variable value like $myvar, and *expr1* through *exprN* are patterns (run the command info bash for details), with the final * like a final "else." Each body must be terminated by ;; (as shown):

```
→ cat script-case2
#!/bin/bash
echo -n "Enter a letter: "
read letter
case $letter in
  X)
    echo "$letter is an X"
    ;;
  [aeiou])
    echo "$letter is a vowel"
    ;;
  [0-9])
    echo "$letter is a digit, silly"
```

```
    ;;
  *)
    echo "The letter '$letter' is not supported"
    ;;
esac
./script-case2
Enter a letter: e
e is a vowel
```

Loops

The while loop repeats a set of commands as long as a condition is true.

```
while command          While the exit status of command is 0
do
  body
done
```

For example:

```
→ cat script-while
#!/bin/bash
i=0
while [ $i -lt 3 ]
do
  echo "$i"
  i=`expr $i + 1`
done
→ ./script-while
0
1
2
```

The until loop repeats until a condition becomes true:

```
until command    While the exit status of command is nonzero
do
  body
done
```

For example:

```
→ cat script-until
#!/bin/bash
i=0
until [ $i -ge 3 ]
do
  echo "$i"
  i=`expr $i + 1`
done
→ ./script-until
0
1
2
```

Watch out for infinite loops, which use while with a condition that always evaluates to 0 (true) or until with a condition that always evaluates to a nonzero value (false):

```
i=1
while [ $i -lt 10 ]
do
  echo "forever"          Oops: variable i never changes
done                      Infinite loop
```

Another type of loop, the for loop, iterates over values from a list:

```
for variable in list
do
  body
done
```

For example:

```
→ cat script-for
#!/bin/bash
for name in Tom Jane Harry
do
  echo "$name is my friend"
done
→ ./script-for
Tom is my friend
Jane is my friend
Harry is my friend
```

The for loop is handy for processing lists of files; for example, filenames with a certain extension in the current directory:

```
→ cat script-for2
#!/bin/bash
for file in *.docx
do
  echo "$file is a stinky Microsoft Word file"
done
→ ./script-for2
letter.docx is a stinky Microsoft Word file
shopping.docx is a stinky Microsoft Word file
```

You can also generate a list of values and loop over them, using curly braces ("Brace Expansion" on page 21) or the seq command (see "Screen Output" on page 257):

```
→ cat script-seq
#!/bin/bash
for i in {1..20}          Generates the integers 1-20
do
  echo "iteration $i"
done
→ ./script-seq
iteration 1
iteration 2
iteration 3
⋮
iteration 20
```

Command-Line Arguments

Shell scripts can accept command-line arguments and options just like other Linux commands. (In fact, some common Linux commands *are* scripts.) Within your shell script, refer to these arguments as $1, $2, $3, and so on:

```
→ cat script-args
#!/bin/bash
echo "My name is $1 and I come from $2"

→ ./script-args Johnson Wisconsin
```

```
My name is Johnson and I come from Wisconsin
→ ./script-args Bob
My name is Bob and I come from
```

A script can test the number of arguments it received with $#:

```
→ cat script-args2
#!/bin/bash
if [ $# -lt 2 ]
then
  echo "$0 error: you must supply two arguments"
else
  echo "My name is $1 and I come from $2"
fi
```

The special value $0 contains the name of the script and is handy for usage and error messages:

```
→ ./script-args2 Barbara
./script-args2 error: you must supply two arguments
```

To iterate over all command-line arguments, use a for loop with the special variable $@, which holds all arguments:

```
→ cat script-args3
#!/bin/bash
for arg in $@
do
  echo "I found the argument $arg"
done
→ ./script-args3 One Two Three
I found the argument One
I found the argument Two
I found the argument Three
```

Exiting with an Exit Code

The exit command terminates your script and passes a given exit code to the shell (see "Booleans and Exit Codes" on page 296). By tradition, scripts should return 0 for success and 1 (or other nonzero value) on failure. If your script doesn't call exit, its exit code will be that of the last command the script runs.

```
→ cat script-exit
#!/bin/bash
if [ $# -lt 2 ]
then
  echo "$0 error: you must supply two arguments"
  exit 1
else
  echo "My name is $1 and I come from $2"
fi
exit 0
→ ./script-exit Bob
./script-exit error: you must supply two arguments
→ echo $?
1
```

Piping to bash

Bash is not just a shell; it's also a command, bash, that reads
from standard input. This means you can construct commands
as strings and send them to bash for execution:

```
→ echo wc -l myfile
wc -l myfile
→ echo wc -l myfile | bash
18 myfile
```

WARNING

Piping commands into bash is powerful but can also be
dangerous. First, make sure you know *exactly* which commands you're sending to bash for execution. You don't
want to pipe an unexpected rm command to bash and
delete a valuable file (or one thousand valuable files).

If someone asks you to retrieve text from the web (say,
with the curl command) and pipe it to bash, don't do
it blindly. Instead, capture the web page as a file (with
curl or wget), examine it closely, and make an informed
decision whether to execute it with bash.

This technique is incredibly useful. Suppose you want to download the files *photo1.jpg*, *photo2.jpg*, through *photo100.jpg* from a website. Instead of typing 100 wget commands by hand, construct the commands with a loop, using seq to construct the list of integers from 1 to 100:

```
→ for i in `seq 1 100`
do
  echo wget https://example.com/photo$i.jpg
done
wget https://example.com/photo1.jpg
wget https://example.com/photo2.jpg
⋮
wget https://example.com/photo100.jpg
```

Yes, you've constructed the text of 100 commands. Now pipe the output to bash, which runs all 100 commands as if you'd typed them by hand:

```
→ for i in `seq 1 100`
do
  echo wget https://example.com/photo$i.jpg
done | bash
```

Here's a more complex but practical application. Suppose you have a set of files you want to rename. Put the old names into a file *oldnames*, and the new names into a file *newnames*:

```
→ cat oldnames
oldname1
oldname2
oldname3
→ cat newnames
newname1
newname2
newname3
```

Now use the commands paste and sed ("Manipulating Text in Files" on page 89) to place the old and new names side by side and prepend the word "mv" to each line, and the output is a sequence of "mv" commands:

```
→ cat oldnames \
  | paste -d' ' oldnames newnames \
  | sed 's/^/mv /'
mv oldfile1 newfile1
mv oldfile2 newfile2
mv oldfile3 newfile3
```

Finally, pipe the output to bash, and the renaming takes place!

```
→ cat oldnames \
  | paste -d' ' oldnames newnames \
  | sed 's/^/mv /' \
  | bash
```

Beyond Shell Scripting

Shell scripts are fine for many purposes, but Linux comes with much more powerful scripting languages, as well as compiled programming languages. Here are a few:

Language	Program	To get started…
C, C++	gcc, g++	man gcc *https://oreil.ly/-kuj1*
Java	javac	*https://oreil.ly/-yvQR*
.NET	mono	man mono *https://oreil.ly/IVenL*
Perl	perl	man perl *https://oreil.ly/LKgdM*
PHP	php	man php *https://oreil.ly/JPmlL*
Python	python	man python *https://oreil.ly/vAunc*
Ruby	ruby	*https://oreil.ly/ifm2L*

Final Words

Although I've covered many commands and features of Linux, there's so much more to learn. I hope you'll continue reading and exploring the capabilities of your Linux systems.

To boost your Linux skills even more, check out my follow-up book, *Efficient Linux at the Command Line*. It goes beyond the basics to make you faster and more effective with Linux, with tons of practical tips and techniques. For more information, visit my website (*https://danieljbarrett.com*).

Index

About the Author

Daniel J. Barrett has been teaching and writing about Linux and related technologies for more than 30 years. His numerous O'Reilly books include *Efficient Linux at the Command Line*; *Linux Pocket Guide*; *SSH, The Secure Shell: The Definitive Guide*; *Linux Security Cookbook*; *Macintosh Terminal Pocket Guide*; and *MediaWiki*. Dan has also been a software engineer, heavy metal singer, system administrator, university lecturer, web designer, and humorist. He works at Google. Visit DanielJBarrett.com to learn more.

Colophon

The animal on the cover of *Linux Pocket Guide* is a *Belgian horse*. The first breeding of these gentle giants was recorded in the 17th century, with the creation of the first studbook in 1886. These horses are descendants of the Great Horse of medieval times. They were developed for industrial and farm work and hauling. They have a gentle, cooperative temperament, are willing to work, easy to handle, and rarely spook. They are also adaptable to a wide range of environments.

Belgian horses have a small head compared to the size of their body. They have a compact, short body with a broad chest and a wide back. They have a straight profile with kind eyes and a thick neck, which is particularly thick on stallions. Their legs are feathered around their medium-sized hooves. They stand between 16 and 18 hands, with males being taller than females. They reach their full size around five years of age and can weigh between 1,800 and 2,200 pounds.

While their predecessors may be extinct, Belgian horses are a very popular breed of draft horse and are not at risk of extinction. Many of the animals on O'Reilly covers are endangered; all of them are important to the world.

The cover image is a color illustration by Kate Montgomery, based on an antique line engraving from Wood's *Animate Creation*. The series design is by Edie Freedman, Ellie Volckhausen, and Karen Montgomery. The cover fonts are URW Typewriter and Guardian Sans. The text font is Adobe Minion Pro; the heading font is Adobe Myriad Condensed; and the code font is Dalton Maag's Ubuntu Mono.

Printed in the USA
CPSIA information can be obtained
at www.ICGtesting.com
JSHW011155120624
64616JS00004B/15

9 781098 157968